D1054243

Market Mapping

How to Use Revolutionary New Software to Find, Analyze, and Keep Customers

Sunny Baker

Kim Baker

McGraw-Hill, Inc.

New York   St. Louis   San Francisco   Auckland   Bogotá
Caracas   Lisbon   London   Madrid   Mexico   Milan
Montreal   New Delhi   Paris   San Juan   São Paulo
Singapore   Sydney   Tokyo   Toronto

Library of Congress Cataloging-in-Publication Data

Baker, Sunny.
 Market mapping : how to use revolutionary new software to find,
 analyze, and keep customers / Sunny Baker, Kim Baker.
   p.   cm.
 Includes bibliographical references and index.
 ISBN 0-07-003688-8 :   —ISBN 0-07-003689-6 (pbk.) :
  1. Marketing—Maps—Computer programs.   2. Marketing research—
 Computer programs.   I. Baker, Kim, date.   II. Title.
 HF5415.125.B34   1993
 658.8'35'0285536—dc20   92-24102
                                                                CIP

1 2 3 4 5 6 7 8 9 0   DOC/DOC   9 8 7 6 5 4 3 2

ISBN   0-07-003688-8   {HC}
ISBN   0-07-003689-6   {PBK}

*The sponsoring editor for this book was Karen Hansen, and the production
supervisor was Suzanne W. Babeuf. It was set in Baskerville by North
Market Street Graphics.*

Printed and bound by R. R. Donnelley & Sons Company.

A [map's] basic purpose is to give the navigator information that enables him to make the right decision in time to avoid danger.

ELBERT S. MALONEY
*Piloting: Seamanship &
Small Boat Handling,
59th Edition*

Contents

7. Using Market Mapping Tools to Analyze New Market Opportunities   155

8. Sales Territory Analysis with Market Maps   171

9. Using Market Mapping for Advertising and Direct Mail Applications   185

10. Using Market Mapping Tools to Evaluate International Market Potential   199

Part 3. Resources for Market Mapping

Acknowledgments

First, thanks to Steven J. Bennett for inspiring us to get involved with desktop mapping in the first place. Special credit goes to our editor at McGraw-Hill, Karen Hansen, for understanding the importance of mapping technology in a global economy and enthusiastically embracing the concept for this book.

In addition, many people from the desktop mapping software companies have graciously offered their time and expertise in support of this project, most notably David Radoff, Director of Public Relations at Strategic Mapping, Inc.; Robert Reading, Vice President at Tactics International, Ltd.; John Hobson, Vice President of Marketing at Urban Decision Systems; and Richard Burger, Director of Communications at PC Globe, Inc. We also appreciate the work of the following people at Strategic Mapping who helped with examples: Sarah Rollins, Robert Norris, Bob Kochenderfer, Jonathan Curtis, Berkley Charlton, Paul Barkin, and Tim Rupp. To all these people and the others too numerous to mention here, we offer our deepest appreciation. Without their companies' innovative products, the business world would be doomed to put its marks on the map with push pins and colored pens.

Introduction—Market Mapping Puts a Competitive Advantage at Your Fingertips

It is estimated that more than 85 percent of the information in corporate databases has geographic attributes—including telephone numbers, zip codes, or addresses. This makes it possible to analyze almost every relationship in business using the impact and visual clarity of maps.

There is simply no better way to visualize geographic data than with a map. With maps you can see *where* things are, not just *what* they are. Remember George C. Scott pondering over the war room maps in the movie *Patton?* Move a few pins around and the whole war changes. Maps are a central component in the strategic planning toolbox for any general, not just those in the movies. In the same vein, maps can and should be an important strategic tool in business.

You probably use wall maps already to display and analyze data in your company. Colorful push pins mark the location of key customers or represent office locations. But maps can do more than hang on your wall. Computerized maps can display otherwise hidden relationships between customers and territories. They can reveal prime business locations and clarify distribution strategies. Maps can be used to analyze promotional alternatives and determine optimal product mixes for different regions.

Information revealed in maps can be the primary input for making major strategic decisions, and modern personal computers put map-based analysis within reach of any company.

As personal computers evolved, not only their speed and number-crunching ability advanced, but their capability to display graphics also improved. Today color output and high-quality graphic displays are standard options on personal computers. The graphic and color capabilities of current personal computers have fueled the development of sophisticated data visualization programs employing a wide range of charts and graphs—and now, maps.

Revolutionary new personal computer software is now available that gives every businessperson the power to unleash the geographic information contained in every database. Software that produces maps on a personal computer is generically called "desktop mapping" software. Market mapping is the ability to display marketing data on the maps produced with desktop mapping software. Market mapping is one application of desktop mapping that is applicable to every business, and market mapping is feasible because of the low cost and sophistication of today's personal computers.

The Market Mapping Revolution

Personal computers have already revolutionized many aspects of business by offering easy-to-use, affordable ways to create documents, analyze financial data, and report on a wide range of corporate information stored in databases. In the same way that spreadsheet programs on personal computers revolutionized financial analysis by making "what if" capabilities available to managers in every department, the new desktop mapping programs are revolutionizing marketing analysis.

Market maps can be created using a variety of desktop mapping programs. Desktop mapping programs employ the data from government, commercial, and self-compiled information sources to create the maps. The maps incorporate symbols, three-dimensional representations, colors, and charts to display trends, locations, and relationships in business data. The information-packed maps allow people to visualize their data faster and with more precision.

Market mapping is by no means new. The capability to analyze demographic and geographic data using mapping software with mainframe computers has existed for decades, but only corporations with giant systems and megabudgets for marketing research could take advantage of the data visualization power of mapping programs. Today, the power of the personal computer is bringing these sophisticated programs down to the desktop level, making mapping analysis available to any business with a personal computer and a color monitor.

What Can Market Mapping Do for My Company?

Market mapping research involves the analysis of populations and demographic statistics—a subset of marketing research that is vital to globally-dependent marketing economies and critical to market-driven businesses at all levels. Here are some of the marketing and business analyses you can accomplish with only a few hours of practice using desktop mapping programs:

- Instantaneously expose demographic trends in your customer base.
- Quickly analyze buying patterns across the nation or the world.
- Redefine sales territories based on the number of potential customers in an area.
- Establish the best location for a new retail store in a city you've never visited.
- Realign your sales force based on shifting populations.
- Discover trends in the marketplace that inspire new product ideas and expose marketing opportunities.

The possibilities for market mapping are endless. Market mapping and desktop demographic analysis work together to enable people involved in all aspects of marketing to make superior decisions at a low cost. Problem solving, based on demographic and geographical considerations, is now as easy as reading a spreadsheet created with Excel or Lotus 1-2-3.

Desktop mapping enables marketing and sales people to generate exquisitely detailed maps and charts that interpret statistics for states, regions, customer populations, and commercial databases. Because maps make statistical marketing data easier to comprehend, the ability to plan and track marketing campaigns is improved. Analysis is greatly enhanced because less time is required to understand the relationships between locations and customers. The companies that make market mapping analysis a central part of their ongoing marketing research program realize competitive advantages that are restricted using ordinary data presentation formats such as reports and listings.

Market mapping research is no longer the domain of the Fortune 500. It is a basic tool for companies of all kinds. With the power and relatively low cost of market mapping, you can't afford not to be part of the revolution.

About This Book

Because the power of market mapping tools is new to many, companies are not sure how to get started or even how to apply the tools to solve specific problems. To answer this need, the book covers the data sources, software tools, and applications of this new and powerful desktop research and data visualization technology in one volume. The book works as both a cover-to-cover introduction to market mapping and as a reference to be grabbed off the shelf to handle a specific type of market mapping research. After reading *Market Mapping* you will know how to recognize demographic trends, visualize distributions for making promotional decisions, and quickly assess market purchase patterns—without leaving the office.

The book covers all the requirements for getting started in market mapping analysis: the computer tools, the information sources, and the procedures to implement real-world research projects, such as reorganizing a field sales force, channeling advertising dollars to different media with alternate demographics, or finding a new retail or office location. To this end, the book is divided in three sections.

The first section of the book provides an overview of the research possibilities and tools available to set up an in-house market mapping research system. Examples from real companies that have successfully used these tools to create a competitive advantage are provided. The basic principles of desktop marketing programs and their functions are presented generically, without focus on one specific program. Various programs with different capabilities are shown to introduce the concepts and illustrate the options available.

The potency of desktop mapping research also depends largely on the databases and information resources used to make the maps and analyses. Thus, an entire chapter is dedicated to information on available data sources, allowing desktop marketers to evaluate and tailor commercial and corporate databases for their own specific research and analysis requirements. This section concludes with a chapter on setting up a desktop mapping research program, with checklists and guidelines for evaluating software, computers, and databases to meet various research needs in a variety of companies.

The second section of the book uses a case-study, problem-solving approach based on real-world scenarios to illustrate the process of market mapping analysis. By working through this series of realistic market research problems step-by-step, with the help of various desktop marketing programs, you will be able to apply the concepts directly to marketing issues in your own business.

The third section of the book is a compendium of sources for desktop mapping data and software products. A glossary of mapping and demographic terms is also included in this third section for general reference.

Who Should Read This Book?

As a book that melds state-of-the-art computing and modern applications of market mapping and demographic analysis, *Market Mapping* is essential reading for any businessperson who wants to improve or expand his or her marketing research and data analysis skills—and this includes:

- *Sales and Marketing Managers*—Managers or marketing professionals in small or large companies can benefit from applying the tools of desktop mapping research and market mapping to their marketing problems. Whether looking for new markets or evaluating old ones, desktop mapping can be used to improve decision-making criteria and identify geographical and demographic patterns not easily determined from other marketing methodologies.

- *Corporate Executives*—Executives need to understand customer demographics and market trends without spending time wading through a myriad of written reports and spreadsheets. Market mapping can give people responsible for setting strategic direction the "big picture" perspective they need. Using market maps to analyze data will save executives both time and effort, freeing them to consider more alternatives and make better decisions.

- *Small Business Owners*—Seventy-five percent of 2000 businesses on a Small Business Administration study completed in 1990 owned personal computers, yet none of these businesses reported using their personal computers for marketing research. Not surprisingly, 51 percent of all new businesses fail within the first four years—largely because of poor market planning. This is a travesty, and it's probably because small business owners are not yet aware of the potential of using their desktop computers for marketing analysis. The mapping tools and on-line demographic resources that can help small businesses visualize their markets, their competition, and the buying power of their customers are now inexpensive and relatively easy to use—so there is no longer any excuse for a small company to be without adequate market research and analysis.

- *Retail Business Managers*—Retail businesses depend on the traffic flow and demographics of a business location. Market mapping tools provide an affordable, easy-to-use methodology for establishing the best location for a retail store. Many retail owners rely on guts and instinct alone. Now they can rely on something more tangible when they decide on a location for their shop, restaurant, or store. Desktop demographic research can also be used by these retail businesses to analyze sales patterns based on locations and demographic criteria, to better focus product mixes, and to improve the impact of advertising efforts.

- *Franchise Planners*—Franchising is a major industry in the United States. There are thousands of viable franchise-based companies in operation. This translates into hundreds of thousands of franchised businesses across the country. Parent companies often provide marketing services to their franchisees, including assistance in establishing a viable location for the franchise or determining the target market areas for promotional efforts. Now, with desktop demographic research and market mapping tools, location analysis can be provided quickly, accurately, and with minimum expense. The analyses can now be completed by the franchisees on their own, as well as by the parent companies.

- *Advertising Agencies and Market Research Firms*—Demographic research is a central component of the services offered by marketing firms and advertising agencies. Desktop mapping research and market mapping programs allow these firms to improve the services to their clients while reducing the overall costs to provide an analysis. The detailed maps and high-quality graphics produced by the mapping programs enable agencies and research firms to make stunning, influential presentations of marketing demographics, trends, and distributions with minimum effort.

- *Business and Marketing Students*—Business students need to learn the latest methods in their fields and desktop mapping research certainly fills the bill. Because of its practical examples and structured approach, faculty and schools can also use the book as a supplementary text in marketing research or general marketing courses.

Why You Need to Get Started Now

It's no longer enough to have the data to manage your business. You must be able to slice and dice it. You must be able to see things in alternate ways to discover the new markets and the new products hiding in your data. Your competition will soon be using market mapping to help visualize the peaks, the valleys, the distributions, the hidden relationships, and the new opportunities in their marketing data. After reading this book, you can too.

Sunny Baker
Kim Baker

PART 1

The Tools and Principles of Market Mapping and Desktop Mapping Research

1

The World of Market Mapping Research

Where should we locate the new office? Where do our customers come from? Which sales region is the most effective? Is there a way to realign the sales territories for better coverage? What international locations have the best profit potential? Where are the best locations for our billboards? Where are the responses to our advertising coming from? What would be the best product mix for a store in Kansas City?

These questions and many more like them characterize the real world of marketing analysis. At the heart of financial success for most companies is the marketing information used to develop insightful corporate strategies and focused tactical decisions. The majority of information used in marketing is geography-specific. Because of this, companies that can visualize and manipulate geographic-based data have a distinct competitive advantage over those that can't.

Until recently, the power to visualize geographic data with the help of computerized marketing and mapping programs was available only to megacorporations with prohibitively expensive and complex mainframe applications. At best, the sales and marketing people in other companies had to rely on outdated reports, convoluted statistics, and indecipherable charts to make informed answers to these questions. At worst, because many marketers can't afford complex research efforts, expensive mainframes, or full-time research departments, geographic market analysis was done by the seat of the pants, if at all.

Now, with desktop mapping programs and a wealth of commercial databases available for ordinary personal computers, companies of any size can implement a cost-effective geographic research program, complete with captivating maps and sophisticated data representations. These personal computing tools put the marketing world at the fingertips of any businessperson so better decisions can be made and a competitive edge can be maintained.

Maps Work Better than Conventional Data Display Methods

A simple example will convince you why maps can help you make better decisions and how you'll be able to see information in your data that is not possible using standard graphs, charts, or listings.

For a moment, consider you are the sales manager for a company that distributes burglar alarms. You are responsible for the region around San Francisco, California. Like most sales mangers, you evaluate reports that include listings of customers by territory and other periodic reports of company sales data. And, like most businesspeople, you already have access to a personal computer, a spreadsheet program, and a database of information on your customers. One of the reports you review every month looks like the example in Fig. 1-1.

REPORT: AUGUST SALES BY CUSTOMER NAME - REPORT DATE 10/4					
CUSTOMER NAME	**ADDRESS**	**ZIP**	**$SALE**	**DATE**	**SALESPERSON**
APPLIANCE MART	33 CERVANTES BLVD	94123	$3563.00	3/5	TED
BUZZ ELECTRONICS	1402 PINE ST	94109	$7352.00	3/21	JANICE
DREAMTIME ADVERTISING	1312 POLK ST	94109	$6345.00	3/14	JOHN
ESOTERIC AUDIO	417 HYDE ST	94109	$5273.00	3/12	TED
EUROPA SALON	55 FLORENCE ST	94103	$5134.00	3/4	TED
EUROPA SALON II	325 FRANCISCO ST	94103	$3213.00	3/28	JOHN
FLOWING FABRICS	1203 SUTTER ST	94109	$2326.00	3/16	JANICE
INFOCOMP COMPUTER	2501 CHESTNUT ST	94123	$9011.00	3/8	TED
JERRY'S COSMETICS	1242 MASON ST	94108	$1289.00	3/2	JOHN
MAC'S PLACE	749 LEAVENWORTH	94109	$2161.00	3/30	JANICE
METRO VIDEO	2199 CHESTNUT ST	94123	$4454.00	3/21	JOHN
MOVIE MOVIE	6 NORTH POINT ST	94133	$2518.00	3/27	JANICE
MY BEAUTIFUL LAUNDRETTE	512 POLK ST	94102	$2482.00	3/11	TED
ROCK'N RECORDS, INC.	1255 MASON ST	94108	$8954.00	3/19	SPLIT: TED/JANICE
SUSIE'S DEALS	1111 CALIFORNIA ST	94108	$4896.00	3/12	JANICE
TED'S TIRES	219 OCTAVIA ST	94102	$5258.00	3/31	TED
THE GOLDEN SWAN	873 BAKER ST	94115	$6389.00	3/1	TED
THE LEATHER LOOK	1761 SACRAMENTO	94108	$918.00	3/18	JANICE
END REPORT					

Figure 1-1. A report showing alarm sales by customer name.

Using the database program on your personal computer, you can sort the data many ways: by name, by zip code, or by the area code of the telephone number. But what does this tell you? Look at the listing in Fig. 1-2 of the same report sorted in zip code order. Do you really know anything more than you knew before? Well, you know which customers are in the same zip code area—that's something, but not much.

You could chart the data as a pie chart so the data would look something like Fig. 1-3.

The graph is clear and concise, but this type of chart still doesn't tell you much, unless you know the locations of the zip codes. In order to understand the chart of zip codes, you need to look at a map and plot out each zip code by hand. If you only had a directory that showed all the zip codes and addresses in San Francisco so you could find them quickly. Well, it's possible. With a desktop mapping program, you can display all your data by zip code with a single command.

REPORT: AUGUST SALES BY CUSTOMER NAME

CUSTOMER NAME	ADDRESS	ZIP	$SALE	DATE	SALESPERSON
MY BEAUTIFUL LAUNDRETTE	512 POLK ST	94102	$2482.00	3/11	TED
TED'S TIRES	219 OCTAVIA ST	94102	$5258.00	3/31	TED
EUROPA SALON	55 FLORENCE ST	94103	$5134.00	3/4	TED
EUROPA SALON II	325 FRANCISCO ST	94103	$3213.00	3/28	JOHN
JERRY'S COSMETICS	1242 MASON ST	94108	$1289.00	3/2	JOHN
THE LEATHER LOOK	1761 SACRAMENTO	94108	$918.00	3/18	JANICE
ROCK'N RECORDS, INC.	1255 MASON ST	94108	$8954.00	3/19	SPLIT: TED/JANICE
SUSIE'S DEALS	1111 CALIFORNIA	94108	$4896.00	3/12	JANICE
BUZZ ELECTRONICS	1402 PINE ST	94109	$7352.00	3/21	JANICE
DREAMTIME ADVERTISING	1312 POLK ST	94109	$6345.00	3/14	JOHN
ESOTERIC AUDIO	417 HYDE ST	94109	$5273.00	3/12	TED
FLOWING FABRICS	1203 SUTTER ST	94109	$2326.00	3/16	JANICE
MAC'S PLACE	749 LEAVENWORTH	94109	$2161.00	3/30	JANICE
THE GOLDEN SWAN	873 BAKER ST	94115	$6389.00	3/1	TED
APPLIANCE MART	33 CERVANTES BLVD	94123	$3563.00	3/5	TED
INFOCOMP COMPUTER	2501 CHESTNUT ST	94123	$9011.00	3/8	TED
METRO VIDEO	2199 CHESTNUT ST	94123	$4454.00	3/21	JOHN
MOVIE MOVIE	6 NORTH POINT ST	94133	$2518.00	3/27	JANICE

END REPORT

Figure 1-2. A report showing alarm sales by zip code.

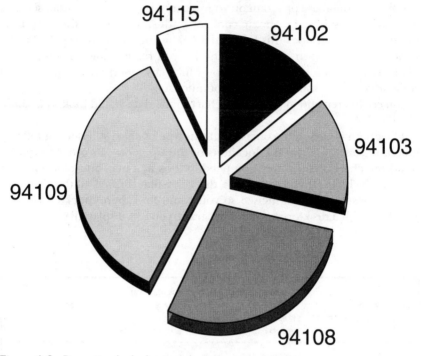

Figure 1-3. Proportional sales by zip code.

Fig. 1-4 is the same data represented on a simple market map produced with a desktop mapping program. You instantly see that most of your customers are in a few clusters.

As you examine the map, you wonder why there are no customers in the western part of the city. You know there are plenty of potential customers in that area. So, you pull up the files of call reports from your sales team and make a map of the calls. Interesting. No one is making calls to the western part of the city. In fact, most of the sales are being made within walking distance of the office. Well, it's time to do something about that. . . .

None of these spatial relationships displayed in the map are readily apparent in the simple spreadsheet or database reports of your data, and you have been studying these listings for months. It is simply impossible to understand the relationships in geographic data by looking at listings. The new insights into your data when displayed on a map leads you to ask questions that make a difference in understanding your business.

After completing your market mapping analysis, you call a sales meeting and give each salesperson a copy of the maps. (It's easy, because you just print the maps on your office printer.) You point out that no one is covering the western part of the city. The salespeople weren't aware of this either.

Now, with the maps, they can do a better job of covering the city and generate new sales in the process—and all because your raw data was transformed into visual information. The information was always there in the data—you just couldn't see it before.

This is the power of desktop mapping. Even in this simple example it is apparent that there are many relationships in business data that can only be visualized in terms of geographic distributions. For most marketing applications, informational maps are superior to nongeographic computer reports like those produced by spreadsheets and database management programs, because you can see relationships in the data that aren't apparent by reviewing listings. It is also possible to summarize large quantities of data on a map that are not easily consolidated in database reports or spreadsheet formats.

Of course, you could have completed the maps by hand, using push pins or markers and overlays to display the customers and territories. This would be slow, and only limited visualization of the data would be possible. The power of desktop mapping eliminates the need to redraw maps each time you make revisions and enables you to easily associate multiple databases on one map. In addition, the storage, retrieval, and display of maps are

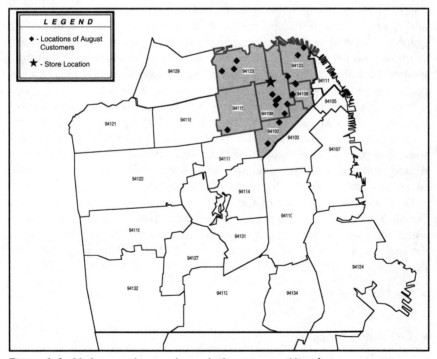

Figure 1-4. Market map showing alarm sales by customer address.[1]

made more efficient. High-quality maps can be easily printed out for distribution to other people or projected from slides in formal presentations. Most importantly, desktop mapping enables you to ask "what-if" type questions about geographic distributions that aren't feasible using a paper map or standard personal computer software.

Market Mapping Is One Application of Desktop Mapping Software

The first mapping software was introduced in the mid-1970s on mainframes and minicomputers, but the process of getting data in and out of large-scale computer systems was expensive in terms of time and money. The first desktop mapping programs linking maps with data on a personal computer were introduced in the 1980s. Desktop mapping is formally defined as the display, analysis, and management of geographic-based data using desktop workstations or personal computers.

Compared to host-based mapping programs on minicomputers and mainframes, desktop mapping costs less for hardware, software, and training. Desktop mapping makes it faster and more convenient to create maps and queries. Because today's personal computers are better at displaying graphic information, the current desktop mapping programs have as much or more power than the programs on mainframes—and there are routines for getting information from mainframe databases so data from any computer can be incorporated into desktop mapping analyses.

It doesn't matter if the personal computer is an IBM-PC or compatible computer or an Apple Macintosh. There are desktop mapping programs for all major personal computer platforms and operating systems, and some companies make mapping software for multiple platforms. The new desktop-based mapping systems are easy to use and affordable—even casual users can display colorful, informative maps in a matter of minutes.

Desktop mapping enhances the ability to work with and understand data. People using desktop mapping software can manipulate and query data using an easy-to-understand geographic interface. The applications for desktop mapping are diverse and numerous. Many of the applications are directly applicable to government requirements and include:

- Land-use Planning
- Crime Analysis
- Regional Planning
- Urban Transit Planning

- Risk Analysis by Locations
- Zoning Administration
- Redistricting of Legislative Divisions or School Districts
- Environmental Studies

But the uses for desktop mapping are not restricted to government applications, even though government agencies have been in the forefront in mastering desktop mapping technology. There are also military, scientific research, banking, insurance, and, of course, many general business applications of desktop mapping technology.

We refer to the major application of desktop mapping research used in business as *market mapping*. Market mapping is the process of using desktop mapping software to display geographic-based data to make better sales and marketing decisions.

Almost every decision in business involves markets. Markets are the consumers, companies, and customers to whom we sell our products. All markets have geographical locations and distributions. In fact, as mentioned before, most data in business involves geographic references. Customers have addresses and phone numbers. Stores have locations. Sales offices service territories. Advertising channels have demographics. Distribution systems use roads and airports. Almost every aspect of getting a product to a customer involves geography—and this means maps can be used to represent the marketing system of any company.

Market maps are geared specifically to identifying and analyzing market information. Through market maps produced with desktop mapping software, it is possible to complete market-related analyses that include:

- Sales Territory Management
- Target Marketing
- Site Selection for Offices and Stores
- Media Planning
- Sales Prospecting
- Trade Area Analysis
- Distribution Planning
- Product Mix Comparisons by Geographic Area
- Competitive Analysis
- Buying Trends of Consumers
- Modeling of Market, Sales, and Distribution Alternatives
- Mailing Lists and Advertising Responses

- Test Marketing
- Sales Call Trip Planning
- Presentations to Customers, Managers, and Industry Analysts

This list is by no means comprehensive. Companies continue to think of more innovative ways to use market maps to display information on customers, consumer behaviors, and sales statistics. From this list alone, however, it is apparent that market mapping could have an influence on most of the major decisions made in business every day.

Businesses in the Know Use Market Mapping to Gain a Competitive Advantage

We are only beginning to understand the wisdom in the old adage "a picture is worth a thousand words." Visualizing market data—through charts, graphs, pictures, and now maps—is one way to simplify the representation and management of data that proliferates at an incomprehensible rate. Data visualization technologies are among the fastest growing and most rapidly developing technological segments of the computer industry—and desktop mapping software is one of the key technologies for visualizing markets and business data.

Using maps to represent marketing data is a powerful way of understanding and communicating complex demographic and geographic relationships. Making demographic data and population trends understandable is a central objective of market mapping research. As we've already illustrated on a simple level, with desktop mapping software and the market maps created, it is possible to manage, analyze, and present your marketing data in ways you've never considered before. Market mapping empowers you to identify unexplored marketing opportunities for increased sales and profitability.

There are foresightful businesses that already use market mapping to perform most of the applications of market mapping described above. These companies range from small retail operations to Fortune 100 corporations. In fact, large corporations have been using market mapping to make better decisions about marketing resources, first with mainframes and now from the desktop, since the 1970s, though it's only in the last few years that the technology has begun to receive widespread acceptance.

Some of the uses for market mapping are unique to specific industries. For example, Federal Express and UPS use mapping programs to direct their trucks along the fastest routes, thus improving customer service and reducing delivery costs. The feed division of Hubbard Milling in Minnesota uses mapping programs to visualize the amount of feed the company can sell in a twelve-state area, based on the tabulation of animal populations and the estimated consumption of each species by county. Comdisco, a firm that specializes in data processing disaster recoveries, uses mapping software to locate new emergency-service centers. Oil industry giants Shell and

---

EXAMPLES OF MARKET MAPPING APPLICATIONS

Retail Stores and Restaurants	• Identifying Locations Based on Area Demographics and Competition • Choosing Advertising Media • Selecting Mailing Lists • Displaying Customer Locations • Analyzing Sales by City, Store, or Salesperson
Manufacturers	• Choosing Manufacturing Sites Based on Costs of Doing Business (Labor, Utilities, Taxes, Property, etc.) • Tracking Assets and Streamlining Product Storage and Delivery • Choosing Advertising Media • Displaying Sales by Office, City, or Salesperson • Analyzing Product Success by City, State, or Region • Understanding Regional Variation in Product Preferences • Analyzing Distribution System
Banks & Financial Institutions	• Identifying Locations Based on Customer Demographics and Competition • Tracking Property Values and Property Loans • Tracking and Managing "Bank Owned" Assets
Insurance Companies	• Pricing Insurance Based on Demand and Area Demographics • Comparing One Area's Pricing and Incidence of Claims to Another
Distributors	• Identifying Potential Customers Locally, State-Wide, Country-Wide, and Internationally

Figure 1-5. Diagram of mapping applications.

Amoco not only use computerized maps for geological analysis related to oil exploration, but also employ market maps to find optimum locations for gas stations in new suburban developments.

Other market mapping possibilities are generic to businesses of all sizes, including the way Manufacturers and Traders Trust analyzes demographic data to display concentrations of customers meeting age and income criteria that can be used to develop new banking products and promotions for specific market groups. A Buffalo-based financial institution also uses mapping software to scout out new branch locations. In similar ways, upscale retailers such as Tiffany's, I. Magnin, and Bloomingdales use information from market maps to analyze lifestyle variables and develop targeted marketing programs. The Arlington, Illinois *Daily Herald* uses demographic data, combined with industry-specific purchasing indexes to show advertisers where their potential customers are in the six counties surrounding Chicago. The paper uses this information to show the percentage of buyers that can be reached and the cost-effectiveness of buying ads in the *Daily Herald*. Apple Computer uses market mapping software to perform geographic planning for sales territories, field resource deployment, and targeting marketing programs. And major consumer-oriented companies like Coca-Cola, 3-M, Colgate Palmolive, and AT&T already employ mapping-based analysis in market research related to consumer purchasing patterns and buying habits.

One of the most market-driven industries of all is advertising. It's no surprise that some of the largest and most successful advertising agencies have adopted market mapping to analyze advertising demographics and establish new marketing opportunities for their clients. The list of agencies using market mapping reads like a "who's who" in advertising, including J. Walter Thompson, Ogilvy & Mather, Saatchi & Saatchi, BBDO, and Foote Cone & Belding, among others. The same can be said for market research firms and major business consulting firms, including pacesetters like Andersen Consulting, Dun & Bradstreet, McKinsey & Co., and DRI/McGraw-Hill. Even local agencies and consultants have jumped on the bandwagon and are using market mapping to expand the services and information provided to their clients. Some of these agencies previously employed the tedious process of producing hand-drawn maps and tissue overlays to present demographic data to their customers—now they can present more options and better-quality graphics in a fraction of the time.

Think of any major market-driven company and there is a market mapping possibility that can assist managers in making better decisions, improving the impact of advertising expenditures and distribution decisions, obtaining a competitive advantage, or reducing the time to market.

Though many companies using market mapping techniques are large and influential, the technology is as important to smaller businesses as it is to larger ones—perhaps more so, because the smaller the company, the less capital there is to fall back on when things go wrong. Small companies often need to compete with larger companies—and market mapping can help smaller competitors identify niche opportunities to make this possible.

There are many small companies that have already reaped the benefits that market mapping can provide. These include retailers who use this technology to identify new locations, improve advertising effectiveness, or do a better job of targeting direct mail and telemarketing efforts. There are small manufacturers who have located less expensive distribution routes and identified cost-effective warehousing alternatives. And, it includes home-based entrepreneurs who use market mapping to stimulate new product ideas.

Market Mapping Possibilities
Compared to Traditional Alternatives

To see how market mapping can be used in a growing company more effectively than traditional report-based research, let's consider a hypothetical case study comparing two companies—one that uses market mapping and one that doesn't.

Jennifer and Jason had an idea for a store called "Earth Works," a retail store that specializes in natural, environmentally safe products for the home and offers a number of gift-oriented products as well, including "nature-oriented" retail items including T-shirts, jewelry, cards (on recycled paper, of course), and books on nature, ecology, and the environment. Susan and George had the idea for a similar store called "Natural Affair" in another city.

Susan and George did what most new retailers do when they get started. They drove around and looked for a location for the store. This was both time-consuming and risky. So, after looking around for a few weeks, they finally asked a broker to find a location for them. Of course, the broker showed them the sites that paid the best commissions and incentives, not necessarily the right sites for their store. The information on actual demographics, traffic, and competing stores in the area was highly subjective. The limited demographic information and reports provided to them were difficult to decipher and comprehend. Finally, they chose a store location on gut feeling and instinct—and because the leasing terms were affordable.

Jennifer and Jason, on the other hand, were avid readers of computer magazines and knew about desktop mapping and on-line marketing research. They decided to use market mapping on their home computer to help them find a suitable location for their store.

After spending a day working through the training demonstrations, they were ready to load the data which they purchased from a commercial information service. Using on-line statistics, Jennifer and Jason found that other nature-oriented stores did well in mid- to high-income areas where the heads-of-household were predominantly college-educated. So, they looked for a location with similar demographics in their area. Then, they overlaid a map of the existing stores and malls in these targeted regions. Finally, they found three general areas worth looking into. After checking out space availability, they found the perfect space in one of their selected areas. The whole process took only a couple of days—compared to a couple of months for Susan and George.

The Earth Works store did great, partly because the demographics and traffic flow patterns Jennifer and Jason had discovered through market mapping proved a perfect match with the product mix and location of the store. But their market mapping efforts didn't stop there. Each customer purchase was logged in a computer database that included the customers' address and phone number. Using market mapping, they used the information from the database to create maps of customer preferences and locations. It was easy for them to see that many of their customers were driving long distances to come to the store. Most of these customers were from an affluent community in another county. Within a year they considered open-

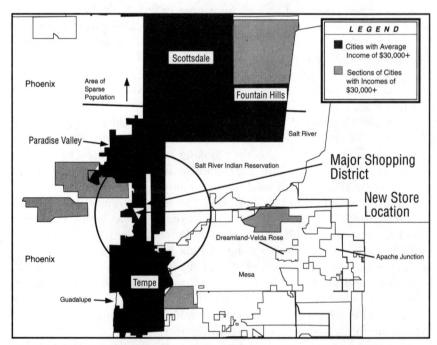

Figure 1-6. A market map showing the selected location of the Earth Works store in relation to income demographics.[2]

ing another store. Once again, they used the on-line data sources and market maps to help them choose their second location, this time in a county with which they were largely unfamiliar.

At the same time, Susan and George were struggling just to make ends meet. They did everything possible to get people in the store—special deals, more newspaper advertising, and even balloons on the outside of the store. Nothing seemed to work. And the customers that visited the store didn't buy much and complained that prices were too high. Since Susan and George knew they had made a mistake in the location, they began looking for a new store site. They needed to move the store before they went bankrupt.

On the other hand, Jennifer and Jason's two stores were so successful, they began to get requests for catalogs from the friends and relatives of their customers who lived in other cities and states—another opportunity for market mapping. Using new sets of geodemographic data for the United States, they were able to target specific cities and zip codes around the country for customers who might be appropriate targets for their products. They also analyzed commercial mailing lists and other information sources using market mapping and were able to achieve very high success rates with their direct mail efforts.

Jennifer and Jason used market mapping to assess the effectiveness of their other advertising efforts, as well, by mapping responses based on demographics and geographic area. This made it possible to target each advertising dollar more effectively to the publications and television stations that worked best in each location.

Of course, Susan and George, like most small company managers, didn't feel they had enough time or money for marketing research. They were still plowing through listings and statistics looking for a new location for the store. They never saw the trends in the data or the new opportunities—because they couldn't visualize the geographic relationships in their customer databases. In fact, they didn't even keep a customer database. They thought it required too much effort for the potential payback.

Susan and George continued to run Natural Affair by trial and error. Unfortunately, they weren't much better at picking the second location. After a few more months of frustration, they decided to close the store and doggedly returned to their old nine-to-five careers.

Well, Jennifer and Jason had an entirely different life ahead of them. Their company grew and the market mapping opportunities expanded. Since their local stores were so successful, they decided to franchise the stores in other cities and states. Market mapping became a central aspect of locating appropriate market locations and promoting the franchise operation in specifically targeted areas. And training in market mapping research was provided to every franchise owner—so each store was able to target promotions and adjust product mixes for its own market needs.

After a few years establishing Earth Works franchises across the United States, Jennifer and Jason decided to go international. Again, market mapping was there to help them locate the best opportunities and areas, in countries they had never even seen before.

As the company continued to grow, it started manufacturing its own products, developing its own brands and distributing environmentally-safe

Business Results With and Without Market Mapping	
Using Conventional Techniques for Natural Affair	*Using Market Mapping Techniques for Earth Works*
Location found by driving around. *Year One*	Location found by using market mapping software and data based on area income and buying habits.
Struggled to survive: Special sales and incentives used to bring in customers, reducing net profit. *Year Two*	Target mailing to promote store. Customer data tracked and mapped as business grew.
Location finally determined to be unsuitable. Started looking for a better location before money ran out. Store moved to new location. Going out of business sale. Back to nine-to-five jobs. *Year Three*	Second store opened to service targeted customers identified through market mapping. Catalog mailings and ads targeted with market mapping were a great success.
Year Four	Franchising of Earth Works across the United States. Market mapping used to select new store locations by identifying where potential customers live in each city.
	Earth Works went international with the help of market mapping.

Figure 1-7. The progression of Earth Works and Natural Affair.

merchandise through other channels. Market mapping was there through every step—helping them locate inexpensive manufacturing locations, new market niches, and improved distribution facilities. When they established a direct sales force to promote the new product lines to retailers and super-market chains, they used market mapping to establish the territories for best market coverage. As competitors came into the market, they used market mapping to analyze the competitors' locations and distribution strategies. When moving into new market areas, they studied the impact of pricing changes by location and market segment.

Needless to say, the company was frequently written up in major business magazines and newspapers as one of the entrepreneurial success stories of the decade. Jennifer and Jason always credited their success to the power of market mapping.

Market mapping was able to take Jennifer and Jason's Earth Works from garage-based idea to multinational corporation with unceasing aplomb. Susan and George never got Natural Affair off the ground because the geographical data they needed to prosper seemed unavailable to them.

Of course, this story is hypothetical and simplified, but the scenario is plausible. Market mapping can't eliminate all marketing mistakes—but it can certainly help avoid the common ones that have to do with locations, territories, targeting, and distribution. And because market mapping has the potential to change the way you look at your business and your customers, it lets you see new opportunities around every corner. Of course, if you don't take advantage of the opportunities, you can't blame the maps.

Market mapping can be used by any business to its advantage—but it alone will not guarantee success. Even with all the wonderful things market mapping can do for you, we don't want you to be misled—market mapping is no panacea. You still need to implement good ideas. You still need skilled management, adequate capital, and quality products. No mapping program can provide those parts of the successful business equation.

The Need to Understand the Geographic Distribution of Markets

The hypothetical example for Earth Works showed how many aspects of a company's success are rooted in an understanding of markets. These markets can be segmented in many ways—by customer size, by buying criteria, by industry, and by other common, shared properties. In fact, most business success depends on understanding the markets for a product or service and then implementing programs to reach those markets. It's not enough for companies to know their own markets either; they need to understand their competitors' markets as well.

Because of the central role of markets in business, marketers and other businesspeople involved with selling products to people are keenly interested in the distribution, density, mobility, age distribution, and movement of market segments or populations. And because the volume of such data is expanding by orders of magnitude every month, it is imperative that the data can be quickly and easily comprehended if companies are to stay competitive and take advantage of new opportunities. The power of desktop mapping offers an efficient and logical way to do this.

Isn't It Hard to Do?

You probably think that a technology with the potential to change your business will be hard to learn. But market mapping isn't any more difficult to master than learning to use word processing software or an electronic spreadsheet program. The common components to any market mapping system, regardless of computer platform, are conceptually simple, and include:

- *Desktop Mapping Software*—Desktop mapping software is used to manipulate and produce the maps. These programs range from simple to complex.

- *Geographic Data or Base Maps*—Geographic data (also called cartographic data) is the actual representation of locations used for creating the market maps. Various map data is available from the software manufacturers to be compatible with their programs. For example, you may have cartographic files for the United States, for zip code areas, for Europe, or for downtown Cincinnati. The types and detail of the cartographic data you use will depend on the locations you are interested in and the detail you require to display your information.

- *Attribute Data*—The attribute data is the data you are interested in analyzing, which can come from a variety of sources, including commercial databases, your own company records, government sources, and independent studies.

- *A Desktop Computer*—Of course you will need a desktop computer to run the software and process the data. In addition, you will need one or more output devices for displaying the maps, usually a printer or plotter, and a color monitor.

In order to get started in market mapping, you will need to learn some basic mapping terminology and become familiar with the types of maps available for market mapping analyses. In the next chapter we provide the background concepts necessary to understand maps in general. Then, in Chap. 3, we explain the mechanics and technology behind desktop mapping that make market mapping possible. You will become familiar with the

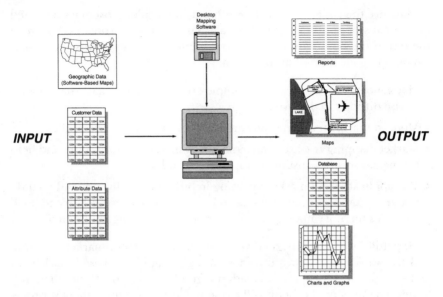

Figure 1-8. The components of a market mapping system.

features, options, and general operation of desktop mapping programs and the mechanics and technology behind desktop mapping.

In Chap. 4, the sources and possibilities for the data used in your market mapping research are revealed. And finally, in Chap. 5, the criteria for choosing the best software and computer equipment to meet your market mapping needs is presented. Then, the basics are put into action and examples of real market mapping applications, complete with step-by-step instructions and sample maps, are provided, to give you a better idea of the kinds of questions you should be asking and answering with market mapping technology. These procedures and examples are contained in Chaps. 6 through 10 of the book.

After reading the book, you will have enough information to explore the possibilities for market mapping in your company on your own and should be convinced that it is a technology you can and must master to be competitive.

Chapter Summary

In this chapter, the underlying advantages of market mapping, compared to traditional ways of viewing data with listings and graphs, have been presented, along with a long list of market mapping possibilities in a wide variety of businesses.

Maps are the easiest way to comprehend and display most market-related data. That's because most market data has geographic roots. As you read the rest of the book, you will want to remember the key points about market mapping elaborated in this chapter:

- Maps allow people to visualize complex relationships in data that are otherwise difficult to discover.

- Modern market mapping software is relatively easy to learn and use.

- Market mapping research can expose new market opportunities and help businesses secure a distinct competitive advantage.

- The applications of market mapping in business are diverse, and include market analysis, competitive research, new product research, trend analysis, sales territory management, distribution planning, and much more.

Hopefully, we have intrigued you with the potential of market mapping and the ways it can help you understand geographically-based markets to make better decisions and take advantage of new opportunities. The following chapters of the book will present the background, theory, procedures, and concrete examples necessary to put the advantages of market mapping to work in your own business research.

2

Mapping Principles and Terminology for Market Mapping

Cartography—The Science of Maps

Mapping—or cartography, as the art and science of mapping is called—has a long and illustrious history. The first maps, produced long before recorded history, were probably lines scratched in the dirt with a stick to describe the locations of food and shelter. Maps were etched in clay tablets used by the Mesopotamians and painted on the tombs of the Pharaohs by Egyptians thousands of years ago. In the third century B.C., Eratosthenes of Alexandria measured the circumference of the earth and was responsible for developments leading to the concepts of longitude and latitude. The first globes were produced and Ptolemy wrote an influential guide to map making, the *Geography*, in the second century B.C. The Romans used maps for administrative and military purposes. The Roman *Orbis Terrarum* became the standard map of the world for many centuries, in spite of its exaggerated representation of the Roman Empire. There is evidence that the Chinese had sophisticated cartographic representations long before these Western accomplishments.

Through the Middle Ages and the Renaissance, hand-printed maps were often elaborate affairs with baroque details on sumptuous papers, but few people could have them. Starting in the fifteenth century, maps could be distributed and printed, although the coloring of maps was still done by hand on the prints. During the seventeenth and eighteenth centuries, France excelled in the development of topographic maps. As exploration continued, more kinds of maps were produced. By the nineteenth century, the development of thematic maps for use in commercial and government applications began to expand. These maps began to use dots, graduated circles, fill patterns, and other methods to represent data.

More recently, the offset lithographic press made available to almost everyone high-quality color maps in the form of elaborate atlases, detailed city maps, accurate road maps, and more. Scientific and technological developments, including aerial photography and satellite information, have improved map details and topographic accuracy. Now we are moving into another new age of mapping possibilities. With desktop mapping and affordable personal computers, the applications of mapping technology are endless.

Mapping has come a long way. Because of the extensive history of cartography, a specialized vocabulary and specific spatial concepts have evolved around maps and map making. These concepts and terms, some of them stemming from ancient Greek and Roman innovations, form the prerequisite knowledge required to master desktop mapping programs. Thus, before you start on your market mapping journey, it's important to take a little time to master the basics. Some of these terms you may remember from school; others will likely be new to you. As you become proficient in market mapping, you will come across them all.

Common Display Attributes of Maps

The word map comes from the Latin *mappa,* meaning cloth or napkin. A *map* is a reduced-size representation of the earth's surface or physical representation of the environment, typically drawn to scale, usually displayed on a flat surface such as paper, or now on a computer monitor. The term *chart* is often used synonymously with the word map, most often to refer to the maps of the oceans used by sailors, or aeronautical maps used by pilots. If a map is of a fairly small area and of a large scale, it is often called a *plan,* such as a house plan or city plan. Information displayed on maps, regardless of size and purpose, has common attributes.

Scale.   First, every map has a scale. Scale is the ratio of distances and areas shown on a map to the corresponding distances and areas on the earth's surface. A large-scale map takes a small plot of land and displays it in detail. A small-scale map shows a large piece of the earth's surface. For example, a small-scale map may have 1 inch represent 500 miles. A large scale map may have 1 inch represent 1 mile. The term small-scale and large-scale are relative; there is no hard-and-fast dividing line between maps called small-scale and large-scale. Scales can be represented as a ratio, such as 1 inch:1000 miles, or by using a graphic scale such as:

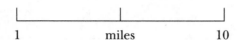

1   miles   10

The advantage of graphic scale representations is that they remain true even if a map is enlarged or reduced photographically.

The scale of a map can be accurate, proportional, exaggerated, or reduced. This is important, because symbols used on maps and the details of the representation all vary with scale. Scale is also important in the interpretation of maps—so it is important to know whether the scale is a true representation of distance, or a contrived representation used to make a point. For example, maps used to show locations in real estate advertisements often use distorted scales to make houses look closer than they actually are to a mall, high school, or influential part of town. In market mapping, you may want to adjust the scale of an area to reflect the importance of the area. For example, the representation of states with the most sales becomes larger than the states with less sales. Of course, it is important to remember that these maps are not geographically or cartographically accurate—you wouldn't want to make a precise location decision based on a distorted scale.

Grids and Coordinate Systems.   In order to find things on a map, a system of lines is often used to help readers locate specific items or locations. The crisscross of reference lines is called a *grid*. The vertical and horizontal lines of the grid cross at points called *coordinates*. Map coordinates are also referred to as *Cartesian coordinates,* representations of locations by x and y coordinates on planes (flat surfaces).

One of the most familiar coordinate systems used to locate geographic elements is that of *longitude* and *latitude*. The imaginary *parallel circles* that run around the earth from east to west indicate degrees of latitude. The latitude of 0° is the equator. Latitude 90°N is the north pole. Latitude 90°S is the south pole. The imaginary line that connects the north and south poles is called a *meridian*. Meridians are half-circles around the earth that represent degrees of longitude. For historical reasons related to the observatory built to assist explorers and navigators, the meridian that runs through Greenwich, England is assigned longitude of 0°. This is often called the Prime Meridian. The degrees of longitude are specified as degrees east or west of the Prime Meridian. For example, Washington D.C. is at 77°W of Greenwich.

One degree of latitude is always about 69 miles or 110 kilometers. However, a degree of longitude varies from 69.171 miles at the equator to 0 miles at the poles, based on the curvature of the earth. Thus, lines of longitude cannot be accurately used for measuring space, only for locating position.

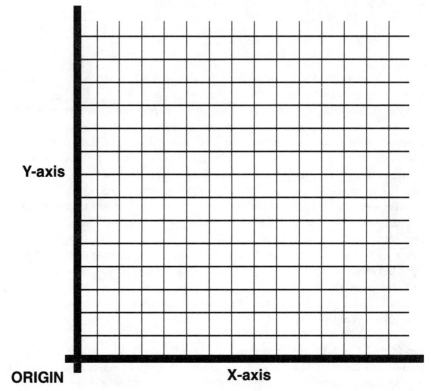

Figure 2-1. A Cartesian coordinate system locates positions by using *x* and *y* coordinates on a grid.

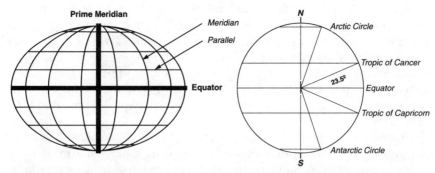

Figure 2-2. Parallels of latitude and meridians of longitude are used to identify any point on the earth.

No two places on earth have the same longitude and latitude coordinates, making the system very precise. Longitude and latitude coordinates can be conventionally represented as degrees, minutes, and seconds. There are 60 seconds in a minute and 60 minutes in a degree. The first series of numbers represents longitude and the second series represents latitude, as in:

78° 37′ 32°W and 39° 22′ 30°N

East, west, north, and south (E, W, N, and S) are not always specified if the location of the map area on the globe is obvious. South and west identifiers are specified in some notations as negative numbers. In computer programs, conventional longitude and latitude coordinates are often specified in decimal degrees, like 78.26° and 39.47°. The formula for converting standard notations into decimal degrees is:

$$\text{Decimal degrees} = \text{Degrees} + \frac{(\text{Minutes} + \text{Seconds}/60)}{60}$$

You probably won't need to worry about this conversion for most of your market mapping work, but in case you find a program that doesn't do the conversions for you, the formula may prove useful.

In most mapping software, data must be assigned longitudinal and latitudinal coordinates, or another coordinate system, in order to be represented by the map. The assignment of such coordinates is called *geocoding*. If a data element does not have a geocode, it cannot be represented on a map, because the computer will not know where to place it on the grid. (We will have more to say about geocoding in the upcoming chapters.)

There are other coordinate systems you will find used in maps as well, including the letters and numbers used to represent the grid of a highway map or city street map. Some mapping programs allow you to specify custom coordinate systems using your own identifiers.

Boundaries. Almost all maps represent boundaries with lines—whether solid, dashed, or dotted. Conventionally, the thicker or more predominant the boundary line, the more important the boundary. Boundaries can represent more than countries, states and towns—boundary lines can also represent sales territories, a booth space in a trade show, or the location of a new building site.

Direction. The orientation and directions shown in maps are important. Though north is usually toward the top of a map, this is not always the case, especially in small-scale maps representing retail locations, trade show booths, or construction projects. In these cases, the maps may be oriented for readability. Because of this, most maps display the compass points to orient the reader to the actual positions of north and south. A bearing is the compass direction of a geographic location.

Distance.   All maps represent distances. Some maps represent distances proportionately and in scale; others do not. When you interpret a market map, it is important to understand the distances being represented; otherwise, the data can be misunderstood and inappropriate decisions can be made.

The compass direction is not the shortest line between two points on the earth—nor does a straight line on a map always represent the shortest distance between two points on the map. This depends on the projection, which we'll talk about later. The shortest line between two points on the earth is along a great circle, and an azimuth is the direction along a great circle at its starting point. A great circle is simply a circle whose center is at the center of the earth and whose radius is the radius of the earth. Of the lines of latitude, only the equator is a great circle. However, all the lines of longitude form great circles when joined with their 180-degree opposites. You need to know this, because most mapping programs measure distance along a great circle, even though the great circle arcs may not be shown as straight lines on a map. When you interpret a large map, you must remember that the distance or scale shown is not always constant.

Symbols and Conventions.   Because some things cannot be represented in scale on a map, map makers use symbols to represent details. Symbols are a pictorial shorthand for representing objects or concepts. Though there are no universal symbols required for maps, there are many symbols and map conventions that are nearly universal, including symbols for roads, railroad crossings, tunnels, boundaries, and other elements. The use of larger type to represent larger populations is also a commonly accepted mapping convention. Desktop mapping programs offer a wide range of symbols, and some programs allow you to develop your own symbols for specific purposes.

Colors.   Colors are part of map symbology and representations. Colors have both conventional and thematic uses in maps. Conventionally, colors represent different kinds of terrain or different countries. In other maps, colors can represent populations, buying preferences, or almost any data element with geographic distribution. Colors can make things immediately obvious that are otherwise difficult to visualize.

Hatch Patterns.   When colors are unavailable or inappropriate, hatch patterns and shading (also called fill patterns) can be used to represent ter-

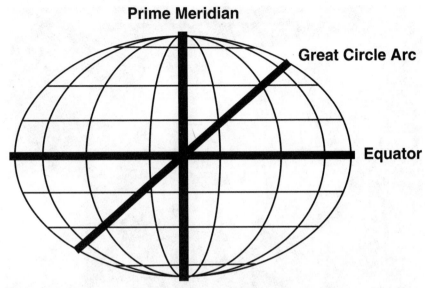

Figure 2-3. The shortest distance between two points on the earth is along a great circle.

rain, populations, borders, or any other mapping element. In computer mapping programs there are a wide variety of hatch and fill patterns available. Sometimes hatch patterns and colors can be combined to represent multiple geographic attributes on one map.

Isograms.   Isograms, also called isolines, are any lines that connect points of equal values. Contour lines are one kind of isogram. In market mapping there are two kinds of isograms that you may choose to use when representing data. Isorithms are isograms that show "how much"—for example, the amount of rainfall, the elevation, or the average temperature. Isopleths, the other kind of isogram, tells "how many"—for example, people, divorces, sales, or stores.

Map Legends.   The legend of a map lists the meanings of map symbols, colors, and other conventions used on a particular map. The clarity and completeness of legends is important, especially if many elements will be represented on a map. Legends may also include a compass indication and the scale of the map. When viewing any map, it is important to pay attention to the legend and the scale indication first, even if you think you are familiar with the symbols and territory. Any desktop mapping program used for market mapping should be able to produce an appropriately detailed legend.

Relief and Contour.   Some maps show the height, shape, and gradient of land surfaces—"the relief of the surface." Relief can be represented by col-

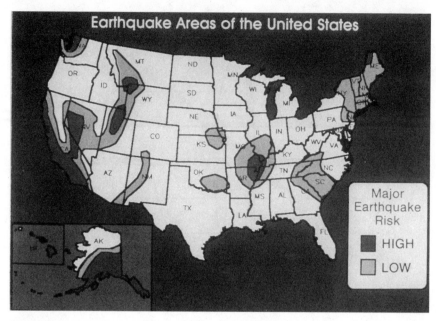

Figure 2-4. A sample map that includes isograms, a legend, and other common map symbols.[3]

ors and lines or recreated in a three-dimensional model. Contour lines are used to indicate elevations on maps, especially on topographic maps. A contour line joins all points in the same height above sea level. On a topographic map, contour lines crowded together on a map indicate a steep slope. Surveyed points may be specified on maps as well, to indicate elevations and precise physical locations.

Types of Maps

All maps share the attribute of representing geographical data, and most maps share a great many other common features as described already. In spite of their similarities, however, there are still many different types of maps with an even greater number of different purposes. There are maps that represent terrain, topographic maps that provide detailed relief information using contour lines and shading, cadastral maps that show land boundaries and subdivisions, and political maps that indicate political boundaries of countries, states, and cities. There are also aeronautical and navigational charts, geologic maps, general atlases, and road maps. There are even flow maps that indicate movements of entities or goods from one geographic location to another.

Most of the maps you will work with in market mapping are part of a class of maps called *thematic maps*. Thematic maps normally illustrate data through the use of visual techniques such as shades, symbols, three-dimensional effects, charts, and dots. Through the use of colors, variable-sized symbols, and different hatch patterns, the relative value of a "theme" can be represented along with its geographic distribution. Multiple "themes" can be displayed on maps as well by using various combinations of symbols, shapes, colors, etc. Of course, thematic maps may be combined with one of the other types of maps, such as political or geographic, to complete a specific analysis.

Types of Thematic Maps Useful in Market Mapping

The kinds of thematic maps available for market mapping research are diverse. Each desktop mapping program offers a different combination of mapping possibilities. Thematic maps can usually represent three kinds of data parameters in various combinations, including proportions, data ranges, and data density. Themes can be created for regions in a map, for lines on a map, or for points on a map. Some of the most common kinds of thematic maps, including hatch maps, density maps, pie maps, proportional symbol maps, prism maps, post maps, multimaps, pin maps, and ranged line maps are illustrated on the next few pages.

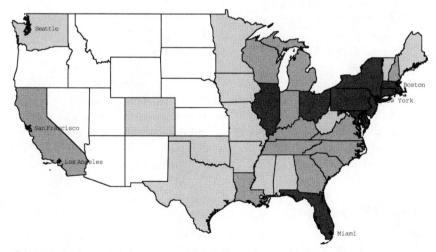

Figure 2-5. Hatch maps display fill colors and patterns for areas as a way to represent data ranges.[4]

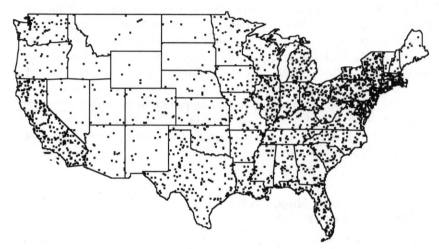

Figure 2-6. In a density map, dots are drawn in each area to indicate the quantity of a variable. Quantities in small areas appear more dense than the same quantities in large areas.[5]

Map Projections and Map Distortion

In spite of their potential for clarity and aesthetic appeal, all maps are distorted in some way. First, they are smaller than the actual geography they represent—so they are an abstraction, not an isomorphic representation of reality. Second, because maps are mostly flat, and because the world is mostly round, the representation of the earth's rounded surface on a flat piece of paper or a computer monitor is necessarily distorted.

The amount of distortion in a map depends on the projection used to create the map. A projection is produced by flattening the globe's spherical surface into a map. To do this, a conceptual transparent globe used to create a map can be placed in many possible angles relative to a source of light. The globe surface is then projected onto a plane (such as a sheet of paper) or a curved form that can be cut and laid flat. Most projections are based on one of the three basic projection surfaces—planar, conical, and cylindrical, as shown in Fig. 2-13.

Types of Projections

You will come across many types of projection possibilities in your mapping endeavors. Each projection type has strengths and weaknesses. In any projection, minimum distortion is found in the area of closest contact, conceptually, between the globe and the projection surface.

Planar projections are made by projecting the globe onto a plane with a *tangent* touching the globe at any point. These projections are also called azimuthal projections. Azimuthal projections correctly show the direction (azimuth) between all points and the center of the projection.

There are three basic kinds of *azimuthal* projections, depending on the position of the light source used to make the projection—*orthographic* projections that have the light source at theoretical infinity, *stereographic* projections where the light source is on the earth's surface opposite the tangent point, and *gnomonic,* where the light source is at the theoretical center of the earth.

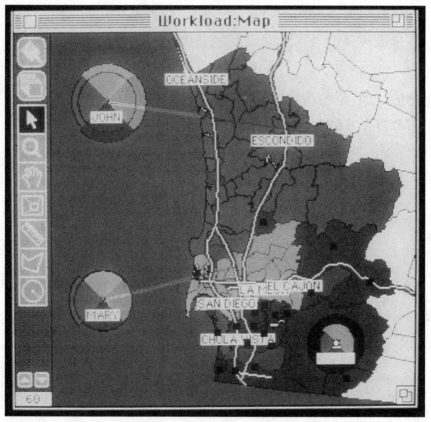

Figure 2-7. Maps can be combined with pie charts to display two or more data variables for each area.[6]

Figure 2-8. Proportional symbols can be used in thematic maps to represent variable data associated with particular areas.

Orthographic projections result in realistic looking globes. The distortion is least around the tangent point and most at the edges of the global representation. Stereographic projections that preserve the shapes of corresponding places on the globe are called *conformal* or *orthomorphic* projections. Conformal projections preserve angles and shapes, but not sizes, over large areas. Parallels and meridians in these projections are at right angles to each other and have the correct positions in these maps, but, to achieve this, the scales of the maps vary a great deal from place to place—and thus, their utility is limited to small areas.

Gnomonic projections maintain straight lines of latitude and longitude, but present large distortions in size and shape. These projections are useful in navigation and the plotting of seismic waves.

The planar projection called the Lambert azimuthal equal-area projection is good for viewing hemispheres and for continent maps. This type of projection is one in which every point is shown, not only at the correct distance, but also in the correct direction from the center point. Equal-area projections preserve the relative areas of objects; thus, two countries with the same number of square miles would occupy approximately the same space in an equal-area projection.

Cylindrical and conical projections have the greatest areas of contact with the globe; because of this, these projections have minimum distortion. A cylindrical projection occurs when the globe is surrounded by a cylinder. The light source can be a point at the center of the globe, or it can be along the polar axis like a straight light-bulb filament. The polar-axis light source produces a projection called the cylindrical equal-area projection. This projection can show the entire world, but the polar regions become quite distorted, forming a long line at the top of the map. If the light source is at the center of the globe, it is called central cylindrical projection. Sizes become greatly exaggerated toward the polar regions again, although the poles themselves cannot be shown.

Cylindrical projections are characterized by straight parallels of equal length with only one parallel being the correct scale; meridians of equal space and length; meridians and parallels intersecting at right angles; and

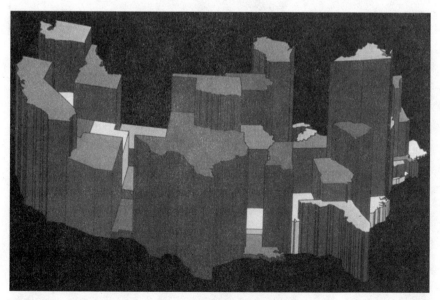

Figure 2-9. Prism maps use height as a way of representing variable proportions of data.[7]

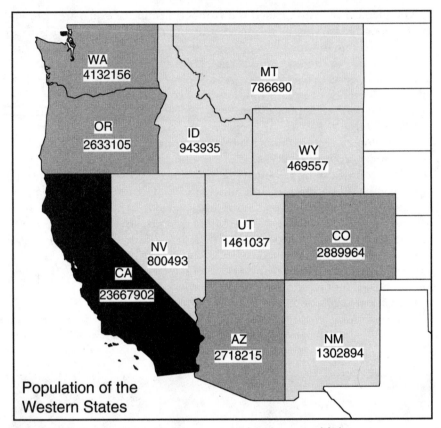

Figure 2-10. In a post map, data values are posted on the map as labels.

basically rectangular images. There are also transverse and oblique cylindrical projections with different characteristics, such as curved meridians. Normal cylindrical projections are appealing because the rectangular grid is easy to use. Gall's stereographic cylindrical projection is a compromise projection that distorts everything a little bit and preserves no single property. This is different from other projections that attempt to preserve one aspect of the map, such as size, scale, or shape, in favor of another. There are some kinds of equal-distant projections that maintain scale between one or two points and all other points on the map, although no projection preserves scale throughout a map.

Conic projections are produced by projecting the grid system on a cone tangent onto a globe along any small circle, usually a mid-latitude parallel. The meridians radiate as straight lines from their true positions, and the parallels are shown as concentric circles. Errors of scale in conic projections are severe enough to reduce the usefulness of the projections. A conic variation, called a secant projection, that has the cone intersect the globe in two parallels produces less scale error. The secant projection is used for displaying mid-latitude countries and continents, especially those in the east and west.

By spacing the parallels, a secant projection can be made equal-area. The Albers equal-area conic projection, for example, is considered one of the best projections of the United States. The secant projection can also be made conformal, as in the Lambert conformal conic projection, which has relatively straight azimuths—that is, a straight line on the earth (actually part of a great circle through the earth) appears relatively straight on the map. There are also polyconic projections that use many cones, each intersecting the earth's surface at a different latitude.

Figure 2-11. Two maps shown on separate layers at the same time allow details to be displayed for a targeted area.[8]

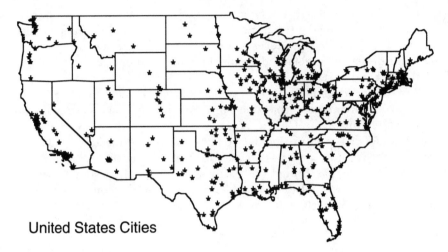

United States Cities

Figure 2-12. Pin maps point out specific locations on a map, using symbols to represent the data elements.[9]

Modified Projections

Modified projections may combine aspects of planar, conical, and cylindrical projections to hold overall distortion to a minimum, or to make a map look aesthetically pleasing. One such projection, Goode's Interrupted Homolosine Projection of the globe, is a good example of a modified projection that

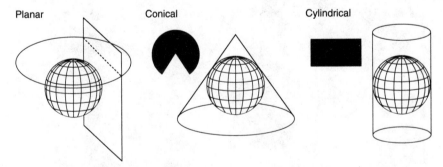

Planar   Conical   Cylindrical

Figure 2-13. To make a flat map, the spherical surface of the earth is projected onto a plane, a cone, or a cylinder as shown. The illustration shows some commonly used orientations of globe and projection surface, although many other orientations are possible. The tangent area in each projection (the area touching the projection surface) is the area of least distortion in the resulting map.

Figure 2-14. An orthographic projection of the earth.[10]

interrupts the projection of the oceans in order to keep distortion of the land masses to a minimum. Another popular modified projection is the Mercator projection, which is a modification of a standard cylindrical projection developed in the sixteenth century by Flemish cartographer Gerardus Mercator. In order to maintain correct proportions, the parallels are spaced at increas-

Figure 2-15. Notice the exaggerated size of the polar regions and the parallel grid in this Mercator projection of the world.

ing intervals toward the poles. The polar regions end up severely exaggerated, but the projection preserves the compass directions as straight lines ideal for navigation. There are various adaptations of the standard Mercator projection as well, involving different tangents and parallels.

The more land being represented in a projection, the more the distortion. It is important to realize the weaknesses of various projections, especially when looking at large geographic areas. Otherwise, the distances and sizes of various locations may be incorrectly interpreted, resulting in less than optimum decisions.

Computer-derived Projections

In addition to storing parameters and representations for many of the common projection types, some desktop mapping programs allow you to define your own projection parameters. The computer calculates the projection display based on the light source, projection surface, tangency line, and distance from the object or any arbitrary *x-y* coordinate system. Computerized projections are actually a set of equations that use parameters of origin and reference parallels, and other specifiers, to approximate actual light-source projections. Most mapping programs also calculate an approximate projection based on the longitude and latitude specifications of an area, which averages the longitude length based on the degree of latitude across the entire map.

A computer-derived latitude-longitude map of the United States. Notice the rectangular orientation of the states.

This map is an Albers equal-area conic projection of the United States. Notice the shapes and proportions are more geographically accurate than in the latitude-longitude projection.

Figure 2-16. Two map projections of the United States.[11]

Projections also have specific coordinate systems associated with them. For example, the Universal Transverse Mercator (UTM) coordinate system is applied to the Transverse Mercator projection. A Transverse Mercator projection can have tangency along any specified meridian. Any location on the map is identified by an *x-y* coordinate with values corresponding to the UTM grid. A given map projection has a coordinate system defined by a map projection and its set of projection parameters. For some market mapping purposes, such as thematic representations, the earth can be assumed to be flat, and the latitude-longitude system can be treated as though it were a rectangular coordinate system.

The projection and coordinate system options provided by your desktop mapping program become more important as your requirements for cartographic accuracy increase. Cartographic accuracy is the degree to which features on a map are located in relationship to the actual geographical positions. This is important if you are locating new facilities or establishing routing requirements. It is less important if you are displaying general information, such as the total population of a state or income levels of a country.

Chapter Summary

In this chapter, you have been introduced to prerequisite concepts and terminology regarding maps and cartography necessary for mastering desktop mapping products in general, and market mapping applications in particular. The many types of thematic maps used in market mapping have also been introduced in this chapter.

Your knowledge of map scales, symbols, legends, projections, and spatial representations will affect the interpretation of maps used in market mapping applications. As you read on, you may need to refer to the important concepts elucidated in this chapter, including:

- The standard map representations of scale, coordinate systems, boundaries, direction, and distance
- The use of symbols and other conventions, such as hatch patterns and colors, to represent various data and geographic components on maps
- The purpose of a map's legend
- The functions and features of political, thematic, geologic, topographic, and other types of maps
- The types of thematic maps useful in market mapping, including hatch, density, pie, proportional, prism, post, multivariate, and pin maps

■ The relationship of map projections and cartographic distortion, and the reason projections must be understood to correctly interpret the data presented in maps

In the next chapter, the structure, functions, and general operations of desktop mapping software will be presented to show how the various mapping parameters introduced in this chapter can be combined to produce informative visual representations of business-related data.

3

Anatomy of a Desktop Mapping Program for Market Mapping Analysis

With the basic concepts and terminology of cartography covered in the last chapter now in the forefront of your mind, the features and capabilities of desktop mapping programs will be easier to understand. As you'll recall, the common components to any desktop mapping system include the mapping software, the cartographic (or geographic) data, the attribute data, and the computer system itself. This chapter concentrates on the first two components of the system—the desktop mapping software and the geographic data. The attribute data sources are covered in Chap. 4 and the selection criteria for choosing software and computer system components for market mapping are covered in Chap. 5.

In this chapter, the operation and capabilities of desktop mapping software are presented as they apply to demographic research and market analysis. As we mentioned in Chap. 1, there are other uses of desktop mapping—including city planning, environmental and weather analysis, crime statistics evaluation, and asset management. Desktop mapping products support these applications, but we will not cover the specific features or data sources used for these purposes unless they apply to market mapping as well.

Desktop mapping software products are special-purpose display programs designed to process geographic data and other information for maximum visual impact in cartographic formats. Desktop mapping software is used to manipulate and produce marketing and business maps used for

41

making a wide range of strategic and tactical decisions. Systems range in capability from simple presentation mapping programs to sophisticated integrated information systems, including not only mapping functions, but also database management, data translation, and even statistics capabilities. The type of program required depends largely on the type and complexity of market mapping research appropriate for your business.

How Does Desktop Mapping Software Work?

In later chapters, we will provide step-by-step guides to the operation of desktop mapping programs used for market mapping analyses. For now, it is only necessary to understand the conceptual operation of desktop mapping software. This conceptual process is generally the same across mapping programs. As you will see later, the difference between mapping software products is not in the concepts underlying their operation, but in the range of features available and in the level of detail and analysis the mapping software can facilitate. Of course, some programs offer unique or specialized features not common to other mapping programs, but we will discuss these in subsequent chapters when their relevance is more apparent.

The utility of desktop mapping programs starts with their ability to represent geographic data on a computer monitor and output it on a printer or plotter or export it to other software. Geographic data (maps) are represented as either raster- or vector-based data. Raster-based systems draw maps as a matrix of dots (or screen pixels), whereas vector-based systems draw maps based on a series of coordinates which are interconnected to form lines, polygons, or points (one coordinate pair). Where vector-based lines surround an area of a map, as does an arc, circle, or polygon, they can be filled with colors and/or patterns.

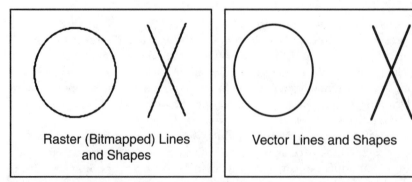

Figure 3-1. Raster dots versus vector lines.

In general, raster systems are used to analyze imagery (such as satellite photos), and vector systems are used for drawing maps or representing maps for manipulation by a computer. Raster maps require substantially more storage space and RAM memory to process. They also display and redraw more slowly and are less commonly used by desktop mapping systems. Raster maps are also very limited in their capacity to be resized for use in a report or presentation.

Because vector-based maps exist as a series of mathematical descriptions of lines and fill patterns, to resize them, new values are simply substituted for the existing ones, making the map and its contents larger or smaller as required. Most mapping software used for market mapping employs vector-based maps exclusively, so we will talk primarily about vector-based mapping programs in this book. However, raster scans of maps can be used to trace features for incorporation into vector-based maps with some software. Once the lines are traced and saved as vectors, the raster image is usually discarded.

Desktop Mapping Systems Link Geographic Data to Attribute Data

Geographic data is stored in mapping software so it can be linked to other data, called attribute data. Desktop mapping software used for market mapping analysis must be able to link its geographic data (base maps) to user-specified attribute data. Software programs differ markedly in their ability to handle and manipulate attribute data—but conceptually all market mapping products link attribute data to geographic data in some way.

Detail in geographic data, linkage capabilities of software, and availability of display functions control the range of map representations that can be produced. Once a linkage is complete, the mapping program allows users to specify the size and features of the map displayed. Depending on the program and the type of data linkage, users can perform functions ranging from drawing filled/shadowed-area maps to performing sophisticated geographic operations and analysis.

As you can see in Fig. 3-2, market mapping depends on linking market- or customer-oriented data to the geographic locations of those data elements. This can be done at various levels; for example, maps may be created from data that shows state-wide product sales, but also contains city-by-city, territory-by-territory, or street-by-street sales data. Most programs used in market mapping applications use a multilayered approach to managing geographic data. Maps often contain features of different layers of data, such as interstate highways, city streets, state capitals, and zip codes. The data to be displayed from a layer can be selected within most mapping programs.

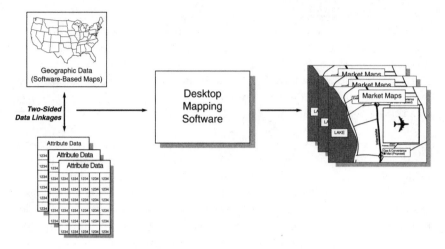

Figure 3-2. In some market mapping programs, linkages work in two directions.

Some systems allow you to store each type of feature in an individual layer to enhance flexibility when working with multiple types of features. So, one map file may contain a city boundary layer, a road layer, as well as a layer that shows hospitals and police stations, or whatever locations you want to display.

The use of layers allows you to group, manage, and graphically depict different classes of features to make analyzing relationships between them more straightforward. Layers can be displayed one at a time or all at once. Characteristics such as color, fill pattern, labeling, line thickness, etc. can be controlled by layer. You can manage these individual layers by hiding or displaying them as needed. Layers may also be individually editable or "write-protected" to avoid making accidental but consequential changes to individual layers or the underlying map.

The Three Components of Desktop Mapping

Desktop Mapping Software

There are a variety of mapping application packages that range in price from a couple of hundred to thousands of dollars. Mapping software is also available for computers ranging from full-size mainframes and minicomputers to laptop microcomputers. Different brands of mapping software run on a variety of computer operating systems, and most manufacturers write programs that run in more than one environment. For example, MapInfo, a popular desktop mapping package, runs under Windows on

IBM compatibles, on Macintosh computers, and on workstations produced by Sun Microsystems, Digital Equipment Corporation (DEC), and Hewlett-Packard. This book is primarily concerned with desktop market mapping products—those mapping applications that run on personal computers like IBM-PCs and Apple Macintoshes.

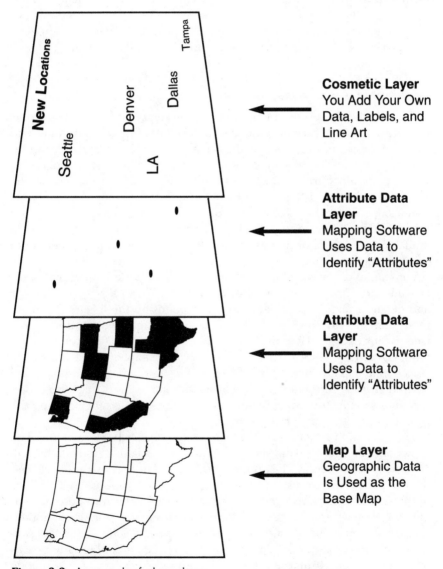

Figure 3-3. An example of a layered map.

In addition to allowing you to graphically represent numerical and alphabetic data on maps for powerful marketing analysis, programs may also allow you to create or add your own maps, modify existing maps as geography changes, add lines and shapes to clarify the map, and complete sophisticated statistical analyses of attribute data before it is mapped.

Once maps are created, most market mapping software allows you to print your maps directly or provides a function for exporting maps in a format compatible with page layout and presentation software. This provides a simple mechanism for communicating the results of analyses completed with marketing mapping to managers, coworkers, and customers.

Geographic or Cartographic Data

The utility of any desktop mapping program depends on the geographic data (also called cartographic data) available for the program and required to create maps of specific areas. This data represents locations and geographic features in computer-compatible formats. Geographic data is generally purchased from the software manufacturer, because the base maps must be 100 percent compatible with the mapping program. (See Chap. 5 for more information on purchasing geographic data from other sources.) The range, detail, and accuracy of the geographic data available for specific programs directly affect the application potential of the mapping program.

For example, you may have cartographic files for the United States, for zip code areas, for Europe, or for downtown Rochester, New York. The type and detail of cartographic data you use depends on the locations you are interested in and the detail you require to display your information. Geographic data describes the location and shape of map features (regions, lines, or points). As discussed in the previous chapter, the features displayed in a map are defined by a series of x-y coordinates. Coordinates are derived from a computer-generated or computer-stored map projection that allows the features on a flat map to be represented as they exist on the round earth with appropriate accuracy.

The geographic data is often referred to as "base maps," since the data shows only basic map data, such as political boundaries, zip code boundaries, or street locations. The number and kinds of projections available, and the coordinate systems used to refer to geographic locations, are functions of the mapping software—and the levels of functionality and sophistication in handling geographic data vary considerably from one product to another.

A set of geographic data, unique to each specific manufacturer, is supplied with every mapping program. For presentation mapping software this may include limited map libraries of countries, states, counties, zip code centroids, and major city locations. In a more sophisticated mapping program, its map libraries may include general libraries of presentation software, but a wide range of additional data may also be available from the manufacturer, including detailed maps of states, cities, counties, complete zip code areas, streets, and even finer levels of detail for individual housing tracts and lots.

Before you buy a mapping program, make sure the correct levels and ranges of geographic data are available for that program from the manufacturer. If you only want to view maps at the state or regional level, this probably isn't a problem—since programs generally come with these maps as part of the basic product. But, if you want to do street-level mapping of a specific city, then city-wide maps including those streets must be available from the software manufacturer or from some other vendor that makes compatible maps.

If the geographic data you need is not available for your mapping program, it doesn't matter how sophisticated the rest of the program is—you won't be able to create the maps you need to complete your analyses unless the program allows you to add your own maps manually. For a city-wide map, this is a long, arduous process. But, if for some reason you absolutely need a street-level map of Coatzacoalcos, Mexico, and no map is available, this may be your only alternative.

Attribute Data

You'll recall that the data you add to cartographic data to create maps for market analysis is called attribute data. This data may be purchased from the manufacturer of your mapping software, created by you, stored in corporate databases, or obtained from a wide variety of government and commercial sources. Attribute data may be supplied as data designed for use by your mapping software or as part of a database or spreadsheet, keyed by you directly from printed sources, or imported electronically via a network or modem.

Examples of attribute data include the population of a census tract, the traffic volume of a highway, or the number of resort hotels and their size and location in Florida. Attribute data remains completely independent of the map itself and of other features in the map.

To be used by mapping software, attribute data is generally stored or translated into database, spreadsheet, or tab-delimited ASCII format where each record represents a map feature and each field contains a variable or attribute about the features. Because attribute data is the heart of your marketing research, the next chapter of the book covers particulars on formats, sources, and options for obtaining attribute data for your market mapping efforts. Ultimately, attribute data is displayed as patterns, dots, colors, or symbols on your market maps.

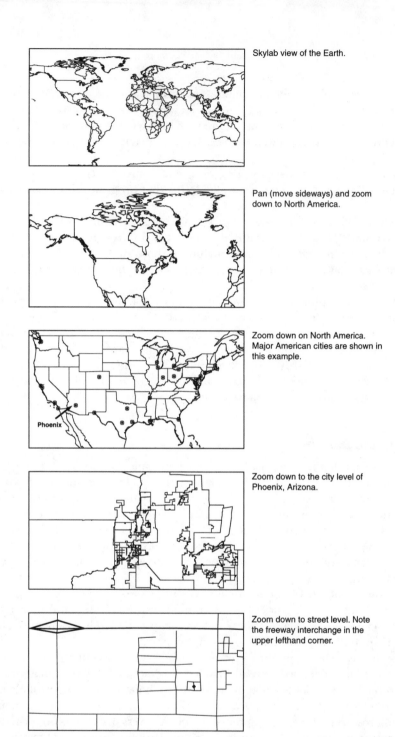

Skylab view of the Earth.

Pan (move sideways) and zoom down to North America.

Zoom down on North America. Major American cities are shown in this example.

Phoenix

Zoom down to the city level of Phoenix, Arizona.

Zoom down to street level. Note the freeway interchange in the upper lefthand corner.

Figure 3-4. Five views of the same map—from Skylab level to street level.[12]

Tip—All Mapping Systems Contain Only Three Components

When working with mapping software and data, at first you may become confused because of the number of "bits and pieces" that seem to be a part of the mapping process. It's easy to become intimidated by the tables, maps, dialog boxes, commands, command sequences, cosmetic factors, map layers, symbols, and even the multiple names of data files. Keep in mind when working in mapping software that there are always only three components to market mapping software (even within the most complicated GIS programs): the software, the geographic data (base maps), and the attribute data. If you suddenly feel lost within a mapping program, sit back a minute and ask yourself which of the three elements you are working with to clarify the process. While you may be working with one, two, or all three elements simultaneously, remembering that everything breaks down into just three components makes the mapping process less intimidating when you're just getting started with market mapping.

The Kinds of Desktop Market Mapping Programs for Market Mapping Analysis

You can distinguish between desktop mapping systems by how the program links maps (geographic or cartographic data) and attribute data. In other words, how the maps and data are linked dictates the level of potential analysis that can be performed. Less sophisticated systems cannot link outside data to maps, while more sophisticated programs provide one-sided or two-sided linkages between maps and attribute data.

Beyond linkage, the ability to perform analyses on attribute and geographic data and express ideas graphically are also characteristics that distinguish one mapping system from another. The more thematic possibilities and colors supported, the more possibilities for displaying your information in a crisp, influential manner for easy comprehension of your business data. Some systems enable you to perform a broad range of presentation mapping as well as a variety of geographic data analyses. Other systems are very powerful when assembling an analysis, but very limited in their presentation capabilities.

Another distinguishing characteristic between mapping programs is the level of cartographic accuracy. Some systems and their maps provide only vague accuracy. When choosing the general location of a new store, an on-screen map error of one hundred feet, more or less, may be irrelevant.

When designing the physical layout of a store, however, this level of error would be unacceptable. Some products are extremely accurate cartographically, allowing you to locate the sides of a building down to precise surveyed coordinates. This second kind of accuracy is rarely required for creating maps for marketing analysis, but it's important when you need to know where to dig to avoid a hitting a telephone cable or water main.

 Definition—One-Sided Links and Two-Sided Links

One-sided links are created when attribute data is read from a table and used to add elements to a map, such as symbols indicating the locations of competitors' stores on a street map. With one-sided links, you make queries such as, "Show me all counties with a median population age greater than thirty-two years."

Two-sided links allow you to add data just like one-sided links, but, once the data is added to the map, two-sided links allow you to ask questions about both the attribute *and* cartographic data. For example, you can select a point on a map and query, "Show me all gas station-based convenience stores within a five mile radius." The results of your search can be displayed on the map and the data from each store can be added to a new table showing the store's franchise affiliation, address, and any other required, available, salient data. This "found" data can be exported to an external database or other program, if required, for further analysis.

A third kind of accuracy is topographic. Maps with topographic accuracy represent physical geography such as hills and mountains. While most "nontopographic" maps show major bodies of water, topographic maps show elevations and "the lay of the land." Again, this kind of accuracy is rarely important unless you are looking for a location for a new subdivision and want to stay out of the "vertical real estate" market.

Based on these general criteria, desktop mapping programs useful for market mapping applications fall into three general categories—presentation-level programs, analysis-level programs, and GIS-level programs. A fourth category, electronic atlases, is also discussed. Electronic atlases are *not* useful for market mapping. We mention them to make you are aware of this kind of mapping software so you can avoid an accidental purchase of the wrong product.

The categories are separated to illustrate the range of functionality and choices available. When you start looking at mapping software you will find that the lines between the categories are not always clear, because as powerful new mapping software hits the market, competition increases. Thus, manufacturers are constantly adding new features and expanding the functionality of their software to take advantage of new hardware functionality, including memory, speed, display functions, and printing technologies—and to remain functionally competitive.

Electronic Atlases

Electronic atlases are display-only mapping systems that are designed to present general information on geographic areas as pictures on a screen. They are useful for educators and general reference requirements. Some of the programs allow hand placement of user-specified symbols on maps, and in some programs maps can be copied and used as clip art for placement in presentations and reports. Electronic atlases may offer colorful, thematic maps in a variety of formats, but are not usually suitable for market mapping applications because they cannot analyze attribute data from outside sources. The content and view possibilities for available maps may be extremely limited as well.

Figure 3-5. Maps produced with electronic atlases display geographic data contained within the program, but offer few anayltical capabilities.[13]

Presentation-level Mapping Programs

Presentation-level mapping programs are used to create specific geographic displays, usually one or two maps at a time, for use in reports and presentations. These programs are capable of displaying a limited range of attribute data on a region, and the resulting images may be pasted into other documents or enhanced in a drawing software package. Presentation mapping systems are not usually cartographically accurate and offer only limited geographic base maps; however, the programs may offer a wide variety of thematic displays, color combinations, symbols, and fonts for labeling map elements. (Thematic analysis is described in the next section.)

For broad, general analysis these programs provide useful displays—but they are not designed for sophisticated "what-if" analysis or street-level location planning. The most useful programs in this category (for market mapping) import information from spreadsheet programs like Lotus 1-2-3 or Excel or databases like dBASE or FoxBase. Some presentation-level mapping programs include capabilities similar to those in page layout programs used for creating documents in desktop publishing; these functions may also be useful when creating other presentation graphics in addition to the maps.

Analysis-level Mapping Programs

Analysis-level programs are desktop mapping programs that allow a high degree of data analysis and display capabilities. The difference between display-level programs and analysis-level programs is one of degree. An analysis-level program is usually characterized by the ability to accommodate interactive what-if analyses or multiple map views displayed simultaneously. These capabilities are important for making informed geographically-based marketing decisions—such as choosing locations, planning mailing campaigns, evaluating sales reports based on several data parameters, or evaluating advertising media.

The majority of market mapping needs can be satisfied with programs from this category, and the range of these products is diverse. Programs are differentiated by number of features, ease-of-use, available geographic data, and specific data management capabilities.

There are five basic functions at the analysis level—thematic displays, street-level analysis, geocoding and data translation, database management, and statistical analysis. Some programs do only one of these functions well—other products offer all of these functions neatly integrated in one package. In addition, where one product may cover all of these bases thoroughly, another may cover them at only a cursory level.

Thematic Display Capabilities.   Thematic mapping functions, which are also available in presentation-level programs, enable you to express

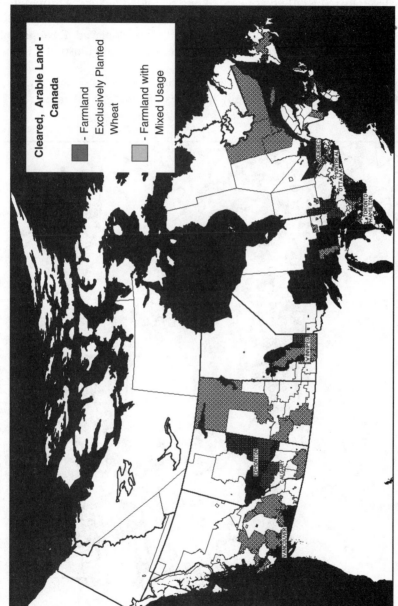

Figure 3-6. Presentation-level maps allow some data manipulation and the creation of attractive color maps.[14]

attribute data using visual techniques such as shading, symbols, dots, and layers. In thematic maps, attribute data is linked to map features at the most basic level, forming either a one-sided or a two-sided linkage. Through the use of color, patterns, shading, or symbol size, the relative value of underlying data and their geographic relationships can be displayed. Examples of the basic thematic map types used in market mapping are illustrated in the previous chapter.

In market mapping you might use thematic maps to display per capita income by census tract to identify locations of different income groups.

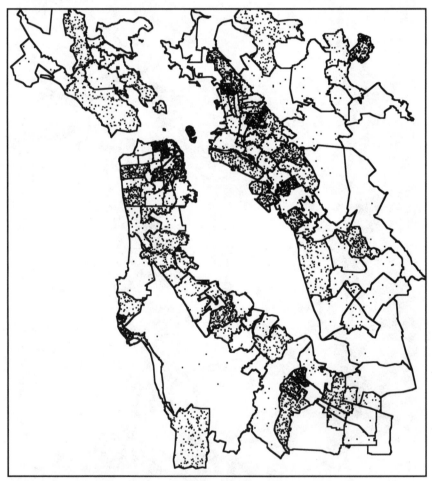

Figure 3-7. Analysis-level maps can plot data brought in from outside sources for complex analysis.[15]

This information is useful for selecting sites for retail stores or different types of restaurants. It can also be used to target sales territories for expensive home improvement products and services.

Software programs that exclusively perform thematic mapping are the most popular type of desktop mapping systems. Most presentation-level mapping programs are thematic-only mapping systems, and as such tend to be limited in their ability to perform geographic and attribute queries and spatial analyses. In advanced analysis-level software, a wide variety of thematic displays are integrated with other mapping functions.

 What Is Geocoding Anyway?

While we've briefly explained geocoding already (and you'll see a step-by-step example of geocoding in Chap. 6), here's a more complete definition for you to work with now. Geocoding is the process of converting data from outside sources into a format compatible with geographic data used by a desktop mapping program.

Geocoding is necessary because even though mapping software is highly "intelligent" as software goes, it is unable to understand data the way you do. If you bring a table of existing customer names and street addresses into a map, you must tell the software to compare the addresses of your customers with the addresses the computer has stored so it knows where to place the location of each piece of data. You must also tell the software what column of data contains the addresses you want to use. Once geocoding is complete, the customer addresses can be placed on the map wherever the software finds a street address that matches its own data. Where no match occurs, geocoding can't be completed without your intervention. So, if you ask a program to geocode a list of addresses for St. Louis to a map of Tampa, only those streets that accidentally have the same name (and address numbers) will be matched.

After data is geocoded, all the data attached to the geocoded field can be represented on the map. When geocoding customer names and addresses to the locations in a city street map, the addresses can then be displayed as symbols or labels on the map.

You can also geocode code new locations in the geographic data. For example, when streets are added to a city map they must be geocoded to the map describing the range of addresses found on each block of the street, the street's name, and any other relevant data, including coordinates for the street, if appropriate.

Street-based Analysis. Also known as pin mapping, street-based mapping functions display locations at the street level based on the geographic data used (such as the United States Census TIGER maps of streets which include address information). Attribute data can be displayed as point data on the map. In other words, the attribute data is linked to points such as addresses of customer sites, store locations, or even fire hydrant locations. Most products with street-level mapping capabilities provide a two-sided link where the user can query and manipulate both attribute data and geographic data within the program.

Some street-based systems enable the user to map and display data for regions by summarizing point data. Also, many of the systems include the ability to map data by address or area of geography (called geocoding) by automatically placing a point at the correct location.

Data Translation and Geocoding Capabilities. Mapping programs offer a variety of translation systems for converting data from a foreign format, such as a database or spreadsheet, into one compatible with the mapping software. There are often two steps to importing data so it can be used by the mapping system. First, data must be made readable by the mapping software by way of a conversion routine that converts data already stored on your desktop computer or through a data extraction routine that connects directly to another computer's database. Programs that accept data from outside sources offer direct translation of data from popular spreadsheets and databases and direct access through network connections and programs like Apple's DAL (data acquisition language), which allow software to connect and extract data from mainframe and minicomputer data sources. (If direct translation is unavailable, you can save your spreadsheet or database into a compatible format with most spreadsheet and database software. See the tip on importing files with delineated ASCII in the next chapter.)

Second, data must be geocoded to be useful to the mapping software. Programs include an intelligent routine that automatically manages the geocoding after you select the parameters for the task. Data that fails to meet the prescribed parameters after the bulk of the geocoding job is done can be manually geocoded or simply ignored at your discretion.

Database Management Functions. Visualization is a key benefit of programs used for market mapping analysis. The more data that can be viewed, the more useful the program. And, the more *ways* data can be viewed, the more useful the program. Of course, as more options become available, programs become more expensive. The types of attribute data you use determine the kind of data visualization functions your mapping program should have. If you will be using only commercially available data, the program must be compatible with these data sources. If you will be using data from your own corporate databases located on a mainframe computer, your systems ability to import data from these formats is important as well.

In addition, you may want to create new databases of information. Some mapping programs include integrated database management programs that can be used for this purpose. These programs can store and manipulate chart, graph, and sort information just like standalone database programs, although they don't have quite the capabilities of the most sophisticated database software available for microcomputers. The major advantage of integrated databases is that they are also able to geocode data and display it in maps and geographical representations.

Statistical Analysis Capabilities.   In addition to providing a range of data management and data translation options, the most sophisticated programs integrate statistical analysis capabilities that include both descriptive and analytical statistical functions, similar to those provided in spreadsheet programs like Lotus 1-2-3 or Microsoft Excel. These capabilities allow you to perform calculations on attribute data and then display the results of the calculations. For example, you might want to average the income levels of specific areas represented in your attribute data and display the results. Typically, the results can be displayed in maps, graphs, and conventional report formats.

GIS-level Mapping Systems

The dividing line between a full-featured analysis-level software product and a GIS (Geographic Information System) is a fuzzy one. Traditionally, GIS systems not only offer most of the functionality of analysis-level marketing mapping software, but also offer a higher degree of cartographic accuracy and

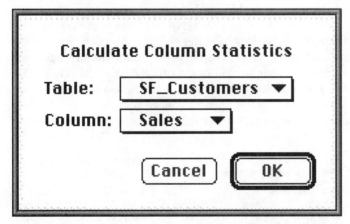

Figure 3-8. Some mapping programs offer complete statistical functions from easy-to-use menus.[16]

precision drawing tools similar to those found in computer-aided design software (CAD systems). These precision mapping products usually combine display, thematic, and street-level mapping functions—and allow finer levels of detailed analysis and drawing capabilities than other mapping software.

Many of these programs allow you to draw your own maps where data is linked in a two-sided manner to an internal database management system. You can query and manipulate both geographic and attribute data within the program. A GIS for market mapping purposes should include all the features of thematic mapping and street mapping systems as well as cartographic accuracy and spatial analysis tools.

Because GIS-level programs include such a large set of functions, they were typically expensive, difficult to use, and required expensive hardware. However, GIS software has recently been made available at lower prices, and the ease of use of desktop-based GIS systems has improved considerably.

Sophisticated GIS-level programs allow the importation of digitized maps and map components and provide a means for tracking street-level assets such as telephone hookups and numbers of lines house-by-house. GIS programs also offer the most sophisticated database tools found in market mapping software. For market mapping, these features are not normally required, unless you need to perform both elaborate marketing analyses and precision location planning.

For example, if you are the vice president of sales for a cable television franchise that handles a large territory, including sections of several states, you might need to analyze both cable subscriptions on a city-by-city basis and cable subscriptions by neighborhood to focus sales strategies. Then, the technical department of your cable company may use the same GIS and data to track cable installations, premium channels, cable layouts, and distribution problems house-by-house.

The power and flexibility found in a GIS-level program allow the development of interactive models and the testing of alternatives to find the best answer to a problem or to monitor the effect of changes over time. A GIS almost always contains functions for creating presentation-quality maps and supports large format and high-resolution output devices, although the degree of presentation sophistication varies among products. Many of the most sophisticated desktop GIS-level products have compatible mainframe and minicomputer counterparts that can share data at a variety of levels.

Additional Desktop Mapping Software Capabilities

Of the three kinds of mapping software discussed in this chapter (ignoring electronic atlases), there are a number of functions and performance cri-

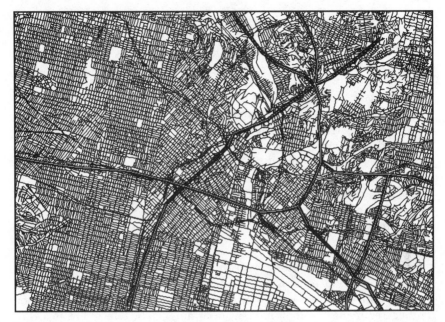

Figure 3-9. GIS-level maps can display streets, houses, and geography with a high degree of precision and a wide range of analytical capabilities.[17]

teria that can be used to evaluate one product with other products in its class. The criteria and functions can then be used to compare prices among packages before making a purchase decision.

A worksheet is included in Chap. 5 to assist you in evaluating software before you make a purchase decision. Like most software, the more complex and complete a desktop mapping product's functionality, the more expensive. With the exception of a handful of the newest "easy-to-use" mapping products, the learning curve for products is proportional to the product's price.

Other Functions in Mapping Programs

As mapping programs evolved, more functions were added that don't fall neatly into any of the categories discussed above. Some of these include the ability to customize maps and to extrapolate data for use in other programs and analyses. Here are several functions that individual programs may or may not offer (and you may or may not need):

- *Drawing and Layout Capabilities*—As mentioned, programs vary widely in their ability to present maps in a finished format. Basic analysis-level programs create simple maps that allow limited changes to map features and their drawing tools are often best described as "clunky." More sophisticated GIS-level programs offer extremely precise tools that take advantage of systems' cartographic accuracy. Unfortunately, to the user unfamiliar with computer-aided design drawing tools, these systems have a steep learning curve if precision is required. Programs between these two extremes offer drawing tools that are both easy to master and capable of a significant range of effects. Tools in most programs are selected by clicking on a tool icon within the drawing tool palette. When precision is required (and available), instead of drawing a line by holding down the mouse and dragging the selected line tool, the precise x-y parameters for the line are entered into a dialog box. This box is used to specify the coordinates where the line should start and stop and how wide it should be. Color or screen values may be specified in this same dialog.

- *Layout Capabilities*—Along with drawing tools, programs offer layout options to enhance maps and symbols. Individual streets, cities, states, and counties can be highlighted with colors, shades, hatch patterns, or other treatments. Symbols in many programs can be selected from a symbol library sold with the program, or added from outside sources. Some programs include a symbol or icon editor. This is usually a grid layout that allows you to create a new symbol one dot at a time in an enlarged format. For actual use, the symbol is reduced, which cleans up the rough edges for display.

Other layout capabilities include support for a variety of typefaces (called fonts), typeface styles (plain, bold, italic, etc.), and paragraph

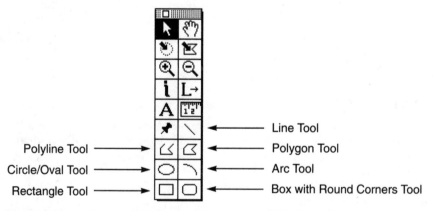

Figure 3-10. Analysis- and GIS-level programs often provide drawing tools for customizing maps.[18]

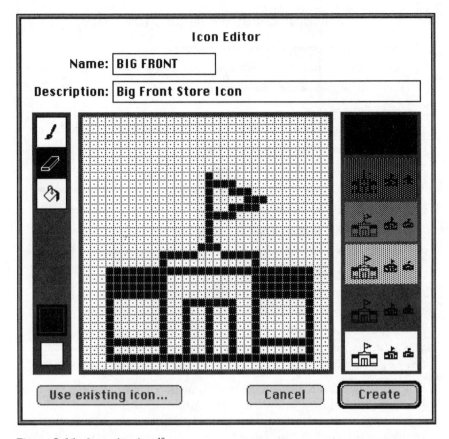

Figure 3-11. Icon editor box.[19]

alignment options such as centering and justifying. Rules, borders, and custom legends are also among the options available.

■ *Graphing, Charting, and Reporting Functions*—Because market mapping software is a nexus for data, often acquired from several sources, analysis- and GIS-level products include tools for creating charts and graphs directly from the data within the program. While rarely as sophisticated as tools found in expensive charting programs, these functions can be quite handy because you can use the data displayed on a map to create simple graphs to further expound or elucidate a point or to prepare a traditional comparison.

Most programs include reporting functionality as well. Data from maps or tables can be output in standard or custom report formats. For example, if you need to show territory-by-territory sales in a map, a

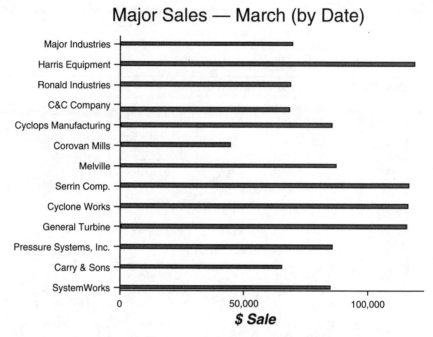

Figure 3-12. Analysis-level programs may have convenient charting capabilities.[20]

printed report can also be generated to provide "hard number comparisons" and additional detail not appropriate to the map, such as the names of active accounts during a period or how much was sold for each of the last five years in the same territory. In most programs, data used for reports can be directly exported for use in word processing documents or page layout programs.

Chapter Summary

In this chapter, we've looked at the general operations of desktop mapping software and the kinds of mapping software useful for market mapping, along with descriptions of the most common functions contained in mapping products.

The features and functions of mapping software presented in this chapter that you need to be familiar with as you proceed in your market mapping endeavors include the following:

- The difference between raster-based and vector-based mapping systems
- The way mapping software links geographic data to attribute data

- The function of layering in mapping programs
- The components of a desktop mapping system, including the software, the geographic data, and the attribute data
- The conceptual differences between electronic atlases, presentation-level programs, analysis-level programs, and GIS-level programs
- Geocoding and data translation functions within mapping programs
- The additional data display capabilities found in some mapping programs, including drawing, layout, and graphing functions

In the next chapter, we'll look at data in more depth, along with sources for locating it and ways to make it compatible with market mapping software. You'll discover that data for market mapping research is available almost everywhere you look—and much of it is free or relatively inexpensive.

4

Data Sources and Data Formats for Market Mapping Research

Market mapping is a powerful technique for visualizing information on customers and markets in geographic terms. Geographic representations make it easier to see relationships between data and the distributions of key elements in a customer population or sales territory. Central to this ability to see relationships is access to accurate, current, and complete information on customers and markets. You can't see relationships in data you don't have. You can't determine trends if you don't have a history of the buying patterns of your customers. You can't out-fox the competition if you don't know where the competitors are selling their products, who they sell to, and where their customers are located. Thus, the entire value and potential of market mapping depends on your access to data on customers, populations, and markets to analyze in the first place.

The success of your market mapping research centers on your access to data on customers and markets, and the goods news is that the amount of demographic data available for market mapping research is enormous. First, almost every company, no matter how small, has a wealth of demographic data on its own customers. Unfortunately, many companies don't even consider this information a valuable asset, but it is. There are lists of customers and their addresses contained in files, databases, bills, invoices, business cards put into weekly drawings for a free lunch at a local restaurant, warranty registration cards, and business cards collected by the sales

65

force. These are all rich sources of geographic-based information on your existing customers.

Company-specific sources don't provide information on new customers and new marketing possibilities, however. For this data you need to use outside sources. Fortunately, there is an abundance of possibilities for this data—in all price ranges from free to prohibitively expensive. These sources include data from the government, from commercial sources, and from independent research. If you have a question, there is probably someone out there who has the data you need for an answer.

This chapter describes these available data options, both commercial and private, in more detail and explains how to customize a database for specific demographic and market mapping research problems.

What Data Do You Need to Make Informed Decisions?

Too many marketing decisions are made without data—managers call them intuition-based decisions. Intuition is still important in marketing, but intuition is better when it is based on complete and valid information. The starting point in any market mapping program is determining the information you need to manage your business effectively.

You may think you have all the data you need already, but for most companies this just isn't true. Think about it for a moment and consider just one familiar example that is critical to managing your marketing efforts: data on your competition. You probably know who your competitors are, but do you really know who your competitors' *customers* are? How many of *your* customers did competitors sell to last year? What is the average income level of their customers? What is different about their customers and yours? Are there differences based on customer locations in terms of age, buying power, attitudes, or preferences? The answers to these questions are as important for a small restaurant as they are for a multinational megacorporation.

If you know all the answers about your competition, *great*—you are one step ahead of most companies. Now see if you can answer these questions:

- Is there a demographic trend that may affect your marketing strategy over the next five years? If so, how will the trend manifest itself geographically?

- What zip code areas have the most buying potential in terms of income?

- Where do the customer profile demographics match your product demographics?

- Who is buying related products in your area? How much did they buy last year? Is the market growing or shrinking?

- How do customer preferences in Chicago differ from preferences in San Diego?

- Who buys more chicken: people in the west of your sales region or in the east?

Now, be honest. Did you have to look these things up? Do you know where to find the answers? Do you even have a clue where to start? If you know, *fantastic*—you can skip this chapter and start mapping. If you have doubts, then read on.

There is data out there to answer all the questions just posed. It's not only the Fortune 500 that can afford answers to these questions, either. The data is accessible to any size business. It's just a matter of knowing where to look for the data that already exists and using it to your best advantage.

As you'll recall, you need both geographic and attribute data for your desktop mapping research. The answers to the following questions will determine the geographic data you need to support your market mapping efforts:

- Where are your products currently sold?

- Where are your sales offices and/or retail locations?

- Are you planning expansion in the future? If so, where? If you don't know where, are you considering a local, national, or international expansion?

- What are the general locations of your customers in terms of countries, states, and cities?

- What new sales locations are you interested in exploring that you have little or no knowledge of now?

The geographic data must generally be available from mapping software manufacturers to be compatible with their desktop mapping products, as we've mentioned before.

Answers to questions like the following will determine the attribute data you require in your market mapping data:

- *Do you need to develop targeted advertising programs aimed at your existing customers?* If you do, then you need detailed information on current customers available in your own corporate data files and databases.

- *Do you need to develop targeted marketing programs aimed at your competitor's existing customers?* If you do, then you need profile data, industry trend data, and location data on the competition's customers and your own.

- *Do you need to find a new store or office location in a specific city?* If new locations are in your plans, you need not only street-level geographic data, but also data on the location of specific businesses related to yours. Other data that will help includes income demographics, land use data, traffic patterns, leasing prices by area, and available building or office sites.

- *Do you need to find new markets for existing products?* If yes, then you need current customer demographics, in addition to general demographics for the areas you are interested in exploring. Data on purchasing patterns, product preferences, and lifestyles is also necessary.

- *Do you need general information on trends and buying patterns to plan for future products?* If so, you need historical data on markets and buying patterns. You need general demographic data on income levels, buying patterns, age distributions, and other general market data for the geographic areas you are interested in exploring, either domestic or international, or both.

- *Do you need to analyze the effectiveness of your advertising and promotional efforts?* If this is important, then you need to use response data from your customers and demographic data and cost data from relevant advertising media, including newspapers, magazines, television, and radio. In addition, you need general demographic data on your sales territories.

- *Do you need to establish new sales territories or analyze existing sales territory distributions?* If sales territories are a concern, you need sales data by territory and sales person, customer data, population data, and perhaps even competitive data.

Once you have determined the relevant questions for your business and the data needed to answer those questions, your search for the best sources of attribute data can begin.

Get Your Own Data Together First

The search for data should start with discovering and organizing the data you already have in your company. Here are some places to look for customer and prospect data that can be used in your market mapping research:

- Your computer databases, whether on mainframes or microcomputers.

- Magazines and journals your company subscribes to. These often contain lists of competitive companies or prospective customers.

- Industry catalogs or resource guides. These include a wealth of information on companies and services for specific industries.

- Business card files. Almost everyone has business card files, and they are often overlooked as data sources. The files may include prospects, competitors, and industry advisors. Business card files are created for market mapping research because they include detailed addresses of people and companies.

- Paper-based files of customer data, bills, invoices, receipts, and credit card transactions. The data is more difficult to process from paper files, because it must be entered manually into the computer, but if you haven't computerized your data files yet, the old file cabinet is a good place to start.

Don't leave any stone unturned. Create a log of all the available data you discover, and detail the following information on the data source:

- The location of the data.
- The person responsible for maintaining the data.
- The general data items contained.
- The time span covered, and the ages of the data.
- The frequency of data updates, if relevant.
- The type of geographic information contained in the data—i.e., address, zip code, telephone number, or other geographic attribute. Remember, you can't map data that doesn't have some sort of geographic attribute.
- The current format of the data. This includes product and file type for computerized data. If the data is not computerized, specify if the format is typewritten, handwritten, on forms, or published.
- The volume of data. The number of records is important in establishing the computer storage requirements and application potential of the data.

A form like the one provided as an example in Fig. 4-1 can be used for logging your existing data sources. The completed log can then be used for locating the data you need for specific mapping analyses.

After you determine the data you already have, you can start. Based on your research priorities and needs, you can see the gaps in your data and look to the following data sources, when applicable, to meet your needs. In addition to the general discussion about sources in this chapter, there is a listing of many government and commercial data sources with their addresses and phone numbers provided in a separate section at the end of this book to get you started.

Current Data Sources Worksheet						
Data Name	Description	Creation Date	Last Update	Geographic Information	Format	Number of Records

Figure 4-1. Current data sources worksheet.

Types of Consumer and Industrial Data

Data available commercially or through the government that is suitable for market mapping research is either consumer-oriented or industrial-oriented information. Consumer information is data recorded on individuals and households. Industrial information is data recorded on companies.

Consumer information includes answers to some primary questions that can be used to determine buying patterns, trends, and preferences, including:

- Who are the consumers? What are their ages, incomes, occupations, and locations? Answers to these questions are often referred to as *population statistics* or *geographic demographics*.

- What do they think? What do they aspire to? What lifestyles do they lead? What are their desires—wealth, status, security, etc.? Answers to these questions are called the *psychographics* of a population.

- What media do they read, watch, or listen to? Do they prefer television or radio? What magazines and newspapers do they read? Answers to these questions are called *media preferences*.

- What do they buy? How much do they buy? How often do they buy? Where do they buy? Answers to these questions are called *purchasing behavior* or *buying patterns*.

Industrial information, also referred to as business data or economic data, answers questions about companies and industries, as opposed to individuals, and includes data that answers the following types of questions:

- What do the companies sell?
- How much of it do they sell?
- What goods, services, and materials do the companies buy?

Type of Analysis	Media Information	Demographics	Psychographics	Purchasing Behavior	Traffic Patterns	Industrial Information	Economic & Trend Data
Market Analysis	●	●	●	●		●	●
Location Analysis		●		●	●		
Product Analysis	●	●		●		●	●
Advertising	●	●	●	●		●	●
Strategic Planning		●		●		●	●
Competitive Analysis	●	●		●		●	●

Figure 4-2. Data required for market mapping research.

- Where are the companies located?
- What trends exist in this industry for sales, growth, profitability, etc.?
- Who are the customers of the companies and where do they come from?

Where does this data on consumers and industries come from? First, every 10 years in the United States, people complete the census forms distributed by the Bureau of the Census. The official census provides a rich source of demographic data on age, sex, race, income, education, occupations, and household structure. In addition, every year a Current Population Survey is sent to a random selection of 50,000 people to establish new trends and changes in demographic data between the complete census. In most other countries, a census is also taken by the governments at regular intervals.

To get at purchase behavior, data is collected every time a person or a company buys something. The transactions are recorded either by the company that sold the product, by the credit card company used in the transaction, or by the bank that provided the loan. Every time a transaction occurs, a statistic is recorded somewhere specifying the type and amount of the transaction.

Information is also gathered through consumer surveys, warranty cards, and other research formats, which ask specific questions on preferences, lifestyles, and demographics. These surveys may be completed by government agencies, by research firms, or by the companies that sell the products. In addition, research firms and agencies produce data projections and estimates—statistical views into the future that establish theoretical trends and patterns in the data.

Psychographic Variables Common in Market Mapping Data

Activities	Interests	Opinions
Sports	Home	About Themselves
Shopping	Family	Social Issues
Local Events	Community	Culture
Memberships in Clubs	Food	Business
Entertainment	Fashion	Economics
Vacations and Travel	Accomplishments	Education
Work	Job or Career	Products
Social Events and Holidays	Television and Other Media	Future Trends and Changes
Hobbies	Recreation	Politics

Ultimately, the data from all these sources is formatted and packaged in some way so the information can be used in marketing research. The packages include combinations of psychographic, demographic, media usage, and purchasing behavior information—because combinations of these data are usually required to complete valid marketing research. Government agencies package the data as reports and databases for a wide range of applications. Research firms package the data to sell in a variety of formats. Companies sell mailing lists and demographic data on their customers to provide an additional source of income. These basic data sources for the packaged data are described in more detail below.

Government Data Sources

Government data sources are vast and relatively inexpensive. Some public data is provided free of charge, though the format may require translation and manipulation in order to work with desktop mapping software. Other data is sold for fees that vary with the format and detail provided.

The United States Bureau of the Census

The Bureau of the Census is the place to start when looking for demographic data for specific areas in the United States; even some international data is available. The Bureau of the Census not only takes a formal census of the United States and its territories every 10 years, but also produces updated population estimates on an annual basis in cooperation with states and counties. The census figures and estimates are tabulated hierarchically for specific geographic subdivisions—starting with the nation, and followed by regions, divisions, states, counties, minor civil divisions (MCDs are county subdivisions), places (usually incorporated areas that do not cross state lines), census tract or block numbering areas (areas containing approximately 4000 people with similar socioeconomic characteristics), block groups (areas with about 1000 people living in them), and blocks (areas roughly equivalent to a city block each).

The 1990 Census, taken on April 1, 1990, involved years of planning. Though census data is available on the United States since 1790, the 1990 census was the most automated, technologically advanced census ever taken and will provide more information on United States populations than ever before available. The data is still being tabulated and is being released in phases for use by government agencies and businesses. There is so much data in the census that the information will take almost 10 years to tabulate completely. The 1990 census is the most accurate view of the

United States population since 1980, the date of the previous census. There have been significant changes in the population in the last ten years. The new census data provides businesses with information to succeed over the next 10 years.

As the census data gets older, more of the data available from the government is interpolated—based on statistical guesses. The more interpolation in data, the less accurate. So, as the year 2000 rolls around, the 1990 census data will be less accurate than it is today. Because of the timeliness of the current census data, this is an especially good time to begin the market mapping research that will lead to your success through the upcoming decade and the next century.

Census Data Formats, STFs, and TIGER Files

The Data User Services Division of the Bureau of the Census provides printed reports on highlights and commonly used data from the census. The Division also provides microfiche, computer tapes designed for use on mainframes, and, now, CD-ROM disks of census data that can be used in personal computers. CD-ROMs are similar to the compact disks that play recorded music, but they are designed to store computer-readable data.

Some of the Relevant STF Files from the 1990 Census

Summary Tape File	Population Data	Geographic Coverage (Varies by STF Letter)
STF 1 A–D	Age, sex, race, household members, housing information	From regional and state to block group levels and congressional districts
STF 2 A–C	Similar data but more detail than SFT 1	From state to block group levels
STF 3 A–D	All data from STF 2, but additional data from the long form including income, education, languages, labor status, and additional housing information	From state to block group level and also ZIP Code information
STF 4 A–C	Same data items as STF 3, but more detail is provided and ethnic information is expanded	From state to census tract and block group levels and by specific urban areas

Paper-Based Data				
1234	1234	1234	1234	1234
1234	1234	1234	1234	1234
1234	1234	1234	1234	1234
1234	1234	1234	1234	1234
1234	1234	1234	1234	1234
1234	1234	1234	1234	1234

Paper

Adequate for small amounts of data; some data can be made computer compatible with optical character recognition (OCR).

Diskette

Good for small to medium amounts of data or for copying large amounts of data to a hard disk through programs that support saving large files to multiple floppy disks.

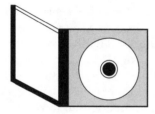

CD-ROM

Excellent for large amounts of data. Requires a CD-ROM reader. Access is slower than with a hard disk.

Magnetic Tape

Excellent for large amounts of data if you are using a minicomputer or mainframe. Data can be transferred to a hard disk.

The available data is divided up into files called summary tape files, or STFs. For example, there is STF-1A, STF-2A, etc. The summary files mask information on individuals to maintain privacy, required by law. Each STF file contains a different aspect and summary of the census data. For example, STF-3 provides sample data down from the long census form and down to the block/group level for income, occupation, and other demographics; STF-3B locates the same information by zip codes and will probably be among the most useful summary tape files for market researchers. STF-4 has more demographic data, but less geographic data. Though the first summary STF tapes were available in mid-1991, the complete STF-3B isn't scheduled for release until 1993. The cost of the census data and files depends on the information and location required. Full demographic information on California, for example, will cost around $850. A complete list of the summary tape files, their contents, prices, and availability dates is available from the Bureau of the Census.

Perhaps the most important aspect of the 1990 census is the TIGER digital map boundary file. TIGER (which stands for Topologically Integrated Geographic Encoding and Referencing) provides digital mapping of the entire country down to the street level. Data from the entire census can be related to these TIGER locations. A number of private data distribution and research firms are reformatting and segmenting the TIGER files to use as geographic data for desktop mapping systems. The potential commercial applications of TIGER will probably outweigh the commercial value of all the rest of the census data combined.

The Bureau of the Census is a huge operation. In addition to releasing segmented data on the census and regular updates to the decennial census data, the bureau has divisions and programs that specialize in maintaining data on almost every imaginable topic. There are specialists and departments for demographics, population and housing data, international data, geographic and product data, political data, business statistics, construction statistics, and much more. There are also regional centers for the bureau in twelve major cities. A complete list of census departments and services is available by calling the general information number for the Bureau of the Census listed in the reference section of this book.

Other Government Data Sources

Besides the Bureau of the Census, there are many other federal government agencies that maintain data for their specific areas of interest that are available for public review. For example, the Department of Agriculture maintains data on food intake and food consumption, among other agricultural related data. The Bureau of Economic Analysis maintains more detailed information on per capita income than that maintained by the

Bureau of the Census, and also records data on business and industries. The Equal Employment Opportunity Commission (EEOC) maintains data on women and minorities, concentrating on job patterns and education. The Department of Housing and Urban Development offers an enormous amount of data through its American Housing Survey, which contains demographic information on home occupants, changes in occupancy over time, housing trends, and other housing-related statistics. The Small Business Administration (SBA) maintains diverse business-related data. Even the Internal Revenue Service (IRS) provides data on income levels and income sources, most of which has been coded to protect the privacy of individual taxpayers, of course. Almost any federal agency offers some sort of tabulated or computer-based data for public use.

Individual states and counties also provide public-use data through their agencies. State and local data comes from departments that maintain state-wide data research agencies (often associated with major universities), and local information agencies. Most states, counties, and large cities have offices for planning and budgeting that offer a wide range of data, in addition to employment development offices, population research departments, and public service departments. Almost every state has a department or group that specializes in business research as well. The list of government departments and information numbers is available in the respective telephone books for particular areas.

International Data Sources

Because international trade and the emergence of the global economy is so important in today's business environment, many companies with an eye to the future will want to complete market mapping research on international locations.

There are a number of sources for international data—data that segments populations on lifestyle criteria as well as national boundaries and cultural criteria. For example, the United States Bureau of the Census keeps an *International Database* with 107 tables with demographic and socioeconomic data for 206 countries and produces a variety of reports. Much of this data comes from the census data collected by developed countries. For less developed countries (called LDCs) the data is gathered, but is not as accurate. The bureau publishes only a part of the vast amount of international data it acquires.

Other sources of international data include the East-West Center in Hawaii, which gathers information on Asia-Pacific populations. The European Society for Opinion and Marketing Research (ESOMAR) is a professional marketing society that specializes in European demographics and market research. The

Euromonitor Consultancy offers many consumer research services and publishes a variety of statistical references on the European community. The Latin American Demographic Center (CELADE), established by the United Nations, conducts applied research and produces publications on Latin America and the Caribbean. Statistics Canada is the Canadian equivalent of the United States Bureau of the Census, producing a wide range of statistics and data on Canadian populations, labor market trends, and income patterns. In addition, the United Nations, the World Bank, and the World Health Organization all produce useful and relevant international market data. There are countless other sources. Information for contacting some of the most common sources for international data is provided in the reference section at the end of this book.

Industry Associations, Nonprofit Organizations, and University Data Sources

The industry organizations and nonprofit organizations that gather data that can be used for market mapping research are too numerous to list. Almost every industry has its own association or institute that gathers market data related to the industry. Examples of such organizations are the American Institute of Food Distribution, the National Association of Home Builders, the Conference Board, and, of course, the American Chamber of Commerce Research Association.

In addition to these industry-specific and general nonprofit organizations, almost every major university has a business department with a research institute that specializes in some aspect of marketing or business research. Some of these university research centers are members of the National Clearinghouse for Census Data Services, which means they own tapes from the decennial census. From these tapes, these university data centers can provide data for anywhere in the United States. Some of the universities complete research (for a fee, of course) for outside clients, and also support the research interests of their faculty members. Some of these university data centers are listed in the reference section at the end of this book. For data available from other universities, check out the business department or library to find out what is available.

Commercial Data Sources

The problem with gathering raw data from government sources—whether domestic or international—is that the data may be very detailed and difficult to decipher. In order to get the data required for a specific marketing problem, it may be necessary to integrate the data from three or more sources. For this reason, there are a number of commercial data companies that organize, integrate, and sort government-supplied data into more useful formats. In fact, most software companies repackage data from a variety of sources to be compatible with their programs.

There are also cadres of companies that complete independent marketing research and sell their data in a variety of formats—including publications, data listings, computer tapes, and CD-ROMs. Other research companies combine government data and independently gathered data into unique data products. Still others sell mailing lists and subscriber information, which can be useful in market mapping research.

There is commercial data available for almost every marketing interest—from lists of specific customers for obscure products to complete demographic studies of the world. In addition to differences in content, commercially available data ranges in quality, format, and price, just like any other product. Supplying data for marketing analysis can be a very profitable business. Sometimes commercial data companies only repackage what you can get for free from the government. Other companies add significant value to the data by making it compatible with your computer system, adding information and variables, and verifying data to eliminate duplications and errors.

Because of the wide range of suppliers, it is important to know your sources before you buy. Your marketing analysis is only as good as the data you put into it. Making the right decisions on invalid data won't make you a cent. Ask questions about the sources of the data, the age of the data, and

A Sample of Commercial Data Available for Market Mapping Research

Automotive Registration Data	Crime Risk Assessment
Hotels, Restaurants, and Nightclubs	Direct Mail Information
Lifestyle Data	Yellow Pages Summaries
Shopping Centers and Commercial Centers	Grocery Store and Supermarket Statistics
Consumer Demand Statistics	Retailing Business Statistics
Market Potential Statistics	Physician and Healthcare Databases
Women's and Minorities Databases	Senior Citizen Databases
Business Locations, Sales, and Other Commercial Statistics	Pricing and Consumption Statistics by Industry and Location
Banks and Savings and Loan Locations and Related Data	Financial Consumer Demand and Other Financial Statistics
Service Industry Statistics	Household Statistics
Traffic Patterns	Distribution Routes

the handling of the data before you subscribe to an expensive data service or spend next year's profits on the rights to analyze a large database. The reference section at the end of this book provides an annotated list of many commercial data companies that supply data products that can be used in market mapping research for almost any industry or customer population.

How is Commercial Data Packaged?

Commercial data is packaged and priced based on content and geographic locations. Prices for data sets range from a few dollars for a single report on one aspect of a small geographic area to thousands of dollars for complete demographics of the United States. Pricing for the same data may vary from company to company, so it's a good idea to shop around if your data requirements are serviced by more than one distributor.

Data is typically sold by specific geographic segments or industry segments that can be identified and specified in many different ways. In addition to census divisions, there are other common terms that describe the geographic divisions used to identify specific data sets. These include:

- *ACORN*—A lifestyle segmentation system that categorizes neighborhoods into 44 unique types, developed by CACI Marketing Systems specifically for businesses targeting specific areas such as finance, insurance, or restaurant services.

- *ADI (Area of Dominant Influence)*—Arbitron is a media and purchase behavior research firm that specifies ADIs as specific television viewing areas.

- *DMA (Designated Market Area)*—A.C. Neilsen, a media research firm that specializes in television behavior, specifies DMAs as television viewing areas.

- *MCD (Minor Civil Division)*—A political and administrative division of a country. Generally, an MCD is a township.

- *MSA (Metropolitan Statistical Area), SMSA (Standard Metropolitan Statistical Area), P/MSA (Primary/Metropolitan Statistical Area), CMSA (Consolidated Metropolitan Statistical Area)*—An MSA is a free-standing metropolitan area surrounded by nonmetropolitan counties, an area with a population of at least 100,000, or an urbanized area with a population of at least 50,000 as defined by the Bureau of the Census. SMSA, CMSA, and P/MSA are various adaptations for defining metropolitan areas and their relative locations to one another.

- *PRIZM*—A lifestyle definition system, marketed by Claritas, that identifies populations by clusters of combined characteristics. PRIZM classifies all United States households into 40 neighborhood types at the block group level using census demographics combined with customer records.

- *SAMI (Selling Area Marketing, Inc.)*—SAMI is a division of Arbitron that tracks product movement for advertisers and retailers of packaged goods. The geographic areas reported on are often referred to as SAMI areas.

- *SIC (Standard Industrial Classification)*—A system used to classify business data by industry, sales, brands, and other criteria.

- *VALS (Values and Lifestyles)*—Developed by Arnold Mitchell and the firm of SRI International in Palo Alto, California, VALS is a widely used lifestyle and psychographic data classification system that describes both social and psychological attributes of populations.

- *Zip code or zip code centroid*—A standard five-digit zip code (with four-digit extension for further location detail) established by the United States Postal Service to facilitate mail delivery. A zip code centroid is an area that surrounds a central post office point identified by the first three numbers of the zip code.

On-line Data Sources

Many data distributors and research firms provide data products over electronic mail systems or commercial information networks like CompuServe, Prodigy, BRS, Dialog, or other services. To access data on-line, you will need to connect to a host system (where the information is stored or accessed) so you can download the information to your personal computer system. This is done with a modem, a hardware device used to transmit and receive information over ordinary telephone lines and with communications software that handles the interchange of information between your system and another system.

On-line access to data is relatively quick, but the convenience of gathering the data on-line using a modem to connect to a host database may cost more. In addition to the costs of the data itself, there may be charges for connect time to the database and access charges for using the information service.

On-line data searches are usually best for searches with immediate, high priority, for regular updates on small data sets, or for placing orders for complete data sets that will be sent to you through conventional mail or shipping companies. The sheer volume of data on-line can make searches difficult and expensive, if not handled properly. To help streamline data acquisition, there are front-end software programs available to develop keyword searches and assist with downloading the data to your computer. To maximize your on-line time, it is important to plan your on-line searches in

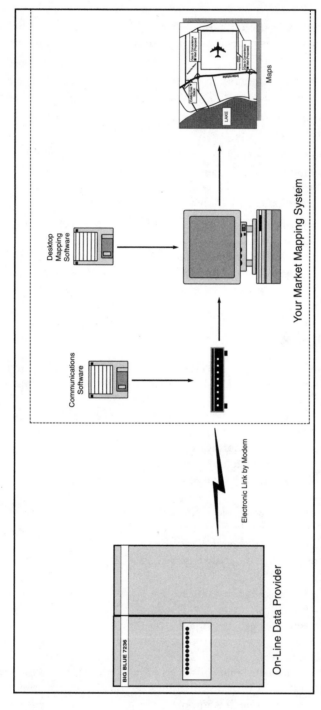

Figure 4-4. On-line data access to commercial databases such as CompuServe can be imported using a modem and communications software.

advance, download one data set or article at a time, and review all material off-line, so you don't run up needless on-line access charges.

If you don't have the time to master on-line searching, there are brokers that can handle on-line data searches for you. For a fee, a broker or research firm will search through all the relevant databases for the data you request on competitors, suppliers, or customers.

A list of the more common on-line services for data acquisition is included in the resources section at the end of the book. To evaluate an on-line service for your particular research requirements, you should first determine your information requirements, and then evaluate the various services based on on-line charges, fixed costs, the number and variety of databases available, and the regularity of updates to the databases.

Data from Independent Research

If you can't find the information you need from the government, nonprofit organizations, or commercial data suppliers, then you can always complete your own independent research on specific marketing questions related to your products and customers. You can design and implement your own research program, hire one of the many marketing research firms around the country, or use the services of an advertising agency that specializes in marketing research.

Completing research for market mapping is like any other business research program. However, you must make sure you gather geographic attribute data such as addresses or zip codes, so the information can be mapped. The basic kinds of research used for gathering market data in general include:

- *Focus groups*—Focus groups involve assembling a group of customers or potential customers in a group meeting, showing them alternative ad concepts, competing products, or other marketing materials, and then having them discuss their reactions to each of the choices. The group is moderated by a focus group specialist. A trained observer takes notes on the reactions, or the group is videotaped and the observations are documented later. Focus groups don't provide conclusive evidence, but they are excellent tools for evaluating the impact of alternative choices among promotional and product concepts, or marketing communications tools, such as packaging, product names, or corporate image programs.

- *Consumer and industry surveys*—Surveys can range from simple to complex and have a wide range of applications. They can be used to test messages, concepts, attitudes, and to define the market demographics.

Survey methodology involves using a well-designed survey instrument (the questionnaire) and mailing it, or otherwise distributing it to an appropriate list of customers or potential customers. For new consumer products, it is not uncommon for surveys to be conducted in malls or supermarkets or distributed door-to-door. In-store surveys include informal surveys at the point of sale that are initiated by the sales clerk or brief questionnaires at the check-out stand or on the back of an invoice.

- *In-store tests*—In-store research programs are used by large consumer product companies inside stores in controlled market areas. Consumers are provided with a variety of test products and merchandising choices. Observations are then recorded about the consumer's behavior. This type of research can also be completed by small companies to test reactions to sales displays, the mix of products on the shelves, or choices on a menu.

Other common research techniques include comprehensive market analyses, consumer panels, purchase monitoring programs, and special trade studies. Most of these comprehensive research programs are suited for large companies and are best handled by agencies or research firms that specialize in promotional and marketing research.

For more information on marketing research options, a well-stocked bookstore or library should have a text on marketing research if you are not already familiar with research design and development. There are also some general references on marketing research and a list of some large research firms at the end of this book if independent research is necessary.

Getting Data into Your Mapping Program

The data you find for your market mapping research will most likely come in one of three formats: printed listings, computer files, or CD-ROM. To be analyzed by a market mapping program the data must be put into a format that can be read or translated by the desktop mapping program.

Data Compatibility and Translation Issues

All printed data must be put into machine readable formats usable by desktop mapping programs. This is usually done with optical character recognition software (OCR) and a scanner, as described later, or handled manually by entering the data into a compatible database management program or spreadsheet program.

If you want to use data from your mainframe computer, you can access this data through a mainframe data exchange program, or use a network system or communications program to gather the data. The mainframe data will need to be translated into an appropriate format. Some sophisticated mapping programs can access the remote database and gather the data directly for importation into the mapping system for you, using systems like DAL (Data Acquisition Language) supported by some Macintosh programs and an ethernet network. Databases that are SQL-compatible can usually share data with one another without much modification. SQL, which stands for Standard Query Language, is a data access and reporting standard that is used by many database software developers to assure compatibility and easy access to data from various computer platforms. Other data gathered through mainframe programs or personal computer database software may need to be translated, using third-party routines or specific translation programs that transform the data into formats compatible with the mapping software.

Data designed for use on IBM-PCs and compatible computers must be translated so it can work on Macintosh computers. There are a number of inexpensive software programs for doing this. Other files can be saved as ASCII or other standard formats and read directly by the mapping software.

Some data is proprietary and cannot be translated for other environments or programs. In this case, the software vendor is locking you into its system. For example, the data files created within many mapping programs can only be read by that single program. Be aware of the data-sharing capability across software products. For example, you may want to use data from your database program, load it into your mapping program, add information to it, and then transfer it back to your database program for other kinds of analysis.

Before you buy attribute data from any source or in any format, make sure it is compatible or can be made compatible with your system. Each mapping program is compatible with different kinds of data files—ranging from simple ASCII compatibility for text files to complete compatibility with spreadsheet formats, database systems, and mainframe files. Some mapping programs won't accept data from other formats at all—you must enter the data directly into the program from scratch. These programs are usually limited to presentation-level analysis. At the very least, a mapping program suitable for marketing analysis should be able to accept spreadsheet data in rows and columns, and translate text-based files in delimited ASCII format (a standard data representation for textual data) into formats suitable for mapping. The more sophisticated programs will do much more than this and make the process of getting data into and out of the system a breeze. After all, the faster you can get the data into the map, the faster you can start visualizing the decisions you need to make.

Tip—Import Data as "Delimited ASCII"

Most databases and spreadsheets are capable of saving files in delimited ASCII. This means the file becomes plain ASCII text with commas or tabs inserted between columns to separate the fields. Such a file format can be directly imported into most mapping software, ready for geocoding. If, however, the file is coming from a program that can't add the tabs or commas directly, save the file as ASCII within the original program. Then add "delimiters" manually from within your word processor. To do this, open the file in your word processor and turn on the word processor's *Show Invisibles* option (this may be called *Show Paragraphs* or some other name that means the same thing). This will allow you to see tabs and paragraph marks to simplify formatting. Use tabs if the file contains commas as part of the data. Once the tabs are added and a hard return (a paragraph symbol created by pressing *Enter* or *Return*) ends each record, the file is ready for importing. Last, save the file as ASCII text with the word processor's *Save As* or *Save As Other* command. If there's a *Save with Line Breaks* option, use it for saving the file. You're now ready to import your "incompatible" file!

Attribute Data Formats and How to Use Them

Attribute data may be delivered in several media formats; your company may own data in several forms. Formats include data stored on floppy disks, magnetic tape, CD-ROM, or paper. Obviously, the easiest format to work with is floppy disks that can be directly read by your desktop computer. Some data sources will provide their data in one of several formats; all you need to do is specify what format you desire when ordering.

For data contained on incompatible disks, translation utilities such as Mac-Link and PC-Link are available. These programs allow you to translate a variety of file formats from one machine to another. Macintoshes equipped with Apple's SuperDrive can directly read DOS-formatted disks, but it takes a translation program to actually convert one file format to another in many cases. Attribute data, however, is usually so simply formatted that a little touch-up with a word processor cleans up the file for geocoding.

For data stored in or imported from a minicomputer or mainframe on magnetic tape, things get a little stickier. Basically, your options lie in either using the creating computer to make the data readable by your microcomputer, or adding the capability to your microcomputer to read the tape. Larger computers can talk to smaller computers directly via networks, or you can send the file via modem from mainframe to micro, and then sort it out with a translation program, if needed. (If you work in a company with a mainframe computer and need to transfer data from it to your microcomputer that's not networked to the mainframe, look around the company to find one that is.) The second option of adding tape-reading capabilities to your microcomputer can be accomplished with one of the tape drives that is PC or Mac compatible. Unless you plan to work with magnetic tape extensively, a nine-track tape drive can be relatively expensive for a microcomputer, often costing more than the computer itself.

Using Optical Character Recognition to Transform Printed Data

There is so much data that is printed or photocopied that you will probably want to get some of this data into your computer so it can be analyzed. Other than laboriously keying the information by hand, a superior alternative is optical character recognition. OCR works by scanning the information on a page of paper and translating it into text that can be manipulated by a computer. There are a variety of OCR systems available, from tiny hand-held scanners that allow you to scan a page in a book, to stand-alone machines that do nothing but convert printed text to electronic data.

OCR software works with scanners to read printed text, and turns it into computer-compatible formats. These files can then be checked and formatted as delimited ASCII or other formats for use in database programs and spreadsheets that can be used directly by your mapping software.

If you have important data that is published on paper, then the purchase of a scanner and some optical character recognition (OCR) software might be a viable alternative for preparing data for your mapping research. There are also service bureaus in most major cities that provide OCR services, if you have a large amount of printed data to translate into computer-readable formats. Scanning and translating printed files can be time consuming, however, so before you buy all your data in printed forms, consider the cost in time for using OCR to translate your data files, if you are comparing the costs of data in various formats. Also, there are some errors than can creep into the data during the scanning and OCR translation process, so you will need to check and verify the data, which also takes time.

The most commonly used system for OCR applications includes a flatbed scanner with a sheetfeeder, and an OCR software package that works directly with your desktop computer. Software may by purchased with the machine, or bought separately from several vendors. When purchasing a scanner without an OCR package, make sure that the software you purchase can directly drive the scanner, or you will have to scan the pages one at a time and import them into the OCR program for conversion.

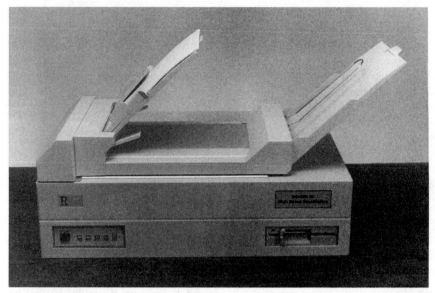

Figure 4-5. Large volumes of data that must be processed with OCR software can be handled with a scanner equipped with a sheet feeder. This unit, integrating a 386-based computer, is a stand-alone scanning station. *(Photograph courtesy of Regent Peripherals.)*

A second consideration when choosing OCR software is the technique it uses to recognize text. Less expensive packages are of the "trainable" variety. That means you must work with the package to train it on each kind of character size and shape, one at a time. Once trained, the package reads the typeface without further help from you. Unfortunately, unless all the data you plan to use is printed with an identical font and font size, you must retrain the package for each new publication you plan to scan, if the type is different. For serious users, these packages are frustrating toys of little use for processing large volumes of data.

The second kind of package, while usually more expensive, is software that has enough intelligence to handle the recognition automatically with almost no intervention from you. This is the kind of package to buy. Examples of this software include Caere's Omnipage, Xerox's Accutext, and Calera's Wordscan. With one of these packages, you simply launch the application, load the scanner's automatic feeder, start the scanning, and go home for the night. In the morning, all of the data will have been converted automatically for you.

If your data is poorly printed or is a seventh-generation photocopy, then all bets are off, even for the best OCR software. While many packages can interpret low-resolution dot matrix output, pages of messy data with characters that are too thick or thin, or pages covered with glitches from top to bottom, may not be convertible without human intervention. (Glitches are small black marks that get into photocopies from dirty glass when copying, or into printed materials from a wide range of sources.) When considering OCR software, bring a copy of a representative document, and try scanning and converting to see what happens. This is a good way to determine a program's ability to recognize poorly copied pages.

Customizing Data for Your Own Research

Using the database management programs and statistical analysis functions available in sophisticated desktop mapping products, it is possible to combine data elements and create new statistics from compilations of data from various sources. Some mapping programs can work with multiple data sources to create a single map, without even modifying the databases. Using functions like name and address matching, it is possible to combine data from various data sources to come up with completely new combinations of data for your research. The value of combining multiple data sources in one map can be very powerful for trend analysis, new market planning, and a variety of other data-intensive research formats.

Chapter Summary

Without data, market mapping is impossible. As you've seen in this chapter, data for market mapping is both abundant and diverse. In this chapter, the wide range of data sources for marketing research and market mapping has been revealed, including:

- Company-specific sources
- Self-generated sources
- Consumer and customer sources
- Industrial sources
- Government data sources, including federal, state, and local data sources, in addition to the data amassed by the Bureau of the Census
- International sources
- Industry associations and organizations

The addresses and phone numbers for many of the sources presented in the chapter are provided in the resources section at the end of this book. The chapter also presented the data compatibility and translation issues that you must consider in order to put attribute data in a form usable by your desktop mapping program.

In the next chapter, information on setting up your market mapping system, including criteria for selecting both hardware and software for your market mapping efforts, will be covered in detail. You can then choose the system best suited for your marketing research requirements and your budget. After setting up your system, you will be ready to put market mapping to work as an integral part of your business research and analysis efforts.

5

Choosing the Best Market Mapping System for Your Business

At this point you are probably convinced, as we are, that desktop mapping is a technology that every person involved with marketing decisions and every business must have access to in order to compete effectively in the fast-changing, globally dependent environment of modern business. Before you jump on the bandwagon, however, there are three decisions you should make prior to buying the software and computer for your market mapping research.

First, you must analyze your requirements to understand what you need from market mapping tools. Having a set of clear objectives helps when selecting software packages and data. Second, you must identify the desktop mapping program and the data to go with it that meets these goals as closely as possible. Third, once you have selected a software package and data, you will need to choose the new hardware required or upgrade an existing computer system to complete your market mapping research system.

This chapter will explain how to define your goals, choose the right mapping software and data, and explain the options for putting your maps to work communicating market mapping information to coworkers, management, and customers.

Understanding Your Mapping Needs

In selecting a market mapping system, your research needs should define your requirements for software, data, and hardware. Unlike purchasing a word processor or spreadsheet, where any quality product works pretty much the same as other products, market mapping products differ greatly in their capabilities and in the kind and quality of data that's compatible (and available) for them. In addition, the quality and sophistication of the maps they produce vary considerably from manufacturer to manufacturer.

A clearly defined goal for your research efforts allows you to choose between products much more easily. For example, a goal of "locate 10 billboard sites in the busiest intersections within all west coast cities containing more than 500,000 people, and then produce a color map of each site at the street level" is very specific. Working backward from this goal, it is easy to identify the right software, geographic data, and attribute data required and a machine to run the software. A goal of "purchasing a mapping system to find billboards" is vague and may result in the acquisition of a system limited in market mapping capabilities or lacking in specific data.

Of course, you want a mapping system that meets *all* of your market mapping needs, so the system should be defined for a number of goals rather than just one. Usually, listing all the goals that must be satisfied over a period of time allows you to purchase a system with the right degree of power and flexibility, rather than one that handles an immediate need perfectly, but is less useful for other projects. We have provided a planning worksheet for this purpose that may help you refine your market mapping research requirements. The ideal mapping system is one that has the flexibility to handle all of your market mapping requirements without serious compromise, one that has a wide variety of compatible mapping and attribute data available, and one with a justifiable purchase price based on the work it will accomplish for you.

To start you thinking about possibilities, here are some common uses of market mapping that will help you establish your own market mapping system requirements.

- *Analyzing situations to make a marketing or business decision.* Example: weighing placement options for retail stores based on the demographics of the surrounding residential areas or looking for new markets and new product possibilities.

- *Presenting information to investors, customers, or executives.* Example: display quotas and performance by sales territory in a formal presentation at a board meeting.

Market Mapping Goal Identification Worksheet

Briefly define the marketing problem or question.

What makes market mapping the best solution for solving this problem or answering this question?

Define the information required to fulfill this need or solve the problem.

Are locations involved in the problem? (Describe)

Is distribution involved in the problem? (Describe)

Using the above information, set the marketing goal for the map (in thirty words or less).

Define the secondary problems and needs that the project will solve or fulfill.

Figure 5-1. A goal-identification worksheet for market mapping applications.

- *Spotting trouble.* Example: if you are a bank executive, you could study maps of competing bank locations to see where your coverage and presence is weak. Or, you could analyze sales performance over a range of market criteria to identify your company's weaknesses.

- *Evaluating business performance.* Example: if you run a chain of retail stores within several cities, a map contrasting each store's retail sales relative to population and income levels is a singularly powerful communications device for comparing levels of relative sales success.

- *Tracking business assets.* Example: if you distribute goods to various locations, maps could be used to track where your goods are stored in comparison to where the market is. Or, a film distributor could use market maps to track where films are physically stored, where they should go next, and how successful they are at generating revenue in each market area.

- *Communicating findings to coworkers, management, and customers.* Example: maps of selected billboards, surrounding traffic patterns, and demographics might be used in a meeting with managers to approve the billboard selections.

Most businesses need a combination of presentation, communication, and analysis capabilities. Since you probably haven't used market mapping as part of your research program before now, you need to explore the possibilities for mapping your business data before you purchase a mapping program.

The Right Mapping Software for Your Applications

While keeping your research goals in mind, begin reviewing software products for both functionality and data availability. As explained in Chap. 2, some products are extremely limited in capabilities, where others are so chock full of functionality that, for the casual user, there is a steep learning curve involved. A general rule of thumb is *the more capable the mapping product, the more complicated it is to learn and use.* This isn't bad—it just means that if you have a lot of mapping analysis to do, you need to allocate a little time for learning the ins and outs of the programs.

Your needs for a market mapping product will likely include several levels of functionality. If your need includes only conveying information to coworkers, an inexpensive presentation or thematic package may meet all of your needs. However, if you want a package with which to make complex marketing decisions based on demographics and internal data owned by your company, a package with powerful querying and analysis tools is required. Or, if you need all of the above capabilities, a more expensive GIS package that integrates presentation tools may be the one for you.

And, while it doesn't concern us in a book about marketing applications, powerful GIS programs can be used to specify locations for power lines, fire hydrants, water pipes, and sewer systems for entire cities. If your company also has requirements for this type of specific location planning, detailed architectural rendering, or topographically accurate space analysis, then a full-featured GIS might be an appropriate choice to complete both market mapping and physical location applications.

 Tip—If Buying a Chef's Hat Could Only Make You A Chef . . .

A common practice among the manufacturers of graphics software is to assemble a real knockout tutorial to showcase a product. Because most people evaluate mapping products by working through at least part of the tutorial before making a purchase decision, software manufacturers sometimes create a tutorial that exceeds the capabilities of the average user. The company may add elaborate color maps and spend extra time adding icons and other elements designed by a professional illustrator. Such a sophisticated map might take you a month to learn how to duplicate, if you could do it at all. Watch out for this problem by carefully analyzing what the program does in the tutorial and then attempting to recreate a map similar to the tutorial maps on your own. This will give you a better idea of how much work went into the demo and how long it will take you to acquire the skills required to do something similar. Another tactic common to less powerful programs is to take you through a snazzy tutorial that shows the program's entire range of functions and leaves the impression that it can do what you see, plus a lot more. In the case of an inexpensive program, study the manual to see what else the product can do, if anything.

What to Look for When Choosing Mapping Software

All mapping software should be evaluated around three parameters: the software's querying capabilities, its presentation abilities, and the data that's available for it—both geographic (map) data and attribute data. Secondary parameters include the mapping product's drawing and colorizing tools. Some packages are also upgradeable by purchasing additional modules or "trading-up" to more powerful packages made by the same company. If such an upgrade is available, ensure that the new program can still access and manipulate the old program's files and work with any data files already in use.

In addition to these basic parameters, some packages are simply much easier to use than others and more predictable in their results. Much like an advanced spreadsheet or page layout program, you may find that you relate to the interface and operation of one program better than another, even though the two programs are comparable in features, data availability, and querying power.

Consider Data Availability and Compatibility First

When shopping for mapping software, the first criteria to consider are data availability and data compatibility. No matter how powerful or easy to use a software product is, if you can't either purchase the right data set or import it from elsewhere, the product is of no use to you. And, while most mapping product manufacturers are adding new data packages to their products, a promise that the data you need will be available in a "couple of months" should be heavily discounted at best.

In most cases you will want a product with a wide range of maps and attribute data available from the manufacturer and the ability to easily import attribute data from standard sources. Some products come with more base maps than others, too, making them relative bargains if the base maps are something you will use. If much of the data you plan to use is contained in your company's spreadsheets, look for a package that makes the importation of this material simple and accurate. If your data must be imported from another computer such as a mainframe, look for a package offering a conversion routine or a direct database link for this information. Also check that the right kind and quality of map data is available because, unlike attribute data, map data for many programs can only be acquired from the product's manufacturer. Of course, you may also want to work with data acquired from other databases and data sources. Naturally, your software's data importation capabilities and file compatibility options will be important considerations if you need to access and manipulate such files.

The Interface Is the Next Major Consideration

You need an interface that is easy to get around in and that supports queries of the complexity required to fulfill your goals. Preferably, this querying process should be simple and intuitive, although power and complexity are often an acceptable combination. Again, look for software with an interface you can relate to, not one that seems odd or that requires layers of menus, endless dialog boxes, or cryptic keyboard commands to accomplish even the simplest tasks. Such hard-to-use software often becomes "shelfware," or it takes the fun out of creating maps because of tedious and repetitious operations. Be equally wary of products that you seem to master in just minutes. This usually indicates a program that lacks power and sophistication, even though it creates impressive maps the first time around.

Overall Functionality Should Be Tested Next

The best way to evaluate a product's functionality is to try it out before buying it. Unfortunately, this is not always possible, because few computer retailers have the right mapping software and data set up for you to try. If you can't try the program, at least work through a prospective product's demonstration program before purchasing it. Almost every mapping software manufacturer offers a disk-based demonstration they will send to you for free or for a small fee. Another way to try the product before making a final commitment is to purchase a mapping product from a dealer, manufacturer, or mail order house that allows you a money-back guaranteed trial period. In a 30-day trial period, for example, you will have ample opportunity to work with a product to create a variety of maps, test the validity of the data purchased, and evaluate the program's interface.

At the very least, study the product's manuals before buying. When using powerful mapping software, with its multitude of functions, the manual is your first point of refuge when you encounter a problem or don't know how to make a function work, so quality manuals are important in getting the most from your investment. A product should have a well-organized manual that explains the product's operation in detail. It must have a credible index and should fully cover the product's functionality. A troubleshooting guide doesn't hurt either. Manuals that are thin, incompetently written, poorly organized, or that ignore some of the product's functions are reasons to pass on the product. Incomplete manuals may also indicate a product that was rushed to market and not adequately tested or debugged. Beware!

As a small part of the decision, consider what kind of post-sales perks come with each package. Some companies offer monthly newsletters with timely technical support information and how-to tips. Others forget your existence until it's time to sell you an upgrade or a new data package at a "once-in-a-lifetime special price."

Consider These General Software Capabilities as Well

When choosing market mapping software, there are several general, technical requirements that should be considered. Sometimes product defects hide under a layer of sophistication and glossy cosmetics, and sometimes these features are easy to miss or simply ignore. That's why we cover them in detail here—because they are important considerations in making an informed decision about the software you'll use for your market mapping analyses.

Projection and View Options.   While maps that focus on a single city are rarely compromised because of projection limitations, unless they lack detail or only zoom to 100 miles above the city, map and mapping products that support a country-wide, continent-wide, or world-wide view should support several projections and various viewing options. Projection and viewing options are important if you need maps that realistically portray the entire earth or if you need a special view of locations, such as a map where Africa is the central continent of the globe, rather than Europe, North America, or Asia.

For example, a typical representation problem in many flat maps of the world is the unrealistically large display of innocuous Greenland. The projection can change a relatively unimportant land mass to one of continent-size importance on a map. When eyes should be focusing on the United States or continental Europe, Greenland looks like the center of the world. If you need to understand distribution distances and location relationships, it is helpful to have views that are accurate representations of land masses in question.

Presentation Capabilities.   In addition to supporting many views of a map, some products allow you to specify a number of different cosmetic approaches to mapping. Simple maps made from lines can be converted to three-dimensional maps, a variety of icons can be used to represent different kinds of businesses, and a choice of type styles, lines, line weights (thicknesses), and colors can be selected.

There is considerable variation among programs in their ability to produce attractive, informative maps. While presentation-level software usually makes great-looking maps, but does little else, analysis-level and GIS packages vary from offering bare bones line-art maps in black and white to full sets of presentation-quality maps with stunning color. If the on-screen rendering of fancy maps is important to you, or if you plan to add your maps to other documents in which attractive cosmetics are important, carefully evaluate presentation capabilities before purchase.

Another factor in this evaluation is consideration of a program's what-you-see-is-what-you-get (WYSIWYG) capabilities. Some programs create maps on screen that look much different in print. Items get moved around, lines change weight (thickness), and type looks jaggy. (Font problems can usually be fixed on-screen and in print with an add-on package, such as Adobe Type Manager on PCs. Macintoshes include ATM as part of their operating software.) Some packages can't add a three-dimensional look to their maps on-screen, but instead wait to fully render the map in print. This makes the product useless for interactive sessions on video. If your presentation requirements include imaging the map at high resolution (described later in this chapter), run sample output before you buy the product. What looks fine on a laser printer at 300 dots per inch may hit a technological brick wall when imaged at 1200 to 2500 dots per inch. Items may not print or may change shape, the placement of design elements may be distorted, or the file may simply produce a useless blank sheet of film.

Data Management.   One of the most powerful capabilities of analysis- and GIS-level mapping software is the ability to take several large, inscrutable files and tables and create a stunning graphic representation of complex data attributes within those files in less than a minute. These representations can be so perfect and quintessential that they almost bring tears to the eyes of people who see the finished map. The distillation of information is so succinct and clear that a child can grasp the comparison as quickly as an adult.

Unfortunately, a few products offer data manipulation facilities that make such work difficult, either because the data manipulation interface is so complex that using it effectively is awkward (to say the least), or it's so over-simplified that a veritable interface-straitjacket limits what you can do with the product.

Test data manipulation functions before purchase by attempting complex, if meaningless, data queries just to see if the program follows your thinking process and interface requirements. Software that requires data restructuring before a map can be produced, or uses commands that resemble computer programming languages should be avoided, unless you are an experienced programmer and you like showing off your technical prowess even when you shouldn't have to.

Market mapping packages that limit your data manipulations to preset formats and sequences can be particularly frustrating when complex market maps are required for a project. These products are like navigating inside a maze with tall walls. You can't see the layout, and the walls won't let you out to explore other options. While at first this kind of program is easier to learn and use, eventually you will feel trapped by its constraints and limited viewpoint. You need a program that is robust, flexible, and still relatively easy to use when making complex data queries.

Layer Management.   As you'll recall from Chap. 3, to produce complex market mapping analyses, layers are assembled on top of each other into a single image or printed map. These layers are handled as separate elements within the mapping software and in some programs each layer can be manip-

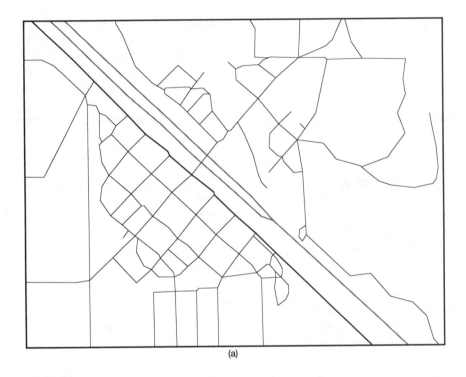

(a)

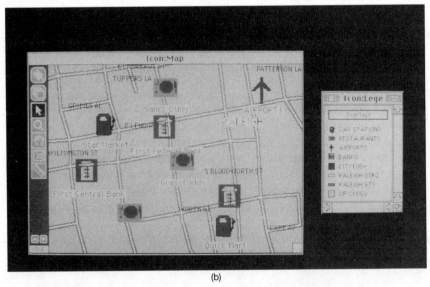

(b)

Figure 5-2. A cosmetically simple map and a more sophisticated map.[21]

ulated in a number of ways. This allows you to add elements, delete superfluous detail, and hide layer elements that complicate a map's key message, but may need to be reintroduced in another map or when another query is made in the same mapping session. The layering capabilities of the software are important, unless your mapping requirements are extremely simple.

Spatial Analysis.   When assembling maps, you want a program that provides detailed control of what goes into the map. You also want a program that can handle diverse geographic queries. If you zoom down to a tight cluster of counties, you want a program that allows you to select and deselect ones that will be used in the map. The program should also allow you to draw a circle and automatically select counties or zip code boundaries contained within the circle. Special features, including point-to-point distance measurement and routing along streets and highways, may be important to you for certain applications. For example, to speed truck-based product delivery, you may want your market mapping program to figure out the fastest and most effective delivery route and be capable of having streets and highways marked out temporarily when under construction. This cuts distribution costs and provides a marketing advantage over competitors using ordinary road maps instead of up-to-the-minute market maps.

Speed of Frequent Operations.   The speed of the product, as well as its functionality, should be considered before you make a final decision on the best product for your market mapping research. Though the speed of a program is partially dependent on the hardware you use, some software products are simply faster to use than others. If time is important to you, like it is for most businesspeople, compare common operations like map redraws and data sorts on the same computer system for the products you are considering.

Selection Criteria
for Presentation-level, Analysis-level,
and GIS-level Products

In addition to the general selection criteria just specified, when your primary requirements center on presentation-level maps you need to look for the following when evaluating software:

- A product that comes with a large set of appropriate symbols. In addition, it is preferable in most cases if the program has the ability to let you create or import your own symbols and graphics into the maps.

- A product that produces attractive maps on the output device of your choice.

- A product that makes export of its maps to other software products convenient. The export file formats must be compatible with the word processor, page layout program, or presentation software you use, and the files must be exported with predictable accuracy. This is especially important if you will be putting the maps into documents or reports for distribution to customers, investors, or other important people.

When you are looking for analysis-level or GIS-level software, the list of features required is more extensive. In addition to evaluating the presentation capabilities of the software, you need to consider all of the following in relationship to your particular market mapping goals:

- *Map Detail and Geographic Accuracy*—Look for a product with maps of the detail and accuracy you require. Mapping programs are either accurate cartographically or they aren't. If your maps will be reproduced for others to see in a report, you may require accuracy. If your needs are strictly analytical, cartographic accuracy may not be important to you. Some products also offer maps with more detail than others. Where many products draw city streets and county and state borders as vaguely accurate jaggy lines, others offer a fair degree of precision. For example, several products we have worked with provide detail of city streets combined with locations of rivers, lakes, railways, highways, and even piers built out into the water. If you are looking for a location for a fast food restaurant or a convenience store, the presence of these geographic elements is vital to *really* understanding your customer reach. The presence of a complex railway system may cut off your trade with people on the other side of the tracks, so knowing the geographic details of an area is vital for certain kinds of location research.

- *Output Options*—Identify all the forms of output you require, including slides, large format maps from plotters, printed maps in black and white, color maps, and maps that can be inserted into presentations or other documents. The printers and other output devices you want to use must be supported by the mapping software. In addition, you will generally want a program that allows you to specify the printed size of the map, the labels and attributes to print, and the colors of all elements (if you are using a color printer); support for PostScript helps if you will be using a laser printer. If you will want to use a plotter for producing your maps in large formats, make sure the program is compatible with the plotter you intend to use.

- *Flexibility and Expandability*—High-end mapping software should be capable of meeting a wide range of goals, as defined earlier in the chapter. When you first try a market mapping program, the ability to manipulate data in a powerful new way may trick you into purchasing a product that makes neat maps, but doesn't meet your needs as you move on to

Market Mapping Software Selection Worksheet

Product Name _____ Date _____

Price: List Price $____ Street Price $____ Dealer Name _____

Geographic Data Availability 1 |—+—+—+—+—+—+—+—+—| 10

Attribute Data Availability 1 |—+—+—+—+—+—+—+—+—| 10

Interface Ease-of-Use 1 |—+—+—+—+—+—+—+—+—| 10

Features/Functionality 1 |—+—+—+—+—+—+—+—+—| 10

Database/Data Management Capabilities 1 |—+—+—+—+—+—+—+—+—| 10

Layer Management 1 |—+—+—+—+—+—+—+—+—| 10

Spatial Analysis Capabilities 1 |—+—+—+—+—+—+—+—+—| 10

Speed of Map Redraws 1 |—+—+—+—+—+—+—+—+—| 10

Geographic Accuracy 1 |—+—+—+—+—+—+—+—+—| 10

Presentation/Reporting Capabilities 1 |—+—+—+—+—+—+—+—+—| 10

Drawing/Map Customization Capabilities 1 |—+—+—+—+—+—+—+—+—| 10

Manufacturer's Reputation 1 |—+—+—+—+—+—+—+—+—| 10

Technical Support Quality 1 |—+—+—+—+—+—+—+—+—| 10

Documentation Quality 1 |—+—+—+—+—+—+—+—+—| 10

Overall Rating 1 |—+—+—+—+—+—+—+—+—| 10

Comments:
_____
_____
_____
_____

Figure 5-3. Product comparison worksheet.

more complicated projects. Ideally, choose a product that makes simple mapping chores fast and easy, but that is also fully capable of accommodating longer, more complicated mapping investigations.

- *Drawing Tools*—A package with basic drawing capabilities is required if you want to annotate maps from within the mapping program. If you need custom symbols for your maps, a symbol editor for creating and manipulating icons (symbols) is useful.

- *Graphing, Charting, and Reporting Capabilities*—If you need to produce conventional charts, graphs, and reports of your data in addition to maps, some mapping programs allow you to create these from within the mapping environment, eliminating the need for other graphic, spreadsheet, or word processing programs. As full-featured visual representation systems, these products save time and effort, because data doesn't need to be transferred from one program to another.

- *Statistical Analysis and Database Management Capabilities*—If you need to perform mathematical or statistical calculations on your data, such as averages, totals, or even complex statistical functions, some mapping programs integrate the capabilities of a spreadsheet program, database management program, and statistical analysis package. These capabilities allow you to perform interactive calculations on your data before and during mapping, making what-if analysis easier and more productive.

 Tip—There's Color and Then There's Color

The majority of mapping software products support color maps. However, "color support" may vary, starting with the ability to add simple colors and crude shadings to lines and shapes and going as far as high levels of color support where maps can be shaded with one of almost 17,000,000 colors and rendered in three dimensions. If you need color support for presentation or video display purposes, test the product's colorization abilities and drawing tools thoroughly before purchase. Note also that some of the least powerful programs still have impressive color capabilities. If you need both versatile color management and a strong suite of analytical functions, carefully test both aspects in a variety of products before you make a final selection.

- *Hierarchical Analysis Capabilities*—For marketing analysis you usually need a program that can work at many levels of abstraction at the same time. In addition, you need a program that allows you to get the right level of mapping detail without a lot of extra effort. Many programs allow you to start at the "Skylab" level and then zoom down to see increasingly small areas with greater detail. With some products, you can't zoom all the way down to the street level or you can't look at data interactively. If analysis at various levels is important, then make sure the software supports interactive zooming and alternate map views from the same data set. Programs that allow you to see multiple windows at the same time are particularly helpful for analyzing trends and market opportunities that involve complex combinations of statistics and data relationships.

- *Compatibility with Other Programs and Data Formats*—Choose a program that allows you to easily export your work to other programs. For example, you may want to take your maps and combine them into a page layout program for reproduction or into a presentation package to create 35-millimeter slides or overhead transparencies. Some programs make this easier than others. Some export maps in a wide range of graphic file formats, making them compatible with more applications. Others save in only one format. So, if your receiving program doesn't accept this format, you'll need to convert the file with a file translation program first. You may also need the ability to export data, reports, and graphs.

- *Quality and Availability of Technical Support*—Look for packages that are adequately supported by the manufacturer. First, you want the program's technical support to be first-rate, especially if the package you are purchasing is complicated. The ideal technical support arrangement is unlimited support by knowledgeable and friendly technicians on a toll-free 800 number. Unfortunately, from some companies you have to settle for a lot less. We test technical support by coming up with a question that only someone who really uses and understands the product can answer. We call at a busy time of the week—typically Monday morning at 10:00 A.M. for most companies—and then see what happens. Note that the automated support systems being installed by some companies are nearly useless for all but the novice user—make sure there is access to a real person when you need one.

- *The Experience and Reputation of the Manufacturer*—Choose a product from a manufacturer that has a reputation for quality and has been in either the data business or the software business for a few years. On-going support for your mapping software is important to you because you will want updates to the data and continued enhancements to be made to your mapping program as technology continues to evolve.

Choosing Geographic Data

After evaluating the software programs in general, you need to determine if the geographic data is available for the types of analyses you want to make. As explained in Chap. 3, geographic data is used by market mapping software to create "raw" or "base" maps. Maps are available for all products directly from their manufacturers. Some companies are also building maps for use with other companies' software. When purchasing from the manufacturer, there will rarely be compatibility problems, but maps from other companies may not be 100 percent compatible. While that's not to say you shouldn't buy them, test them fully before losing your return privileges. Test at several zoom levels and check all cities or counties for obvious errors or anomalies.

A defective map may look fine at Skylab level but will exhibit strange idiosyncrasies when you zoom down. For example, one third-party map of the San Francisco Bay Area must have been drawn after the 1989 earthquake. The San Francisco side of the Bay Bridge doesn't connect to the Oakland side on the map. In fact, the ends were about 10 miles apart in the middle of the bay. In addition to obvious problems like this one, when purchasing geographic data you should also look for these attributes:

- *Cosmetic quality.* If you plan to mix third-party maps with ones sold by the software manufacturer, compare them for visual similarity if cosmetic continuity is important to your project. The third-party maps may be completely different in style, detail, and color. If you are considering the purchase of TIGER maps and data, study competing products carefully. They vary considerably in quality.

- *Information layering.* When purchasing map data, if you need to break apart salient features such as counties, check that the data allows you to separate them from each other onto layers or break them into independent maps.

- *Comprehensive data.* Some geographic data is not complete and some is not accurate. To test integrity and completeness, perform a series of "find tests." Load the data and look at it. Most sophisticated mapping software allows you to use an intelligent "find" command or dialog to look for locations without assembling a complex map. For example, if you are looking for city-street-level cartographic data, and know the city, search for small alleys and streets to ensure completeness. Look also for a street called "unknown." If there are many areas listed with this name, it will be difficult to geocode and display a significant portion of your attribute data.

- *Precision and cartographic accuracy.* If you require maps that offer a high degree of precision cartographically, or if you need topographic information to assist in your site planning efforts, load the product's maps and view them on a monitor. Then, attempt to compare the electronic representation to conventional printed maps to judge detail and accuracy. Physical topographic maps can be purchased from government agencies and specialized map retail stores for comparison with the electronic versions. Keep in mind that cartographically accurate maps don't necessarily contain any topographic information, and topographic maps may not contain detail such as street grids. Some mapping programs allow you to link layers of topographic and street-level detail to maximize the analysis possibilities. This level of linkage is not necessary for everyone, but those who need it should verify that the geographic files are compatible, as well as accurate.

How to Select Attribute Data

The types and sources of attribute data were covered in detail in the previous chapter. As emphasized in the chapter, attribute data is central to the success of market mapping research. For this reason, it is important to study available data options carefully. Ideally, you want to purchase as much data as possible from the company that manufactures your market mapping software. Why? Because attribute data sold for a particular mapping product is directly compatible without conversion or data translation. Almost every desktop mapping manufacturer offers a wide range of attribute data that has been covered from other government and commercial sources. This is often the same data you can buy directly from other suppliers, but because it has already been converted for compatibility with the desktop mapping program, it is more convenient to buy from the software manufacturer. Surprisingly, the data is not always more expensive when purchased from the software maker.

As mentioned in Chap. 4, data is priced according to its level of detail and the amount of information provided. (As we mentioned previously, pricing policies among data sources vary greatly from company to company. What one source sells for $5000 may cost $800 somewhere else. That's why shopping for price is a good idea before purchase.) To save money, consider purchasing data in packages when this option is available. In most cases, combination data sets can be purchased for less money than separate components. Data may also be priced according to its timeliness. For example, the complete 1990 census sorted by zip code is available for some mapping programs at a very high price. Obviously, by the time the census is taken in the year 2000, the prices for the 1990 data will take a nose-dive.

In addition to price and compatibility, the following factors should be considered when buying or using attribute data for your market mapping research:

- *The Source of the Data*—Both the company selling the data and the original source of the data should be considered. Is the company reputable? How long have they been in business? If the company is unfamiliar, ask for a list of reference customers.

- *The Detail Level of the Data*—Carefully analyze what you are buying. In some cases you may be purchasing expensive data that contains far more information than you need. Or, it's possible to purchase data that lacks necessary information. For example, one package that we used includes detailed street addresses, but for some odd reason has only partial zip codes.

- *Compatibility with Your Mapping Software*—Ensure the data's compatibility with your software. Yes, we're saying this again because it's central to the success of your market mapping efforts. Most data requires simple geocoding that can be handled with a fair degree of automation in most packages. However, data stored incorrectly for coding must be manually reformatted. While almost all attribute data can eventually be reformatted for proper compatibility with your software, in the case of the large volumes of data used for market mapping this could take weeks. Reformatting can also introduce errors that could negate the value of the data completely.

- *Age of the Data*—Timeliness of data is almost always a factor in the value of marketing data, so make sure that the seller can clearly document the age of the information and the frequency of the updates.

- *Usage Rights*—Does the data have unlimited usage rights and do you have the right to copy and reproduce the data? Some data comes with restrictions that limits the ways it can be reproduced and distributed unless additional fees are paid or permissions obtained; other data can be copied and reused as required.

Doesn't It All Cost a Lot? Well, Consider the Alternatives . . .

While, at first glance, competent mapping software and comprehensive data capable of high-level marketing analysis may seem pricey, in skilled hands these products greatly improve your marketing efforts and reduce the amount of money wasted on ineffective programs and uninformed decisions. Consider, for example, a national chain of coffee shops looking to open their first of four new restaurants in a city far from corporate headquarters. Conventionally, someone has to get on a plane, work with an unfamiliar leasing agent, and choose a sight based largely on instinct. If the choice turns out to be less than ideal, the firm's entire program for the new city will be in jeopardy and millions of dollars may be wasted.

Using mapping software and data priced under $4000 to handle the research, the firm can direct the leasing agent to look for space in very specific areas after carefully reviewing the target city's demographic profile by neighborhood and examining areas where no direct competition exists—without even leaving the headquarters office. By strategically placing the first restaurant based on the analysis of a mapping program and subsequent review of selected sites, the company will have a much better chance of locating in the right area with the right kind of customers. Mapping software can even help identify eating habits useful in adapting the menu for geographic food preferences that will make the restaurant more profitable over time.

With market mapping, intelligent, repeatable analysis augments raw intuition. While $4000 for the software and data in this example is a fair amount of money, it's much less expensive than just taking a chance based on luck and the word of the leasing agent. Anyway, the software and data can be used again to locate sites for the other restaurants—the plane fares and other travel charges in a conventional analysis are unrecoverable.

Hardware Requirements for Market Mapping

To use market mapping software effectively, you must have the right kind of computer for the job. Presentation-type packages can run on almost any computer with a grayscale or color monitor, but sophisticated analysis-level and GIS-level programs require a fast computer with a large hard disk to handle the processing-intensive tasks and storage requirements typical of these packages.

While the most obvious approach, and one that is certainly the least expensive, is to use a computer you already have, you may need to purchase a new system to run an important mapping application that's not compatible with your present system. Once the domain of massive mainframe systems, there are two microcomputer platforms that most desktop mapping software runs on—the IBM-PCs and compatible computers and Apple Macintoshes. Other high-speed desktop computers, often called workstations, can be used for mapping as well. For example, the SPARCstation from Sun Microsystems is much faster than either a PC or a Macintosh, but there are only a handful of mapping packages that run on the system. While some mapping program manufacturers offer versions for more than one kind of computer, not all do. For this reason, it's better to find a superior program first and then select a computer for it. For sophisticated mapping programs, even if you already have a computer of the right persuasion, if it's an older model it may need substantial upgrading to effectively process maps and data.

As the most popular computer platform in the world, there are IBM-PCs and compatible computers in almost every office, store, or business. For that reason, a large number of market mapping programs run on the PC platform.

The Macintosh is also a strong performer when it comes to mapping because of the computer's graphics-oriented environment. There is a lot of capable mapping software available for this platform, and the Macintosh's desktop publishing capabilities allow you to create stunning black-and-white or color publications right on the desktop that can easily incorporate even the most complicated maps. This can be done on the PC platform as well, but the Macintosh is considered a superior environment for desktop publishing applications. Using the highly standardized Macintosh graphics file formats, copying maps from one application to another is easy and reliable. This is helpful when you want to move a map from your mapping software and paste it into a report or presentation for distribution to other people.

Regardless of manufacturer, the right computer for running mapping programs handles data fast enough so you can create several variations on a map in a matter of minutes. A poky machine makes the mapping process slow and may render the process so cumbersome that a powerful mapping program becomes ineffective or frustrating. One data-intensive map we assembled in a little more than two minutes on a fast IBM-PC compatible with an Intel 80386 processor took nearly an hour on an older 8086-based system. The same is true for Apple Macintosh computers—the models with faster processors like the Motorola 68030 and 68040 are a better choice for mapping applications than those equipped with slower 68000 processors.

Tip—Test a System's Actual Market Mapping Speed with the Software

A simple way to check out whether a system is fast enough for designing maps is to load the mapping software you plan to use and create a map or report similar to the complexity of those you plan to assemble. This provides you with a real-world appreciation for the machine's speed or lack thereof. You can also use this technique to compare two products' performance on similar tasks or to compare the speed and interface of the IBM-PC version of a product to that of its Macintosh counterpart.

Storage Requirements

When purchasing or configuring a computer for use with mapping products, you need to take into account how much RAM the product requires and purchase a large enough hard disk to accommodate the program, maps, and data. Market mapping software programs tend to be fairly large and take up a fair amount of room on your hard disk. In addition, your system must have enough RAM memory installed and available to allow applications to open and run smoothly. Tactician, for example, occupies almost 1 megabyte on disk (not including the data), and the Macintosh version asks for a minimum of 2.5 megabytes of internal memory just to run. Presentation-level products are not as large and don't use as much memory as the more powerful programs.

RAM Requirements.   Most computers are sold with a minimum configuration of RAM storage. (RAM storage is the internal memory used by your computer when processing information.) For mapping products above the presentation level, minimum RAM configurations won't be adequate for most applications. If the program launches at all, it will spend a considerable amount of time swapping chunks of itself in and out of memory as required—which takes time and slows the mapping process. With this kind of arrangement, drawing and redrawing maps will be a slow procedure at best and system crashes may result. To find out how much memory should be available, consult the manufacturer or read the manual. Take into account the amount of "overhead" memory requirements of your operating system and any other programs that will be used simultaneously. If you do need to add memory, RAM prices have plummeted in the last few years, so upgrading is relatively inexpensive, as long as your computer is upgradeable in the first place.

Hard Drive Requirements.   Unless your program reads the bulk of its data from a CD-ROM, or is a low-level product that processes only small data files, you need to purchase a fairly large hard disk to accommodate the data files you'll want to use. Depending on the kind of product you are working with and the amount of data required, you may require a hard disk with 50 to 200 megabytes of storage capability available to accommodate the mapping software, its data, your computer's operating software, and any other programs or data you require. Some program maps themselves take up a fair amount of space, especially if you create numerous "what-if" scenarios and save copies of them for future reference.

If you are using a program that creates raster format maps, storage requirements for these maps can be huge. Remember that in raster format each dot of the map is represented individually in memory. Collectively, the dots create the image, bit by bit. Most modern programs use vector-based drawing where each line and element is represented mathematically. This format results in maps that require far less hard disk space and memory to store. They also print faster and can be scaled in size with little change in quality.

Because mapping programs spend a lot of their time reading data from the hard disk, purchase the fastest disk you can afford, particularly if you're planning on creating complex maps. Access times vary from a slow 35 milliseconds to as little as 5 milliseconds. Look for a hard drive with 20 millisecond access time or better. Another alternative is to add an accelerator board to your system. Several companies make these boards and they can more than double the speed of a hard disk in accessing and storing data. For creating complex maps, this can be a major advantage, especially if you plan on displaying maps on video while interactive changes and queries are being suggested by managers or customers.

 Tip—Need More Room on Your Hard Disk?

Many of the mapping programs we've used are compressed on a floppy disk(s) and use an installer routine to unpack and load the files onto your hard disk. Programs that use an installer also place tutorial files and data on your drive whether you want them there or not. Once you have been through the tutorial, discard it to free up extra space. The tutorial for one program we use takes up ten megabytes of space for the data. If you have a lot of hard disk room, this isn't a problem, but since the tutorial has absolutely no application after you master the product, there's no reason to save it if you need disk space for your own maps and data.

CD-ROM.   A format growing in popularity for distributing data for mapping products is CD-ROM. CD-ROMs look identical to the compact disks used for music reproduction and these shiny silver platters are capable of holding a huge amount of information. Unfortunately, the data access standard for CD-ROM was established around the time that the standard was set for audio CDs and results in slow access to the CD-ROM when locating and reading information from the disks.

Like hard disks, CD-ROM access times are measured in milliseconds. The players for this read-only format typically take 350 to 900 milliseconds for accessing data—much slower than even the pokiest hard disk. For this reason it may be tempting to transfer the disk's data to your hard disk. That's fine if you have one big enough and if you move only the files you need, since most CD-ROMs contain more than 150 megabytes of data (usually much more than this). Keep in mind that not all the mapping software we've worked with is smart enough to look for its data on your hard disk. If the program expects to read the data from a CD-ROM, that's where it will look for it first, and it may not look at your hard disk at all. Some programs allow you to tell them where the files are and some don't.

Most CD-ROM players can play audio CDs as well as ones containing map data. However, it is not advisable to use them for this purpose because, like all CD players, the laser has a finite life and wears out after several years of use. The cost of replacing the laser invariably justifies tossing the unit and purchasing a whole new player. At this writing, street prices for the least expensive CD-ROM players are five times more than the cheapest audio CD player, so wearing one out playing music makes little sense. Of the CD-ROM players we've listened to, most have mediocre sound quality anyway.

Color Monitors

Most mapping programs support color—and you will want to use a color monitor with high-resolution color reproduction if you have the option. On an IBM-PC or compatible computer, this means a VGA or Super-VGA board used with a monitor that displays at least 800 × 600 pixels of resolution, and more resolution if possible. On a Macintosh, this means a full-color monitor and display board capable of supporting the monitor size you select and 16.8 million colors. In some configurations, a monitor and the board to drive it can cost more than the computer—especially if the monitor is large and high-resolution. The larger the monitor, the more information you can display—so buy the biggest, highest-quality color monitor you can afford to make your mapping efforts more productive and visually satisfying.

A Digitizing Tablet for Adding Your Own Geographic Data

Because change is inevitable in the world around us, some mapping products support digitizing tablets that allow you to enter a custom map and add or change the geography of streets and locations as cities evolve and freeways are built, or as states, counties, or countries change their boundaries. These devices allow you to place an image of a map on the tablet's surface and trace it with either an "electric pen" or with a "puck" (a puck looks like a mouse device but is smaller and has more functionality). Pucks are also called "cursors" by some tablet and mapping software makers.

Tracing maps can also be accomplished with a mouse and no tablet, but the process is much more difficult because a mouse lacks absolute coordinates. Each time you pick it up and move it, its relationship with the screen position changes. With a tablet, if you place the pen at the bottom of the tablet's work area, the on-screen cursor always shows up at the bottom of the screen. This one-to-one relationship makes tracing with a tablet much easier than working with a mouse. As elements are traced on a tablet and entered in the software, they are geocoded so they can be manipulated by both you and the software.

Figure 5-4. Digitizing tablets allow you to add detail to existing maps or create your own. *(Photograph courtesy of Kurta Corporation.)*

To choose a tablet (if your desktop mapping product supports one), look for:

- *Light Weight*—Many people put tablets on their lap to get the best control angle for drawing. One tablet we own weighs 10 pounds because it has a heavy internal power supply. After a long session, your knees begin to buckle with so much weight.

- *Sturdy Construction*—The pens or other pointing devices and the tablet should be solid and well-built from quality materials. One tablet manufacturer that we borrowed a tablet from made a cordless pen so flimsy, it broke into pieces the first time it was dropped on the floor. Pens and pucks *do* get dropped—especially the cordless ones.

- *Full Compatibility with the Mapping Software*—While most tablets integrate easily with a computer's hardware and software, a few that include complex software drivers suffer from incompatibility as the operating system for the computer evolves. When in doubt, call the mapping product's manufacturer for tablet recommendations and software compatibility *before* purchase.

- *A Clear Plastic Layer for Tracing*—To trace an image or map, the original is sandwiched between a plastic overlay and the tablet's actual surface. Pressure-sensitive tablets popular for color painting and graphics programs may work with your market mapping product, but may lack this important plastic overlay. You can add your own, but unless it's firmly in place when tracing and fully removable when using pressure-sensitive painting software, it will cause reproduction problems or get in your way when you're not mapping.

 Tip—Talc Makes Tracing Much Easier

When tracing elements on a tablet, you may find that your hand tends to jump from place to place rather than making smooth movements along a roadway or other element being traced. A simple fix for this problem is to dust your hands with talcum powder before starting your tracing work. The talc absorbs hand moisture and provides you with "ball bearings" for making smooth, even movements when tracing. If you do a lot of tracing, make sure that the talc doesn't get in your computer or inside a mechanical mouse.

A powerful innovation that's not yet widely available in desktop-based systems is the ability to import maps or other graphics by scanning them with a desktop scanner for use by the mapping software. This simplifies adding new elements because you can scan aerial photos of neighborhoods or maps printed on paper (be careful of violating copyright!) and then trace and geocode streets and other elements. The tracing converts the information in a bitmapped scan into the vector formats (mathematically described lines and shapes) used by most mapping programs. Unfortunately, tracing over scanned maps on screen isn't much easier than using a tablet. So, if you own a scanner but not a tablet, and your program allows you to trace scans, at least you won't need to buy a tablet. However, some kind of intelligent autotrace feature, such as that available in Adobe System's Streamline product, would be a nice addition to programs that support on-screen tracing of scans. Such a feature would cut the time from raw scan to finished map substantially. We expect to see such improvements in map tracing and importing capabilities in the near future.

Putting Your Maps to Work

Unless your maps are strictly for personal analysis, you will probably want to put your maps to work communicating your findings to others. Options for showing off your work include output to printed form, incorporation into other computer-generated documents, output as slides, or direct presentation using your computer and video-display technologies. In this section we will explain the output options available to you to make your maps highly persuasive to other people.

Hard Copy Maps

The most sophisticated market maps are beginning to show up in expensive annual reports, corporate brochures, and ads. Even a basic black-and-white map can add interest and credibility to proposals and reports. Because of their visual impact, you too will want to output your maps in hard copy formats and include them in a variety of publications and presentations.

The most obvious output option for market maps is to print them on a printer connected to your computer. Maps can be output on dot matrix, laser, or color printers; however, they look their best on laser and color printers in most cases. Dot matrix output, even from a "high-resolution" model, is only adequate for proofs or informal documents. This is also true of many inexpensive ink jet printers.

A laser printer produces clear, clean maps that can be used in professional-looking presentations or pasted into other documents for reproduction. If you are printing on a PostScript laser printer, crisp lines and type are easy to achieve.

Color printers produce stunning maps, but their purchase price and cost per page are higher than a black-and-white laser printer. Color printer output can be duplicated for distribution on one of the new generation of color copiers found at most large copy centers. The quality is so good from the new color copiers that you'll be hard-pressed to tell which is the original and which is the photocopy.

You may want to place a map into a page layout program such as PageMaker, Ventura Publisher, or QuarkXPress. Using a page layout program allows you to integrate your map with text, other maps, and just about anything that can be printed on paper. From these programs you can print your document directly or have it imaged, ready for publication. Imaging involves having the file containing the map printed on a special piece of equipment called an imagesetter. While most laser printers print at only 300 dots per inch, leaving type and angled lines with a slightly jagged appearance, an imagesetter produces output between 1200 and 4000 dots per inch on film or on coated paper. Output this clean and detailed is suitable for reproduction at a quality print shop. Color maps can be directly color separated as well, using an imagesetter and special software, but the job should be handled or discussed with someone knowledgeable about color desktop publishing before attempting this.

Imagesetters are quite expensive and require special knowledge to be operated and maintained effectively. Rather than buying one of these for your company, you can rent time on an imagesetter from a business called a service bureau, listed in the *Yellow Pages* under *Typesetters* or *Desktop Publishing*. Many large print shops rent imagesetter time as well. Film output runs between $12 and $20 per page, depending on the shop you choose and the number of sheets of film you run. Imagesetter output can be processed directly by any print shop.

 Tip—When a Map Fails to Image, Try Some Workarounds

If you want quality reproduction of your maps from imagesetter output, you may find that some maps won't "image" when you take them to a service bureau. Try these workarounds to solve this frustrating situation.

- Place the map inside of a reliable page layout program instead of running output from the mapping software.

- Convert the map to another file format. Try converting it to a reliable format such as EPS (encapsulated PostScript). EPS supports both raster and vector format images and talks directly to the PostScript interpreter that drives the imagesetter. Unfortunately, EPS map files tend to be larger than those stored in other formats.

- Open the file in a drawing program such as Adobe Illustrator, CorelDRAW, or Aldus Freehand. Save the file in this new format and try imaging again.

- Ask the service bureau for help. Questions will be answered for free at most bureaus, but there is usually an hourly charge for serious help. However, it's often cheaper and less frustrating than running and rerunning expensive film.

Presentation Tools

In addition to being able to produce printed output of your maps, you may need to produce your maps in a format suitable for a formal presentation. A number of options are available, ranging from slides and overheads to interactive video sessions where the map is displayed or projected on a huge screen in an auditorium.

Slides and Overhead Transparencies. The easiest presentation formats to produce are 35-millimeter slides or overhead transparencies. To produce slides and overheads, maps can be processed directly from the mapping program or incorporated into presentation software such as Aldus Persuasion or Microsoft PowerPoint.

Overheads can be printed directly by most laser and color printers, although laser-printed overhead transparencies may appear grainy when projected and color 8″ × 10″ overheads produced on transparency film are

Figure 5-5. Film recorders accept color output from personal computers for imaging 35-millimeter slides.

costly. Slides are a popular presentation medium in many organizations. They are colorful and easy to transport. To create them, maps can be sent to a film recorder, a special-purpose device that connects to your computer. Slides are output to the film recorder and the image is captured with a 35-millimeter camera mounted in the unit. The 35-millimeter film is then processed conventionally into slides.

Quality film recorders cost between $4000 and $12,000, so you may prefer to rent time on someone else's machine. Many service bureaus offer this service, charging between $3 and $18 per imaged slide. Several companies also offer slide services for the entire United States that let you send in your presentation files through the mail or over a modem connection. The companies then return the slides to you, sometimes in as little as 24 hours.

Computer Presentations.   One of the most effective ways to display colorful maps is through interactive video sessions where maps are shown on video monitors or projection televisions. For example, the marketing department of a company may assemble a series of maps and then project them from the computer for a staff meeting. Then, during the meeting, they can plug in different sets of data or ask the mapping software to widen or narrow the searches as required. As changes are made, new maps are created immediately for all to see. To accomplish this, the computer can directly drive a specially equipped monitor, a projection television, or an LCD projection unit tied to a computer which can be placed on an overhead projector. The maps produced during the interactive sessions can also be captured for use in video presentations, and individual map frames can be saved for review or reproduction.

 Tip—Capture Color Maps on a Film Recorder for Color Printing

While it's possible to generate film for reproducing color maps with your computer, it involves extensive knowledge, expensive color separation software, and practice. An easier way to capture a color map for reproduction in an ad, brochure, data sheet, or annual report is to print it to a film recorder. Once the map is imaged on 35-millimeter film and the film is processed, the picture of the map can be converted by your print shop into a format suitable for black-and-white or color reproduction. The only limitation is enlargement size. For high-quality reproduction, don't enlarge the 35-millimeter image to a print size larger than 5" × 7".

Building a War Room for the Ultimate Market Mapping System

Tactics International, Ltd., headquartered in Andover, Massachusetts and the developers of Tactician, a high-end desktop mapping program specifically designed for marketing and business mapping applications, has been actively promoting the concept of the "war room" to corporations as a way of dealing with communication problems inherent in business and sales. Business war rooms are based on the premise that "marketing is war." Much like generals and their staff plan their most important strategic moves in rooms surrounded by maps and displays of critical geographic information, the war room concept supports the notion that businesspeople should also view data and strategic information in special environments designed to support superior communications and improve the group decision-making process.

In a business war room, information workstations in the form of high-end Macintoshes, PCs, or graphics workstations that integrate the capabilities of decision support systems (DSSs), executive information systems (EISs), and geographic information systems (GIS-Level Mapping Systems) are tied to a complex of videoscreens and display systems in a specially equipped room, ranging in size from a board room for a dozen people to a major conference center with seating for hundreds.

The desktop workstations in a war room are provided direct access to the data contained in corporate databases through networks and other communication channels. The workstations can then be used to interactively view and manipulate corporate data, competitive information, and marketplace statistics. The results can be displayed as maps, charts, graphs, and reports in multiple views on war room screens and monitors. Complex data is instantaneously turned into clear information in a comfortable environment.

Companies, like GTE for example, are already using war rooms to analyze market segments, develop sales strategies, and evaluate alternate distri-

Figure 5-6. A war room for a major corporation incorporates mapping technology at the heart of strategic decision-making.

bution strategies. The visual, mapped information is also used for making compelling sales presentations to major customers.

Setting up a war room using sophisticated mapping products as the central, integral component is a relatively expensive proposition in terms of computers, networks, data, and display technologies. But for the companies that have adopted the concept already, war rooms have meant the difference between lackluster performance and outstanding profitability. For corporate visionaries who want to lead their industries into the next century, the war room concept is something to consider as a superior option for analyzing and communicating important concepts and strategies in a group setting.

The Things No Market Mapping System Can Do

As powerful and efficient as desktop mapping programs are, many aspects of the marketing and decision-making process are not within the computer's realm. Using market maps makes data visualization easier and reveals hidden relationships in data files that are not otherwise accessible, but the following are things the computer can't and shouldn't be allowed to do:

- *Mapping Software Can't Gather Data*—You will have to decide how much and what type of information you need for your market mapping analysis. You or members of your business team will still need to determine data sources and gather required information. The computer only helps compute and display the information after it is available.

- *Mapping Software Can't Make Your Decisions*—The computer can make it easier and faster to look at alternatives, but it is ultimately you and your business team who will have to make the choice among alternatives and take responsibility for decisions.

- *Mapping Software Can't Solve Problems that Require Subjective Judgments*—Sometimes human intuition is the most important ingredient in business, especially when dealing with people. People require understanding. Software is programmed and not intuitive. It only reports back what you put into it. You still have to manage the conflicts, solve the problems, and use your own judgment when deciding between two alternatives.

- *Mapping Software Can't Find the Errors in Your Input*—If you put biased, incomplete, or erroneous data into desktop mapping software, it will output biased, incomplete, and erroneous maps and charts. Don't blame the computer for human error. The best way to eliminate this problem is to check the data source and verify the maps before they are distributed.

- *Mapping Software Can't Communicate for You*—Mapping software is great at producing visualizations that look good and contain a wealth of detailed information, but there is more to communicating than sending out a map. You still need to speak and work with people face to face, no matter how much information is contained in the maps.

- *Mapping Software Probably Won't Save Money by Reducing the Need for Personnel*—Automation almost never really reduces the personnel costs on a project. The software can make you more efficient and make decision-making more effective because information is better, but desktop mapping software will not significantly reduce the need for marketing people, although it might reduce some of your research bills from agencies and third-party suppliers.

Chapter Summary

In this chapter, we've examined the hardware and software components for desktop mapping and provided criteria for selecting products for your market mapping and business research needs. To begin your search for the best system, talk to computer store personnel, read computer magazines, and ask friends and colleagues about the programs they use. Then, when choosing your desktop mapping system, you should remember the following steps from this chapter:

- Determine your research requirements and objectives first.
- Consider data availability and compatibility before you buy anything.
- Establish your personal criteria for evaluating the program's interface.
- Test software functionality before you decide on a software program.
- Evaluate the attribute data available for the software.
- Determine the hardware configuration required based on the power of the central processing unit, necessary input and output devices, and storage options.
- Establish the presentation and publication formats required for your maps and match the program's output file formats to the output desired.

When you are ready to make a corporate commitment to market mapping, the chapter has also presented the concept of the "business war room" to consider as an option. Wars rooms are starting to appear in many major corporations to help improve communications, enhance corporate planning, and generally improve strategic decision-making.

In the next five chapters, which comprise Part 2 of the book, we'll show you how to put a market mapping system to work to assist you in making specific marketing decisions. First, we demonstrate how to work with market mapping data and software to assemble a map step-by-step. Then, the chapters that follow show you how to use market maps for a variety of other applications.

After finishing the book, you'll be ready to select a program and get started in market mapping. Follow the step-by-step guidelines for implementing the market mapping process you will read about in the following chapters. With each success, you will contribute to the business, the economy, and your own career—no mean feat for just learning how to create a few maps.

The Power of
Color in Market
Mapping

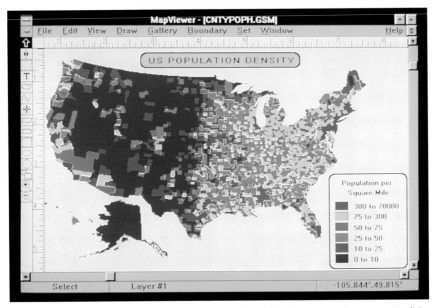

This map of United States population density created with MapViewer is a fine example of the types of presentation-level maps that can be produced with products that cost less than $300.[22]

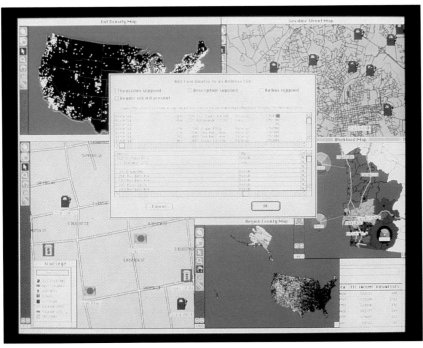

Tactician is a powerful mapping system with data management and decision support functions. Here data is being geocoded for further analysis. Note the multiple display possibilities for the maps created with this program.[23]

Another map produced by Tactician demonstrates how complex statistics from multiple databases can be integrated on one map using colors, symbols, and shading for easy visualization of complex concepts.[24]

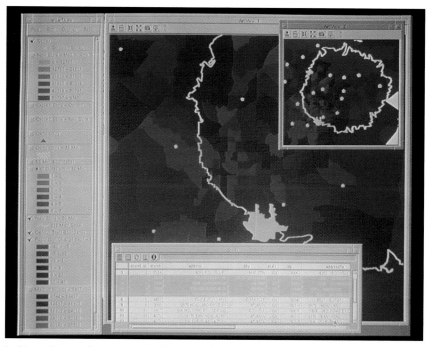

In this sophisticated map created with ARC/Info, stores and regions are classified by the demographic attributes of the population.[25]

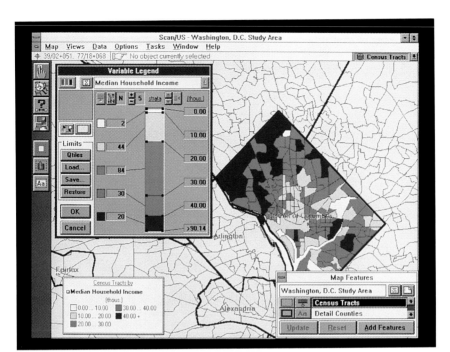

This market map, produced with Scan/US, displays demographics for Washington, D.C.[26]

This map produced with MapInfo analyzes branch sales and customers in San Francisco. MapInfo Corporation produces MapInfo products for a number of computer platforms.[27]

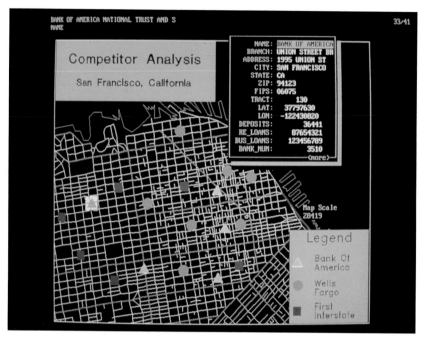

The powerful products from Strategic Mapping offer a full range of mapping possibilities for PC-compatibles and Macintosh computers, including Atlas GIS, Atlas MapMaker, and Atlas Pro. Here competitive locations are being analyzed for a bank using the company's Atlas GIS product.[28]

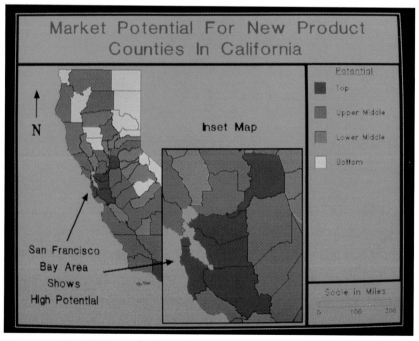

In this map, Atlas GIS clearly displays product potential by county in California.[29]

PART 2

Step-by-Step Applications of Market Mapping Analysis in Business

6

The Market Mapping Process—Step-by-Step

You've just seen that each desktop mapping product offers a different set of tools and operations, some more appropriate for market mapping applications than others. Still, underneath all these interface differences and feature options, all mapping products within a given category remain conceptually similar in their operation. Individual products use a variety of methods for geocoding data, working with data, and selecting parameters for individual maps, but, to complete a market mapping analysis, a similar step-by-step methodology is usually followed, regardless of the specific product. This chapter will introduce you to the steps in market mapping methodology that are shared across programs and computer platforms.

In this chapter we use MapInfo, a product available for IBM-PCs and compatible computers as well as Apple Macintosh and other platforms, to take you through a sample market mapping session using our recommended step-by-step methodology for market mapping. We could have created the example just as easily with a number of other products—so our choice to use MapInfo here is largely arbitrary. If you are familiar with San Francisco, you will discover that the restaurants we use in the example are hypothetical, but the street locations are accurate.

Until you become fully proficient in market mapping, photocopy the diagram of the methodology and tape it to a wall near your computer. That way, if you suddenly feel lost or confused in the middle of a mapping session, study the methodology to identify where you are, and follow the steps as they are described in the chapter.

Tip—Be an Explorer!

The step-by-step methodology we outline here is a guideline to use when you have known problems to solve or immediate marketing objectives. However, another way to understand your data is to simply play with it. Mapping software that is adept at interactive mapping, like Tactician from Tactics, International, for example, lets you explore what there is to see in your data while working interactively with your mainframe and desktop-based information. Just load some geographic data and start displaying attribute variables on the maps. Then start asking questions that are inspired as the maps expose new relationships. The answers will lead to new questions and new maps. Ultimately the geographic visualizations will lead to the discovery of possibilities you would have never seen without the maps.

As you study the methodology, note that the initial steps for market mapping with analysis- and GIS-level products are identical to those for presentation-level products, but the final steps differ. While presentation-level products can be used to make decisions if the right data is available, GIS- and analysis-level programs are capable of analyzing choices and looking at data from a wide range of views and formats. For this reason, there are additional steps for interactive marketing analyses with more sophisticated products. When mapping becomes an interactive process, involving map "tuning" and alternative data combinations, higher-order mapping products not only assist you in making marketing decisions, but almost make decisions for you. Using visual analysis, complex relationships hidden in tables of data become instantly clear to anyone with eyes to see.

Market Mapping Step-by-Step

In this section, we'll use an analysis-level product, MapInfo, to demonstrate the steps in the market mapping methodology. While the next chapters showcase the general process and steps for visualizing marketing data with maps, they don't show every step as we do here. In this chapter we'll show all the "nuts and bolts" of the market mapping process. While not every market mapping product works exactly like the one in the example, the steps for producing most market maps are identical, although other mapping products have a different look and feel, and may or may not have all the capabilities available in the example given here.

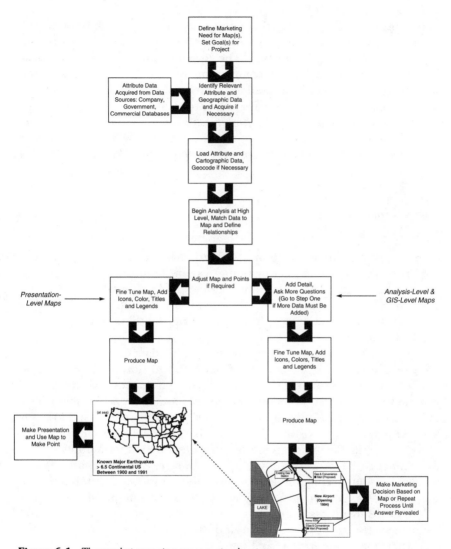

Figure 6-1. The market mapping process step-by-step.

Step One—Define the Marketing Need or Initial Question to Be Answered

The first step in any market mapping analysis is to define the marketing need or to focus on an initial question to be answered. Although new questions may be exposed as you complete your marketing efforts, it's still important to have a clear starting point when you begin mapping. In our example, we are looking for a location for a large "cafeteria-style" restaurant in downtown San Francisco. The location must preferably be near Market Street with no direct competition from other large, low-priced restaurants. It must not be located too close to pricey Union Square either, or the project will be too expensive to be profitable.

So, the goal of the project is to *"find a location suitable for a large cafeteria-style restaurant where the lease is affordable. It should be as close to Market Street and as far away from the direct competition as possible."*

Step Two—Acquire the Necessary Data

Once the goal or initial question is defined, the next step is to acquire the required data for the market mapping session. Both the geographic data and the initial attribute data requirements should be established. As you continue your research, you may find that you need additional data—but don't worry about that now. Just list everything you think you will need to meet your defined goals.

In the example, we had to acquire geographic data on San Francisco at the street level, which was available from MapInfo Corporation. Next, we needed to get attribute data that contained addresses on existing restaurants in the area, and also showed the square footage of each location. This data allowed us to identify and compare existing competitors and look for a location away from existing restaurants that compete with ours.

A commercial database was located that describes all restaurants for the San Francisco Bay Area including square footage, type of cuisine, owners and key personnel, and estimated annual sales. Unfortunately, this database was relatively expensive and we didn't feel the vast amount of data it provided was really necessary for this project. Instead, we used data acquired from a current issue of a restaurant industry journal that contained a special article on restaurants in San Francisco.

Inconveniently, the data from the journal was in a print format and not directly accessible by computer without entering it manually. To minimize the time and errors associated with keying data manually, we used an optical character recognition program to scan and convert the data into a format suitable for geocoding. After checking the text for errors, we opened the file in a word processor to prepare it for use by our mapping software.

The OCR software converted the printed copy into text that was able to be manipulated on the computer. After throwing away the superfluous title text from the document, we added tabs between the fields. Tabs are the standard way data is transferred between databases or spreadsheets to map-

Restaurant Industry Survey
Market Street Area of San Francisco

Restaurant	Address	Square Footage
Drumm Street	440 Drumm St.	2200
The Beagle	99 Beale St.	6063
The Bear	449 California St.	8200
Big Joe's	124 Market St.	4200
Bill's Place	370 Market St.	4552
Cal Pub	657 California St.	4400
Carrie's House	70 Main St.	6300
Clay Bar & Grill	301 Market St.	4800
Davis Pub	299 Davis St.	1100
Franco's Crab Cooker	101 California St.	1700
Hill & Company	165 Beale St.	3200
Hollywood Alley	269 Beale St.	1900
John's BBQ	66 Spear St.	5520
La Cocina del Puerco	201 Main St.	3300
Las Margaritas	301 California St.	3300
The Little Drummer	151 Drumm St.	3300
Mackken's Pub	299 Front St.	3000
The Market on Market	601 Market St.	1900
Melson's Rest.	77 Spear St.	4400
Mom's	501 Market St.	7200
The Plowshare	399 Market St.	6600
Old Ed's	410 Market St.	3300
Spear Cafeteria	101 Spear St.	11800

Figure 6-2. The raw data of the restaurants in the Market Street area.

ping software. Tabs allow the mapping software to break the data into clear columns that the program can geocode for ready use in a map. Commas also work within most programs, or you can use a single character of your choice. Note that data in this format can be imported to most spreadsheet or database programs as well.

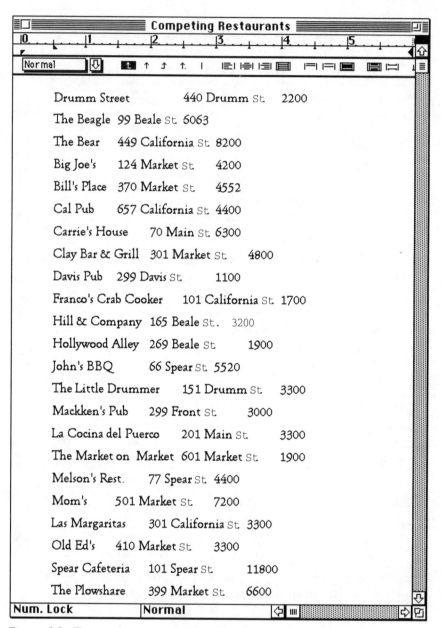

Figure 6-3. The raw data captured with OCR software and edited in a word processor—
ready for incorporation into the mapping program.

Step Three—Load the Data into the Mapping Program

Now that we have the geographic data (a map) and the attribute data (the list of restaurants, their addresses, and square footage), we are ready to open the mapping software. The geographic data is directly readable by the market mapping software, so it's a simple matter of opening the map and zooming down to the street level in the relevant part of San Francisco. In this case, we've asked the program to add the San Francisco street data as another layer that relates to a map of the United States and the Major Cities data, which we already have open, as shown in Fig. 6-4.

For some mapping needs, the data is inferred while the map is still projected from a high altitude. For example, when studying sales for a large chain of grocery stores with multiple stores in all cities, you might start at a high level comparing chain sales by city. At a high level, you can compare the total sales of each city's stores to totals from other cities. Then, you might zoom down to individual cities to see which stores sell the most in each one. For the purposes of this example, we can skip the high-level analysis because we are concerned only with San Francisco.

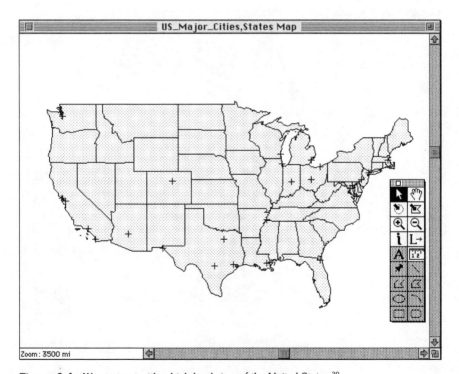

Figure 6-4. We start out with a high-level view of the United States.[30]

As you can see in Figs. 6-5 and 6-6, as we zoom down, the streets become larger and more detail becomes apparent. In the lower left hand corner you can see the distance above the earth specified as miles. Our cartographic street data is only for San Francisco, so the street grid stops immediately at the border of the city. In the diagrams, which have been captured directly from the computer screen, you also see the MapInfo's tool palette. The tools on top are for navigation and searches. The "grayed out" tools at the bottom are for drawing. We'll get to them later in this example. Remember, the layering and zooming features may not be this sophisticated if you are using presentation-level mapping software.

To make the map easier to understand, we ask MapInfo to label the streets for us. Labeling is easy and automatic in most programs, although sometimes the labels are placed arbitrarily in relationship to other elements. In this example, note that the labels run over other streets because the type is too big. However, by setting the typeface size down, most of this minor inconvenience can be eliminated.

The next part of getting the data into the system is to load the data file with the restaurant information so the data can be placed on the map. To

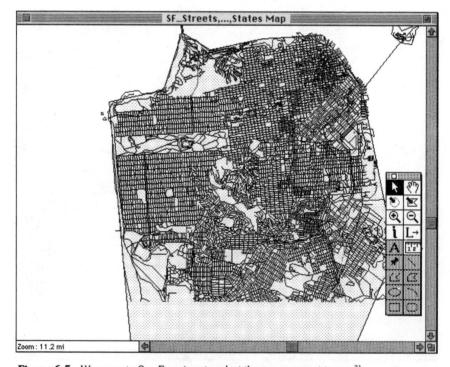

Figure 6-5. We zoom to San Francisco to select the area we want to use.[31]

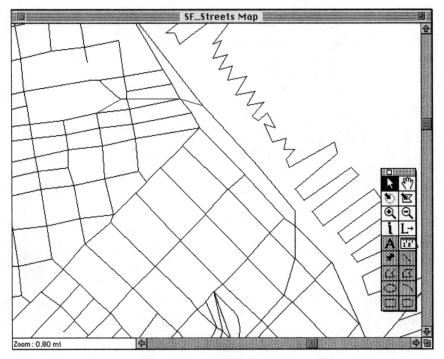

Figure 6-6. Zooming to the Market Street area displays the street grid.[32]

do this, we must import the file and then geocode it to be compatible with the map and the mapping software. The file has been stored on our hard disk, so we simply enter the name of the file from within MapInfo using the *OPEN* command. To geocode the file in this example, it's simply a matter of telling the program to look at the addresses in Column Two of the data and match them to the street locations stored with the geographic data already open in the program.

In this example, all of the data was successfully (and automatically) geocoded, because each address matches a street and street number in the map of San Francisco and the address data that accompanies it. Once the data is brought into the mapping software, it is represented in a table that can be viewed with the *browser* in MapInfo. Most mapping programs have a mode similar to the browser that incorporates functions and operations similar to a simple spreadsheet or database program and allows you to review the attribute data available for your maps as rows and columns.

If a restaurant address had failed to match because it was located on a pier without a normal street address, we could have manually geocoded the actual address so the program would have known where to place it. If the

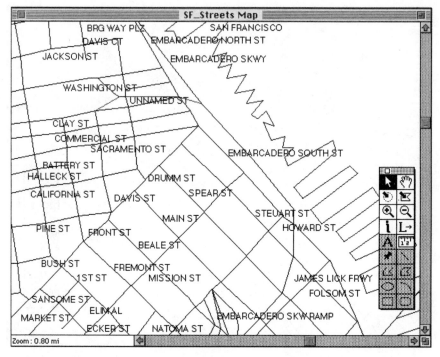

Figure 6-7. We add street name labels automatically to better understand the map.[33]

address was located on a street built since the geographic data was created, we could have added a new street to the map and street numbers. As an example of inaccurate geographic data related to the age of a map, notice that the Embarcadero Skyway, which was severely damaged and later demolished following the earthquake of 1989, is still present in this cartographic representation of the city.

Step Four—Map the Attribute Data

In this example, we want the map to show us the locations of competing restaurants within the Market Street area. That information allows us to look for a location that is suitably distant from direct competitors or, if no suitable location is found because there are too many competitors, make a marketing decision to look at another part of the city.

Once the restaurant location data is geocoded, we ask the program to display each restaurant location on the map. To do this, we "map the data." This is done by adding a new layer to the map. This invisible layer displays the symbols that mark each restaurant location. By adding (or activating) the new layer, the program places information in the correct positions over the active street map layer. In complex analyses with a lot of data, additional attribute layers can be rearranged on top of each other to create different views or turned off altogether to visually simplify the map. (Layers and layering were discussed in Chap. 3.)

At this point we have a map, although it's somewhat basic and does not yet present a clear understanding of the existing competition. It's also difficult to read. As you can see, the labels for the names of the restaurants, streets, and the streets and symbols themselves are visually complicated and look unattractive. To work around this problem, we eliminate the street names. That way, the important data is easier to see. The labels may be added again later as required, either for individual streets or for the entire map.

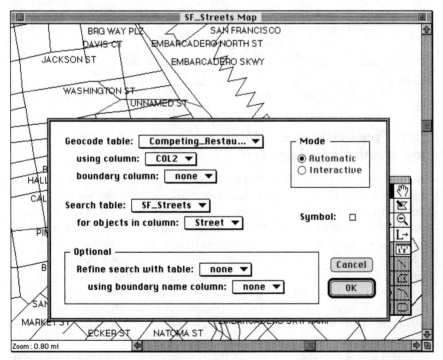

Figure 6-8. The restaurant data from an industry report is geocoded for the Market Street area by MapInfo.[34]

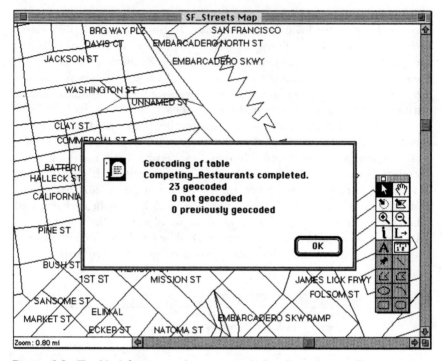

Figure 6-9. The MapInfo program has now matched each restaurant address to its own database of San Francisco street addresses.[35]

Step Five—Adjust the Map and Symbols If Required

Once a basic map is in place with data, you will probably want to adjust the view and refine the symbols. At this point in our example, we decided we needed to adjust our map for a more precise view of the area we are studying. We zoom out just a little to include a few more entries on the map and make the surrounding access streets and freeways more visible.

Next, we needed to make the data easier to understand. Adjustments in symbols, fills, and colors with the product mapping tools may make maps more understandable and, consequently, more powerful as communication tools. A well-constructed market map explains a complicated comparison with little more than a glance from someone who is unfamiliar with the map's content and data.

As you can see in the first view of the restaurant data, there are competitors to be dealt with everywhere. At a glance, it appears unlikely that we will be able to find a suitable location away from a cluster of competitors, unless we move away from the Market Street area which was our first choice for a new location. After studying the square footage of each restaurant in our data table, it is apparent that not all of the competitive restaurants are running large operations like ours, but from the current map it's impossible to tell the relative size of each location.

Using the power of market mapping, we discerned the real competitors from the smaller operations and studied their locations in relationship to Market Street. The table we copied from the industry report showed restaurants' square footage, as well as their names and addresss. The square footage data was already imported into the mapping software, but so far we hadn't used it. This column of information was integrated into the map to clarify the competition's size and help us separate large restaurants from small ones. To do this, we used the square footage data (Column Three) to show the size of each competitive location, as well as the restaurant location.

Based on the square footage data, we asked MapInfo to change the simple square symbols used on the map to proportional diamonds that represent the size of each restaurant. In this case, we assigned four ranges for

SF_Streets Map

Competing_Restaurants Browser

COL1	COL2	COL3
Drumm St.	440 Drumm St.	2200
The Beagle	99 Beale St.	6063
The Bear	449 California St.	8200
Big Joe's	124 Market St.	4200
Bill's Place	370 Market St.	4552
Cal Pub	657 California St.	4400
Carrie's House	70 Main St.	6300
Clay Bar & Grill	301 Market St.	4800
Davis Pub	299 Davis St.	1100
Franco's Crab Cooker	101 California St.	1700
Hill & Company	165 Beale St.	3200
Hollywood Alley	269 Beale St.	1900
John's BBQ	66 Spear St.	5520
The Little Drummer	151 Drumm St.	3300
Mackken's Pub	299 Front St.	3000
La Cocina del Puerco	201 Main St.	3300
The Market on Market	601 Market St.	1900
Melson's Rest.	77 Spear St.	4400
Mom's	501 Market St.	7200
Las Margaritas	301 California St.	3300
Old Ed's	410 Market St.	3300

records 1 – 21 of 23

Zoom: 0.80 mi

Figure 6-10. We open the program's "browser" to check the imported data.[36]

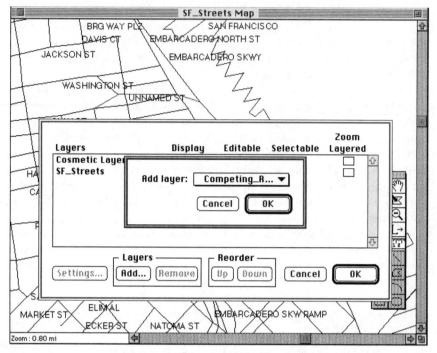

Figure 6-11. Next, the restaurant locations and names are added as a new layer to the map.[37]

restaurant size. MapInfo then displayed the locations with appropriately large or small symbols. Now, with just a glance, the real competitors stood out on the map. Smaller restaurants that were not direct competitors were effectively ignored to help clarify the analysis.

With the restaurants quantified according to square footage, a pattern was visible that wasn't obvious from just looking at the table of data. A number of the other "competing" restaurants were specialty restaurants or "bar and grill" operations. Also, the really large restaurants were mostly on one side of Market Street where the lease prices are lower. This analysis tentatively suggested that the other side of Market Street, away from competing large restaurants, was the superior location. But how far north did we need to look and how much did space cost in the area?

Once the symbols were adjusted, it was easy to see that many of the restaurants were too small to be considered direct competition. To make the map easier to read, we adjusted the symbols once again to make the "noncompetitors" even less prominent on the map. (To further simplify the process, the market mapping software automatically generated a legend that explains the values applied to each symbol.)

Step Six—Ask More Questions to Refine the Analysis

We then had a complete map that clearly showed the competition and separated the smaller, less competitive restaurants from the larger ones. We still didn't know exactly where we should open our new facility, however. To clarify the criteria, we needed additional data. The obvious questions were, "What suitable space is available in the Market Street area?", and "How much does the space cost?" Again, we didn't need to purchase data, although we could if we wanted to. Instead, we got the information from a few leasing agents who represented the area we targeted.

Once the data was collected from several phone calls to agents, the new data was processed by repeating Steps One to Three and adding a new layer to our map. We also used the Shading dialog to change the new symbols to ones that were able to be interpreted with just a glance, as we did for restaurant square footage. In this example, we were looking for space that costs under $12.50 per square foot, since space priced any higher was just too expensive for our needs because of the low-cost meals we serve.

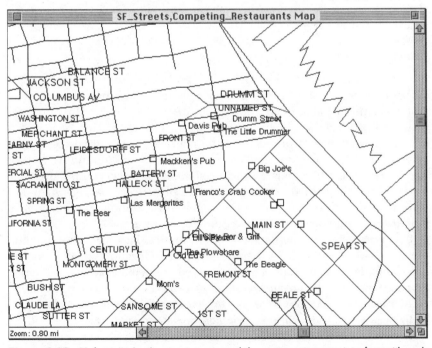

Figure 6-12. Unfortunately, the street names and the restaurant names interfere with each other.[38]

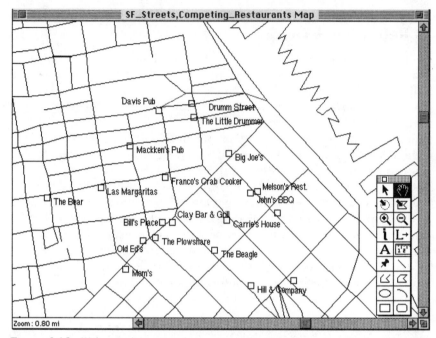

Figure 6-13. With a single command, we remove the street names to make the map easier to read.[39]

We were also looking for space that probably cost more than $9.50, because several leasing agents informed us that space priced lower than that was either located in an undesirable area, or needed roofing or other structural work before being suitable for a restaurant. However, we left inappropriately priced property on the map to show where a competitor might possibly move in. Smaller, noncompeting restaurants were also shown, because, while we largely ignored them for direct competitive comparisons, we still needed to be aware of their presence, especially when they appeared as clusters close to a space under consideration. Too many small restaurants could have diminished our market share.

Upon reviewing the map, the obvious location from a space/competition viewpoint was located at 77 Drumm Street. The location was not close to any other large competitors and provided immediate access to Market Street. It also had the advantage of being located on the more upscale side of Market Street, but not so far north that leasing rates increased substantially because of the location. Nineteen Spear Street was also a possibility because of its close proximity to Market Street and its attractive lease rate, but 44 Drumm Street was closer to Market Street and farther from major competitors. The only other possibility was 14 Market Street, but this location was technically out of the Market Street area and closer to the piers and the Embarcadero. This area was not a dining/shopping district, but one of townhouses and warehouses.

To simplify the choice, labels for competing restaurants were cleared from the map. To highlight the location, a circle was drawn with the circle tool. This tool is available by selecting it from the floating tool palette shown on the right side of the map. Tools are available for drawing and for adding labels. In addition, the "i" tool (info tool) can be used to click on an unlabeled symbol to establish its identity and relationship within the data file.

Labels were added for other compatible space for comparison purposes. At this point, if the mapping analysis is for your personal use, you would probably print a copy of the map and stop work because the choice of location is clear. The mapping data was then saved as a *workspace* in MapInfo. This is a file that links all of the geographic data and attribute data to make returning to the map easy. The program also remembers the view you were using to make access to the same environment more convenient when you start your next mapping session.

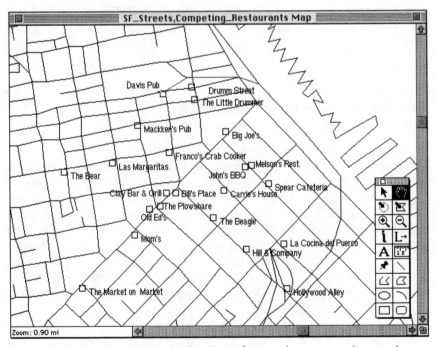

Figure 6-14. We adjust the view slightly to better focus on the target area by using the pan and zoom features.[40]

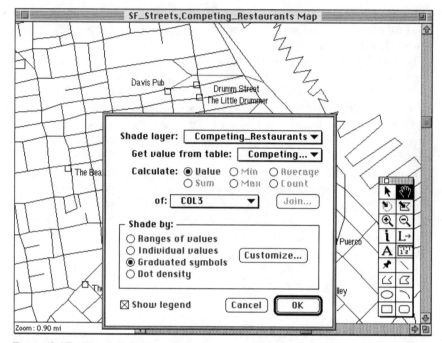

Figure 6-15. We asked the program to use proportional symbols to indicate restaurants with more square footage.[41]

Step Seven—Fine-tune the Map for Maximum Impact and Clarity

In the analysis we just completed, the resulting map clearly demonstrates the ideal location, but for purposes of presenting it to others to solicit their feedback on the location selection process, the map could be enhanced cosmetically. While the product we used in this example offers limited presentation capabilities, it is still a powerful tool for communicating mapped information with only a little additional work on your part. To enhance a map, first go back to your original goal. Review it to determine what the map should communicate and what information is secondary. In this example, our goal was to *"find a location suitable for a large cafeteria-style restaurant where the lease is affordable, as close to Market Street as possible, and as far away from the competition as possible."*

To enhance the map, we must clearly demonstrate the following:

- The location is as far away from a competitor as possible, while still remaining in the specified area.

- The location is close to Market Street.
- The leasing rate is affordable without settling for less desirable space farther from Market Street, or locating close to a competitor.

 Tip—Clean Up Maps with Compatible Drawing Programs

Depending on the market mapping software you are working with, you may want to clean up your map or add additional details with an outside drawing program. To work with your map in another program, export it in a compatible format and then open the map within the new program. This allows you to fix problems, fine-tune type, add color, and make changes of all kinds. The advantage of modifying the map in a familiar drawing program, rather than in the mapping software, is that you may be able to use additional drawing tools and avoid working around any typographic constraints common in mapping programs. Also, you may be able to choose from a much broader range of effects, colors, fill patterns, and line treatments.

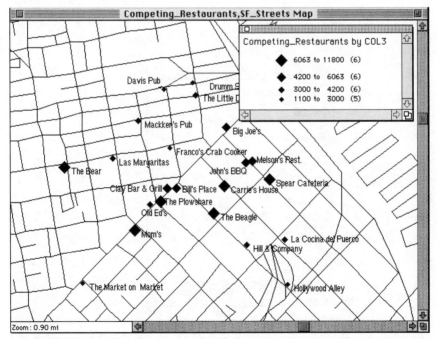

Figure 6-16. The new symbols revealed that there were only a handful of large, competing restaurants.[42]

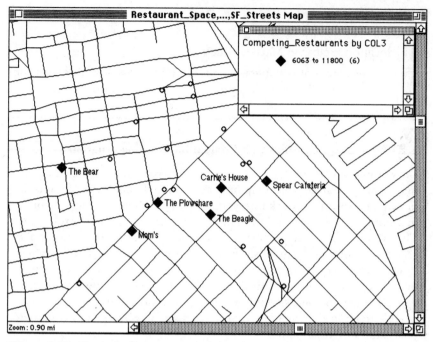

Figure 6-17. To clarify the map, we made small restaurants even less prominent in the display.[43]

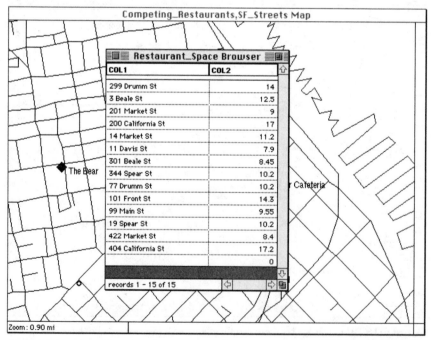

Figure 6-18. A list of available space was imported and geocoded for inclusion in the map.[44]

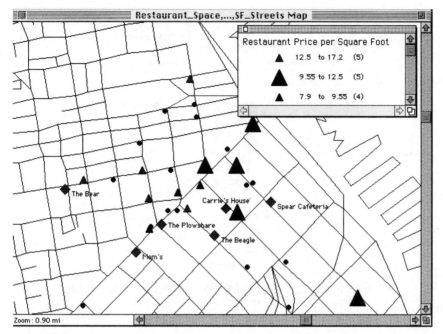

Figure 6-19. The available space was represented with proportional symbols representing the relative leasing price.[45]

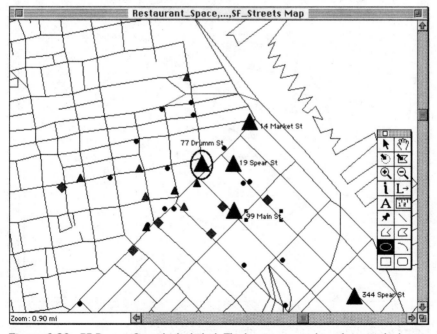

Figure 6-20. 77 Drumm Street looked ideal. The location was right and so was the leasing rate.[46]

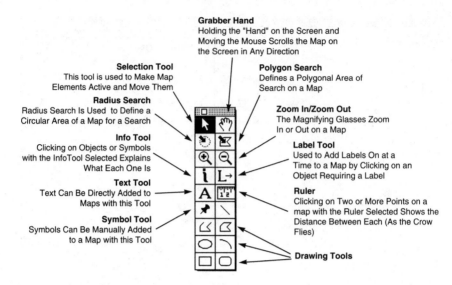

Grabber Hand
Holding the "Hand" on the Screen and Moving the Mouse Scrolls the Map on the Screen in Any Direction

Selection Tool
This tool is used to Make Map Elements Active and Move Them

Polygon Search
Defines a Polygonal Area of Search on a Map

Radius Search
Radius Search Is Used to Define a Circular Area of a Map for a Search

Zoom In/Zoom Out
The Magnifying Glasses Zoom In or Out on a Map

Info Tool
Clicking on Objects or Symbols with the InfoTool Selected Explains What Each One Is

Label Tool
Used to Add Labels On at a Time to a Map by Clicking on an Object Requiring a Label

Text Tool
Text Can Be Directly Added to Maps with this Tool

Ruler
Clicking on Two or More Points on a map with the Ruler Selected Shows the Distance Between Each (As the Crow Flies)

Symbol Tool
Symbols Can Be Manually Added to a Map with this Tool

Drawing Tools

An Example Market Mapping Software Tool Palette

Figure 6-21. The tool palette with callouts for each tool.[47]

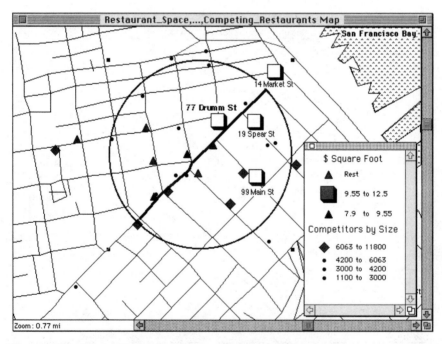

Figure 6-22. We simplify the map further so its message will be clear.[48]

Reviewing the map, we make minor changes to highlight these requirements, while eliminating extraneous detail wherever possible. We also make minor adjustments to make the map easier to understand. For example, drawing the circle around the target market will focus viewers on the area of interest. Shading San Francisco Bay helps orient viewers to the map. A little fine-tuning is done to refine the symbols and the view as well. If we have more time, custom icons shaped like our company's logo could be used, and we could produce a number of different views of the map to help familiarize other people involved in the decision with San Francisco's various neighborhoods and the competitors in each area.

Step Eight—Output the Map or Import It into Other Documents

While you can print your maps directly on a laser printer and photocopy them for a meeting, or output them on overhead transparency film for a presentation, you may instead want to export them and incorporate them

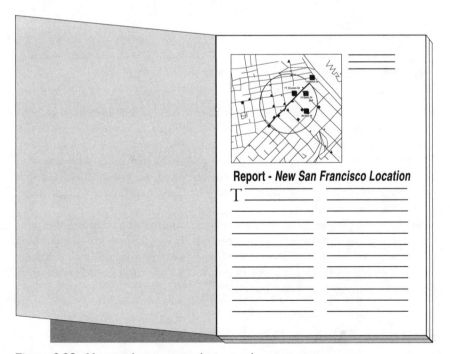

Figure 6-23. Maps can be incorporated into page layout programs.

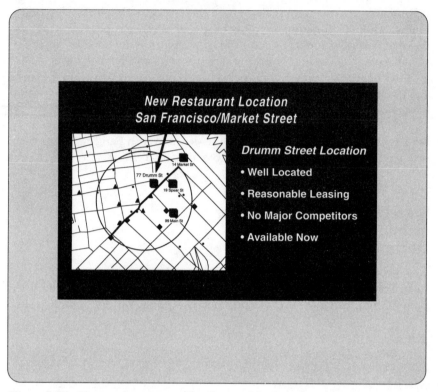

Figure 6-24. Maps can be output as 35-millimeter slides for presentations.

into presentation programs or page layout software. Depending on the market mapping product you are working with, you may be able to save the map and its tables and even produce charts and graphs from the mapping information, and then move your files from the mapping software into another program for further manipulation. Most mapping products use a *Save As* command or an *Export* facility that saves map files in one or more popular formats for this purpose.

In our example, we have used the export command to convert the map into a stand-alone graphic format called PICT. We have provided examples of the map we created as a slide used in a presentation and as a diagram inserted into a formal document that could be used to communicate with coworkers, managers, or customers.

Step Nine—Make a Decision!

The purpose of market mapping software is not so much to create attractive maps, but to help you make the right marketing and business decisions in a timely manner. While your maps may eventually find their way into brochures, corporate presentations, or manuals, once maps are created and subsequently refined, they should be used to assist you in correctly guiding your company to success and profitability. Unfortunately, as you become proficient at mapmaking, it's tempting to spend all of your time in front of the computer exploring mapping tools and improving your mapping skills. Watch out for this seductive trap! Use your mapping ability to understand your markets, make strategic decisions, and review alternative action plans—not to create pretty pictures for hanging on the wall.

How Would the Example Work in a War Room Environment?

The focus of this chapter was to take you through a simplified market mapping session for making a real-world decision, with the end results being a hard-copy map or printed presentation to distribute to others. If, however, you were using market mapping tools in an interactive war room environment, you would follow the steps in pretty much the same way. (The war room concept was explained in the last chapter.) Most interactive war room sessions begin with a base map and data, as described in the first steps in the methodology. This map is then modified as various people in the meeting ask questions and make suggestions. In a war room, the maps can be produced interactively by adding new data, changing views, and revising calculations. The discussion revolving around the maps leads

---

 Tip—Carefully Test the Equipment Before Mapping

Interactive computer-to-video sessions with maps are one of the most power marketing tools available. However, before scheduling an interactive war room session, spend time testing everything to make sure that it works as expected. One session we observed involved a "mapping system operator" watching the session on a computer monitor while typing commands and making changes to the maps. The managers in the meeting watched her efforts on a projection television while asking for changes and making suggestions. Unfortunately, the computer's monitor board proved completely incompatible with the one that drove the projection television. Since this set-up wasn't tested previously, forty-five minutes were required to identify the problem and change the monitor and board, while meeting participants twiddled their thumbs. Avoid this problem by testing even the simplest system well in advance of the meeting.

to further changes and queries and the results are displayed on monitors and screens for all to see.

Preparing for a war room session takes a greater degree of planning than individual mapping sessions in terms of anticipating the possible data sources and questions that may be asked. In a war room session you want to have as much data as possible available before you start the session—and should also have custom icons and symbols predefined to make the maps attractive. If attribute data from many sources is required, have as much of the data geocoded as possible before the session begins. If you have a clear understanding of what kinds of questions will be asked, either prepare maps required to answer the questions beforehand, or practice making the kinds of changes and tests that may be requested during the meeting.

Chapter Summary

In this chapter, you saw how to produce a relatively complex market map using one set of geographic data and two sets of raw data that required geocoding before the information could be mapped. As mentioned at the beginning of the chapter, not all analysis-level or GIS-level market mapping products work exactly the way MapInfo does in the example, but most of the mechanics of market mapping are represented in conceptually similar ways in other software products.

As you read through the examples in the following chapters, you should recall the basic market mapping steps that were presented in this chapter:

- Defining the marketing question to be answered through the market mapping process
- Determining the data to be used and acquiring the data
- Loading the geographic and attribute data for use by the mapping program
- Mapping the attribute data to the geographic data through geocoding and layering functions in the software
- Making adjustments to the map and assigning desired symbols to the attributes displayed
- Refining the analysis by asking new questions and creating new maps until you get the answers you need to make a business decision

In the next chapters, we'll examine additional market mapping applications using this same step-by-step methodology. These examples will expand your understanding of mapping products and demonstrate how you can put them to work analyzing your customers and building your business.

7

Using Market Mapping Tools to Analyze New Market Opportunities

One of the most powerful applications of market mapping is to analyze a new market before making a major commitment of time and money that may be unwarranted. Market analysis with mapping software can be used to substantially reduce risk when entering a new market or expanding an existing one. When properly used and carefully studied, market maps point out the best use of resources and provide risk assessment that makes go/no go decisions much easier. When analyzing a market for expansion, new data may need to be purchased; sometimes it may seem expensive, but the cost of data and a few hours of mapping analysis is far less expensive than entering a market and pulling out later because the business just isn't there.

In this chapter, two different market opportunities are presented. The first hypothetical case involves the addition of a new product line and the second example involves expanding operations based on customer data.

Scenario #1—Distributing Microbrewery Beers

You're the owner of a medium-sized distributorship for beer and wine that handles the New Haven, Connecticut region of the country. Until now, most of your business included selling specialty wines and a handful of premium beers, most vinted or brewed in Europe. Business has been steady and your company has had moderate success, but you would like to see your revenue increase by building up new business and customers. Unfortunately, with the existing product line, there is little growth potential. You already sell wine to most of the liquor stores and restaurants in the area and you have several competitors that handle similar products. None of the competitive companies are growing much either.

A second problem, one that worries both you and your competitors, is that sales of wine and beer have been flat for several years as Americans choose to drink less for safety and health reasons. In fact, at the request of one of your large restaurant customers, you considered adding premium single malt scotches to your product line, but a cursory investigation showed that only one customer had any interest in the products and probably wouldn't buy more than several cases a month—not nearly enough volume to go to the trouble of adding the product line.

One area that has caught your interest after reading an article in a trade journal for beer and wine distributors is a rapidly expanding section of the beer market—the sales of beer produced by very small breweries using old-fashioned brewing techniques and top-quality ingredients. Called microbreweries, these special breweries are small operations, often run by couples with a few part-time helpers. Producing a hundred gallons of beer or ale at a time, instead of 100,000 gallons like major breweries, their focus is on quality rather than quantity. Because the quantity is limited, distribution is usually limited to local markets around a few towns and a major city or two. And, since these beers are made the old-fashioned way, trade must be brisk, because the hand-made brew has a short shelf life and quickly spoils if not refrigerated and consumed within two months after bottling.

According to the published research on microbreweries, upper-middle-class consumers are purchasing these beers in growing numbers. Being stronger in flavor than conventional American brews and most of the European beers available commonly in the United States, microbrewery beers are at first an acquired taste, but quickly develop a loyal following. These beers are also of interest to consumers because they are brewed and distributed on a local scale, so buying a microbrewery beer directly supports the local economy.

After reading the article, you decide to look into these beers as a possible growth path for expanding your business. Before you can proceed, you must find out what beers are available that meet the following criteria:

- Priced right, so you and the restaurant or liquor store profit from the sale of microbrewery beers.
- Made locally, so purchasers feel they are buying a local specialty, rather than a nationally distributed beer.

- Available all year. The trade journal article explains that some micro-breweries produce beer on an irregular basis and you won't want to handle a product that's not continuously available.

- Meets the taste, look, and texture criteria of expensive beers. According to the article, some microbreweries make poor quality beer and you certainly don't want to represent those.

After making a few phone calls, you find that there are indeed several local microbreweries anxious to do business with you. You have each contender drop off samples for you to taste and compare. Tasting reveals that of the six microbreweries identified, five produce excellent beers, and the ones from the sixth aren't all that bad. Now it's time to see if this expansion makes sense or not.

Conventional Analysis for Adding Microbrewery Products

Conventionally, a distributor adding a new product line establishes a credit line with the new manufacturer, acquires the product, and then attempts to sell it to new and/or existing customers. If the product sells, the distributor orders additional product and keeps it as part of the product line. If it doesn't sell or moves slowly, the product is dropped from the line. Unfortunately, this process can be expensive, time consuming, and can cause a variety of headaches. For example, the distributor may incur substantial costs in advertising a new product, wasted sales calls, and the purchase of undesirable inventory. There is also the touchy issue of dropping a product when faithful customers are already purchasing it.

Offering microbrewery beers and then dropping them might alienate restaurants who buy the new beers, promote them, get customers to like them, and then suddenly find they can't sell them any more. Not only may business be lost when the beer products are discontinued, but also the restaurant may take *all* of its business to another distributor who still handles the beer. When this happens, by cutting one new product line, you lose the microbrewery beer sales *and* the restaurant no longer buys your wines or remaining beer products—a major blow to your profits.

Analyzing Product Potential with Market Mapping Tools

Instead of plunging head-first into a new beer line with a substantial risk of failure, market mapping techniques can be employed to analyze the market to see if the product line looks viable and potentially profitable. To do this, you need to identify sections of the New Haven area where such beers will sell. According to the well-documented article which reinforces your own knowledge of the market, these beers are purchased by upper-income people who also happen to like beer. If your mapping analysis shows that most areas in your market contain lower- and middle-income families, microbrewery beers most likely won't do well and adopting the product will lead to failure.

Step One—Define
the Marketing Need

As with any marketing problem, the first step toward solving it is defining the problem as succinctly as possible and setting a goal for your analysis. Without a completion goal, there's no way to tell when the analysis is complete or correctly implemented. After consideration, you determine the goals for the microbrewery project to be as follows:

> Primary Goal: "Quantify the existence and size of the microbrewery beer market for the areas we distribute to within the New Haven area. This involves identifying population concentrations with the right demographics to purchase beer made by microbreweries."

> Secondary Goal: "Expand the analysis to identify the appropriate restaurants and liquor stores in the target areas to sell the beers if the initial market analysis appears positive."

Step Two—Identify and Acquire
the Data Required
to Create the Map

To perform the analysis, you must first acquire the geographic and attribute data you need. There are five pieces of data required to complete this map analysis. They are:

- A map of New Haven and vicinity including zip codes compatible with the market mapping software you plan to use. In this case, you will use Descarte, an analysis-level mapping program marketed by PC Globe, Inc.
- Attribute data showing the income levels of New Haven and vicinity.
- Attribute data showing the areas of New Haven and vicinity that spend more than $70 a year on beer and ale.
- Attribute data outlining the liquor stores in the area.
- Attribute data listing the restaurants with liquor licenses that serve beer.

In this case, the geographic data is available from Descarte's manufacturer, PC Globe, and so is the income data. Beer sales data is purchased from the same magazine in which you saw the article on microbrewery beers. You also use your own database of liquor stores and restaurants in the area.

Step Three—Load the Geographic and Attribute Data

The next step is to load the data into the mapping program so the analysis can begin. The first thing to be loaded is the base map. Then you zoom to an appropriate level so you see all the zip code areas in your distribution territory, but not in irrelevant areas of Connecticut. Next, using the radius command, you click on New Haven to make it the center of a selection and draw a circle that encompasses zip codes for 10 miles around the city.

This selects the zip codes that comprise your distribution territory. Next, you import the data bought from the magazine into a format compatible with Descartes software and load the other attribute data that's directly compatible.

Step Four—Define the Data Relationships

Now that data is available for use with Descartes, you define the relationships to be displayed on the map. In this example, you want a map that shows the

	Store Name	Address	City	Zip	Telephone
11	Auroras Package Store	673 Main St.	East Haven	06512	203-467-5693
12	B & L Package Store	45 New Haven Rd.	Seymour	06483	203-888-1527
13	Bakers Package Store	646 Ferry St.	New Haven	06513	203-562-0959
14	Barile's Bottle Shop	1226 Whitney Av.	Hamden	06517	203-248-3446
15	Basks Liquor Cabinet	432 Shelton Av.	New Haven	06511	203-787-4513
16	Bayview Package Store	149 Welches Poi...	Milford	06460	203-874-5923
17	Beacon Spirit Shop	113 N. Main St.	Beacon Falls	06403	203-723-1880
18	Beer Taps Unlimited	55 Meadowside Rd.	Milford	06460	203-878-4601
19	Best Buy Liquors	165 Cherry St.	Milford	06460	203-874-3836
20	Bills Package Store	195 Seymour Av.	Derby	06418	203-734-7934
21	Bobs Bottle Shop	13 Water St.	Guilford	06437	203-481-9383
22	Boston Plaza Spirit Sh...	326 Boston Av.	Stratford	06497	203-378-9511
23	Bottas Foxon Package S...	914 Foxon Rd.	New Haven	06513	203-467-7175
24	Bottle Shop	486 Orange St.	New Haven	06511	203-865-4590

Classes Sort Order Summaries Go All Store Records

Figure 7-1. Attribute data of New Haven area restaurants, liquor stores, and population demographics is imported and geocoded.[49]

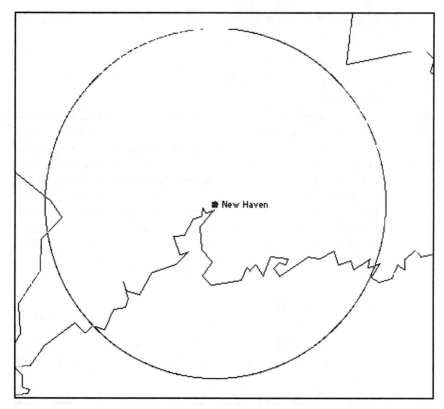

New Haven

Figure 7-2. A circle indicating the 10-mile distribution area is drawn around New Haven.[50]

locations of people making more than $50,000 a year and spending more than $70 annually on beer. To accomplish this, you specify a series of simple formulas that tell the mapping software how to manipulate the data and add it to the map display.

In the Descartes dialog box, the results of three functions are captured in baskets. (Baskets in this program are used to hold data following searches, sorts, math operations, and other processes. The baskets are a unique feature of Descartes. They are similar in function to the tables most other mapping products create that look like spreadsheets. For example, the "browser" and data manipulation routines in MapInfo, which you saw in the last chapter, are similar to the basket functions in Descartes.) The first operation you request locates areas with a median income greater than $50,000. The second function locates areas that spend more than $70 annually on beer and ale. Then the results of the first two queries are put in a single basket that holds the results, ready for mapping. Finally, you create the map by moving the data into the map using simple Descartes commands.

Make a Decision

The resulting map clearly shows a large area of the New Haven vicinity that drinks enough beer and has the right income profile for your needs. Most importantly, when reviewing your primary goal you find that the map clearly identifies a large potential market with the right demographics within the market area your company services. Deciding to add the microbrewery beers to your distribution product line is easy to justify based on the map.

You can easily meet the secondary goal of locating restaurants and liquor stores for distribution, because the data used for the analysis contains the names, addresses, and phone numbers of all restaurants and liquor stores. You simply ask Descartes to map these locations by name.

As a result of the analysis, the outlook for adding microbrewery products is positive and the mechanics of making the expansion were easily defined with the mapping software. This mapping session took less than half an hour after the data was acquired and produced excellent results.

For the purposes of this example, you are done—but you could complete even more in-depth map-based research on this market opportunity. For

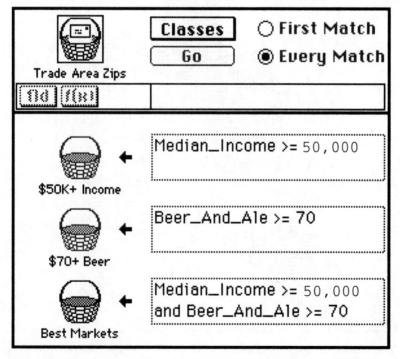

Figure 7-3. Data variables to be displayed on the map are specified within Descartes.[51]

example, you could find out exactly how many people live in the areas that meet the sales criteria. You could also map the restaurants and liquor stores that exist in the best area for the market demographics, along with actual names and addresses for each one. If you use a territory-based sales force, you could draw the territories on the map, add the locations of each potential customer, and hand the maps to each member of the sales force along with the list of target addresses and phone numbers. Street-level maps could be used as handy references for calling on prospects and clients and for routing delivery trucks as well.

Now, let's look at another scenario where market mapping helps identify a different kind of market opportunity.

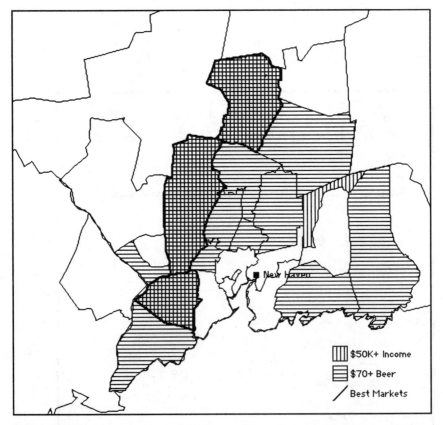

Figure 7-4. The finished map looks promising. There is an adequate number of upper-income beer consumers to justify adding the microbrewery beers to the product line.[52]

Scenario #2—New Locations or More Promotion for Gino's Pizza Restaurants

You are the marketing manager for a national chain of pizza restaurants that offers delivery within a two-mile radius of each store. You know you have a problem with the Grand Rapids, Michigan stores. The market is expanding and the competition is fierce. The question is whether you should open more restaurants or spend money promoting the ones already there. Based on the population of the city, the sales of pizzas within the city aren't in line with total sales in similarly sized cities. You made several trips to the city to get a better feel for the problem, but came back empty-handed each time. Some test promotions were tried, but the net increase in sales was not impressive. Maybe a real advertising blitz is required, but that costs as much as opening another restaurant. What should you do—advertise or expand?

Market mapping can be used to identify many kinds of distribution issues and opportunities for expansion within a market. A problem that retail chains face on a regular basis is the choice between adding stores to improve distribution or increasing advertising to build awareness of the stores already open. Choosing the wrong option is often a ticket to bankruptcy court. This problem is becoming more serious for many companies as their markets become increasingly competitive and difficult to comprehend. Thirty years ago, if you wanted to open a new hamburger stand, a drive around the city to locate a viable location was all that was required, because few competitors existed. Today, there may be five competitors selling the same food within three city blocks. How can you work around this kind of competitive pressure without assistance from a clairvoyant or spending $50,000 to $75,000, or more, on marketing research? Easy—use market maps to help you decide what to do.

When used to analyze promotion versus expansion decisions, market mapping represents masses of data unlike any other tool. While you could spend months comparing spreadsheet information on sales, competition, advertising rates, and span of influence, a market map helps you visualize the same data and allows you to make a decision in minutes.

Conventional Expansion versus Promotion Decisions

This classic quandary is a source of grief for anyone who has to make the choice. The usual approach is to spend more money on promotion first and then wait to see what happens. If sales don't increase, and opening a new store to provide access to neighborhoods not currently served is appropriate to the business, that's the next step. While sometimes opening more stores is a solution, in many cases the money spent on the expansion and the time focused on expansion activities, instead of day-to-day business, sink the entire operation.

Rather than keeping a weather eye on sales, inventories, and customer satisfaction, time is spent driving around looking for suitable space, negotiating leases, managing construction firms, and setting up the new store. With management's lack of attention on operations, food and service quality may plummet. This results in alienated customers and reduced revenues. In most businesses, once customers go to the competition, it's extremely difficult to lure them back.

Expansion/Promotion Decisions with Market Mapping Tools

Using market mapping, careful analysis of the customer base in relationship to existing stores is easy. If you run a chain of discount drugstores, for example, this kind of analysis can be used to display customer addresses to visualize the drawing power of your stores in outlying areas. You can also look to see where your competitors are in relationship to your stores, current customers, and potential customers. If a group of potential customers exists that is not being served by you or your competition, a new store in that vicinity probably makes sense. If the maps clearly show that no need exists for another drugstore, then boosting advertising may be the proper business decision, rather than opening a store. This same logic is true in the pizza business.

Step One—Define the Marketing Need

In this example, you need to understand the relationships and distributions of your current customers and competitors' customers. Then, depending on what you find out, you can make a decision to expand operations or increase promotions. You specify your primary goal for this analysis as, "After identifying customers that purchase pizza in the Grand Rapids area, decide whether this group is adequately served by pizza restaurants." The secondary goal is to "Use the maps generated by the research to choose a new location, if appropriate."

The analysis should allow you to see the entire pizza market for the city without pouring over financial reports or driving around the city in an attempt to understand your restaurants and the competitors'.

Step Two—Identify and Acquire
the Data Required
to Create the Map

To complete the analysis, you must first acquire the geographic and attribute data you need. There are four kinds of data required to assemble your analysis of the pizza market in Grand Rapids, including:

- A map of Grand Rapids and its outlying suburbs, including detailed street and freeway information.

- Attribute data showing pizza consumption by neighborhood.

- Attribute data showing addresses of customers who visited Gino's restaurants or had Gino's pizzas delivered three or more times last year.

- Attribute data showing your competitors' restaurants as well as your own.

In this case, the map is available from Strategic Mapping, the manufacturer of Atlas GIS, the desktop mapping software you selected for your analysis. The attribute data describing pizza consumption is obtained from a private data supplier that specializes in restaurant data. The locations of your pizza restaurants and your competitors' stores are available from your notes and the *Yellow Pages*.

Step Three—Load the Cartographic
and Attribute Data

The next step is to load the data into the mapping program so the analysis can begin. As always, the map data is loaded first. Next, the attribute data is made available for Atlas GIS to analyze. Addresses of Gino's customers are readily available from the company's mainframe computer. You use a modem to transmit the data to your PC and a conversion routine to translate the data into a compatible format. The pizza consumption data is purchased in a format compatible with Atlas GIS. The locations of the pizza restaurants are added manually within the mapping program because there are only a few names and addresses to enter.

Step Four—Define the Data
Relationships

To begin the mapping process, you geocode Gino's sales data and have the program map it. You also ask Atlas GIS to display Gino's locations as dot patterns and draw a circle around each location equal to the two-mile delivery zone around each store. In your initial map, it looks like your current stores service the area consistently and the results point out that increasing pro-

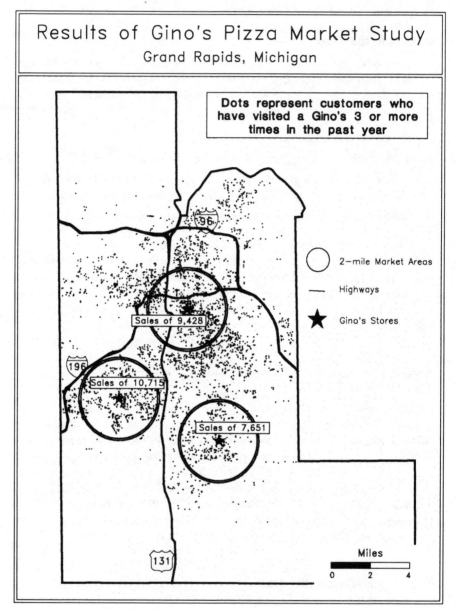

Figure 7-5. A map based on Gino's data shows existing customers.[53]

motion is still a possible solution for expanding sales. Next, it's time to look at the total number of potential pizza customers to see if they are in different locations than existing customers.

Step Five—Adjust the Map

Now you have Atlas GIS create a map of potential pizza customers for the Grand Rapids area. You also add your competitors' stores and draw a radius around each to get an idea of the areas they serve. Instantly, you see several areas not served by a pizza restaurant. You mark these with a symbol and add a two-mile radius around each. You also ask the computer to calculate how many potential pizza sales each area represents and instruct the program to label each one. Several of the new sites offer good potential—so it's not a promotional problem after all. Instead, the map shows that you need to open new restaurants to better service the population of Grand Rapids.

Step Six—Add New Data or Ask More Questions

The next thing you must do is find a suitable site in the appropriate target area. After choosing the area of largest market potential to analyze, you ask Atlas GIS to display data of available restaurant sites as close to the center of your newly identified market as possible. The data comes from your leasing agent and you key it in manually since only a few sites are available within the circled area.

Make a Decision

You reach a decision by comparing leasing rates to pizza consumption potential. One site looks particularly attractive. It's close to the center of the market area and the leasing price and terms are reasonable. The proposed location doesn't compete with your existing restaurants and is far from any competitors. So, you decide to open Gino's new restaurant at 2741 Leonard Street NW.

As a result of this analysis, the classic promotion-versus-expansion problem was analyzed quickly and effectively. The market maps also made choosing a new location easy, as we demonstrated before. The new restaurant is well-positioned for success and will bring Gino's pizza sales in Grand Rapids into line with other cities with similar populations. Maybe next year you'll look at Grand Rapids again using fresh data and choose one of the other sites for yet another new restaurant.

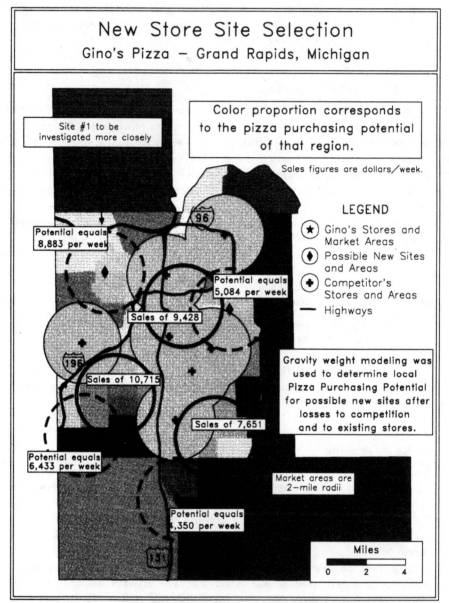

New Store Site Selection
Gino's Pizza — Grand Rapids, Michigan

Site #1 to be
investigated more closely

Color proportion corresponds
to the pizza purchasing potential
of that region.

Sales figures are dollars/week.

Potential equals
8,883 per week

Potential equals
5,084 per week

Sales of 9,428

Sales of 10,715

Sales of 7,651

Potential equals
6,433 per week

Potential equals
4,350 per week

LEGEND

(★) Gino's Stores and
    Market Areas
(♦) Possible New Sites
    and Areas
(✚) Competitor's
    Stores and Areas
—   Highways

Gravity weight modeling was
used to determine local
Pizza Purchasing Potential
for possible new sites after
losses to competition
and to existing stores.

Market areas are
2-mile radii

Miles
0   2   4

Figure 7-6. A map created with purchased data shows "pizza potential" and existing pizza restaurants.[54]

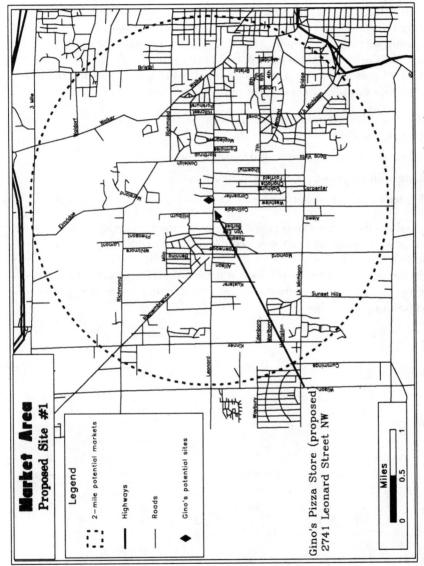

Figure 7-7. Gino's new restaurant is selected for its location within a large potential market with no nearby pizza competitors.[55]

Chapter Summary

In this chapter, we've shown that desktop mapping is a powerful tool for analyzing new markets and customer buying patterns. Map-based research like that described in the examples allows you to save money and focus marketing efforts in directions that build a business with minimum risk. With mapping software and timely data, unassailable evidence of market conditions and sales potential is assembled in just minutes.

Other applications of market mapping that use techniques and data similar to the examples in this chapter include:

- Relating demographic characteristics to buying patterns across geographic locations.
- Establishing buying trends in diverse market locations
- Determining growth potential in new locations
- Understanding competitive reach and distribution

Analyses like these can be used to focus promotional efforts, determine new product potential, improve competitive positioning, and enter new markets.

In the next chapters, we will look at further market mapping applications used to answer business questions and investigate a range of hypothetical business opportunities.

8

Sales Territory Analysis with Market Maps

When used to analyze sales territories, market maps provide unrefutable, visible evidence of the number of prospective customers and the revenue results for each salesperson in a territory. This allows territories to be assigned and adjusted based on business criteria rather than unreliable "seat-of-the-pants" rationales or arbitrary geographical divisions.

Conventional decisions regarding sales territories are usually based on a mixture of instinct, the power of the individuals involved, and convenience. Other factors, such as state or country borders, also come into play in most territory partitioning schemes. Obviously, the components in this territory mixture don't always make good business sense. Throwing darts at a map is almost as good for dividing up the territories as these traditional schemes.

In some cases, the person splitting the territories never spent any time in the field and never visited the states or provinces incorporated in a territory. For example, looking at a map of Canada, it would be easy to assume that because the massive province of Alberta takes up nearly one-twentieth of North America that it should be its own territory. However, anyone who has ever visited Alberta knows that the bulk of the province consists of wheat fields, grasslands, and not that many people or companies compared to the similar-sized but more heavily populated province of Ontario. If a province is given to each salesperson in Canada, the territories are inappropriately balanced if they are created solely on political boundary criteria.

When territory divisions are assigned, however irrationally, the sales managers watch the sales numbers in an attempt to get a grip on how well the partitioning went. If problems occur, territories are laid out yet again, and the sales force goes through another period of push and shove in an attempt to maintain its customer base and sanity. During all of this upheaval, the best salespeople often find jobs elsewhere because of frustration with their changing assignments. The energy required to constantly move territories around often cuts into sales because the participants spend time moving offices, studying paper maps, and arguing over boundaries, when they should call on accounts, sell products, and make money. Rarely do they have time for both.

Sales Territory Management with Market Mapping Tools

Bypassing the dart board technique and the arbitrary geographic assignments described above, informed sales managers consider the power of market mapping a much better method for analyzing sales territories and establishing partitions. Not only are the territories much easier to understand and assign, but the salespeople and managers don't argue with substantiated facts displayed in market maps like they do with the arbitrary assignments used by many companies. Market maps created for territory analysis are used to reinforce decisions because they graphically reveal the underlying basis of the analysis more clearly than ordinary printouts of regional sales figures, pie charts, and quota comparisons.

Scenario #1—Sales Territory Management for a Medical Instrument Manufacturer

In this case you are the sales manager for a company that makes medical instrument systems sold primarily to private doctors' offices and small practices where less than five doctors share a medical facility. Your region currently includes three southern New England states, for each of which you have one salesperson—Jean, Mike, or Sam. Right now you have a problem that needs immediate attention. Not only are Mike's sales not meeting quota, but his performance is dragging down the profitability of the entire region. Mike is a veteran salesperson for the company with a strong record until assignment to his present territory. He claims that his lack of success is because the territories are broken up by state, not by sales potential.

With Mike's sales figures failing to meet expectations and the confrontational attitudes of the other two salespeople when you discuss the possibility of moving territories around, you feel caught in the middle. And, since you were recently transferred from the California office and are completely unfamiliar with New England, you aren't sure what to think. In addition, your boss hinted that he may split your region and give one state to another sales manager whose region is performing more consistently. What should you do?

Step One—Define the Marketing Need

In this example, defining the goal is comparatively simple. You want to analyze the sales potential of each territory and look for an imbalance among the number of potential customers available to each salesperson. This will confirm or refute Mike's claims and provide hard evidence for moving territories around or keeping them as assigned. The results of your analysis should also convince your boss that you really have the situation in hand and no reductions to your region are appropriate or necessary. Thus, the primary goal is to "Analyze and (if necessary) equalize sales territories based on potential sales volume." The secondary goal is to "Produce market maps and data which can be used to demonstrate why sales territories should be redistributed or left as they are."

This analysis will allow you to discuss Mike's job and territory with credibility. If the numbers show that his territory lacks the potential he claims, then you can recognize his argument and make adjustments. If Mike's argument is disproved then, you may need to discuss his working style and look for other ways to improve his performance.

Step Two—Identify and Acquire the Data Required to Create the Map

To complete the analysis, you must first acquire the geographic and attribute data you need. There are two pieces of data required to assemble your map. They are:

- A map of the region that is compatible with the market mapping software you use. In this case, the product is again Descartes from PC Globe, Inc. The map and software should also allow you to assign territories by county and/or zip codes.

- Attribute data that shows the sales potential of each county in each state.

In this case, the map is available from Descartes' manufacturer, PC Globe. The attribute data describing sales potential by county in terms of the number of small physicians' practices is obtained from a private data supplier that specializes in medical industry data. Instead of purchasing data for your region only, with the approval of your boss, you purchase data for the contiguous United States, so other sales managers can perform similar analyses for their regions.

Step Three—Load the Cartographic and Attribute Data

The next step is to load the data into the mapping program so the analysis can begin. The map data is loaded and then you zoom to an appropriate level so you can see the three relevant states to be studied. Next, you select the counties in each salesperson's current territory.

Last, you import the attribute data that contains the sales potential in dollars based on the number of doctors' offices in the counties in the three states.

Step Four—Define the Data Relationships

In this example, you need to tie the potential sales data to the counties shown on the map. Then, using the data by county, you produce a simple bar chart that shows how much total sales potential each salesperson has with the current territory partitions. It takes only a glance at the map to see that Mike has a legitimate grievance. His territory, while consisting of an entire state (Rhode Island), is not only physically smaller, but also has far fewer potential customers according to the purchased data.

Step Five—Adjust the Map

Now that everything is set up, you can reassign counties to other salespeople interactively. Because the data is tied to the map, making interactive changes to the territory partitions changes the bar chart to display the potentials of alternate territory divisions. In this case, Sam has too much territory. Moving counties from Sam's territory into Mike's begins to equalize the picture because as the counties are reassigned, the chart showing sales potential in relationship to salespeople is immediately updated. Naturally, adding counties close to Mike's existing territory makes the most sense. As shown in the finished map and chart, by moving several counties from Sam's territory into Mike's territory, an almost exact balance of prospective customers is achieved. Jean's territory remains unchanged because its number of prospective customers is right in line with the new "adjusted" territories for Sam and Mike.

		Classes	Sort Order
		𝔾𝔬	Summaries

All County Records

✓	↑ ...	County	State	Potential ($)	
1		Fairfield	CT	4839000	
2		Hartford	CT	4818000	
3		Litchfield	CT	726000	
4		Middlesex	CT	663000	
5		New Haven	CT	4164000	
6		New London	CT	1020000	
7		Tolland	CT	312000	
8		Windham	CT	372000	
9		Barnstable	MA	1029000	
10		Berkshire	MA	750000	
11		Bristol	MA	1923000	
12		Dukes	MA	75000	
13		Essex	MA	3324000	
14		Franklin	MA	237000	
15		Hampden	MA	2007000	
16		Hampshire	MA	480000	
17		Middlesex	MA	7236000	
18		Nantucket	MA	18000	
19		Norfolk	MA	4092000	
20		Plymouth	MA	1713000	
21		Suffolk	MA	2883000	
22		Worcester	MA	2961000	
23		Bristol	RI	96000	
24		Kent	RI	1053000	
25		Newport	RI	375000	

Figure 8-1. Attribute data of sales potential in the three states, by county, is added to the mapping program.[56]

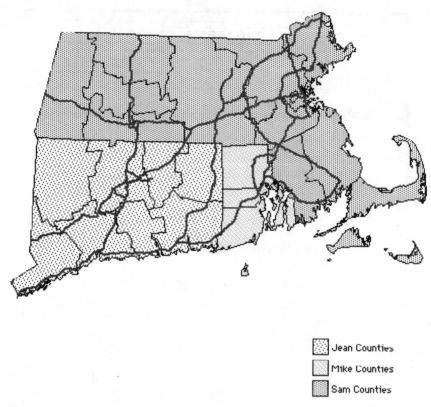

Jean Counties
Mike Counties
Sam Counties

Figure 8-2. The current sales territories are assigned by state.[57]

Make a Decision

Now that it's been graphically demonstrated that Mike was shorted on customers and Sam has the lion's share of prospects, you can announce and justify the new territory adjustments. Sam may argue loudly that his territory is being taken from him unjustly, but he can't argue with the numbers and charts produced by the mapping software. Jean will be pleased that no changes were made to her customer base because it was already the right size.

To take the project to its logical conclusion, lists of the new territory assignments by county name are printed along with copies of the market map, visually showing where territories start and stop. These can be used in meetings as presentation tools and to show other managers how they can use the power of market mapping to solve their own territory management problems.

As a result of this analysis, a good salesperson is assigned an appropriately sized territory. Sam had so many prospective customers that he couldn't call on all of them in a timely manner. Now Sam has a territory that is more manageable. The maps produced with Descartes convinced everyone that the change made good business sense, and after the reassignments the region's sales figures began to climb back toward quota as Mike began calling on customers that Sam didn't have time to pursue in the old territory structure.

Scenario #2—Assigning New Sales Territories for an Expanding Farm Equipment Manufacturer

This scenario is another example of territory management, but this time you use Atlas GIS from Strategic Mapping to complete the analysis. In this example, you are the vice president of sales for a farm equipment manufacturer that is experiencing rapid growth with a line of low-cost, high-quality farm machinery. The equipment is selling briskly because hard-pressed farmers are looking for less expensive solutions for replacing worn-out equipment. The use of new lightweight materials in the equipment allows you to build it for less money, and the lighter equipment requires substantially less energy to operate—a win-win situation for both your company and the farms that purchase your products.

You are having a problem with your salespeople wasting too much time driving through several states to reach customers; the salespeople are cen-

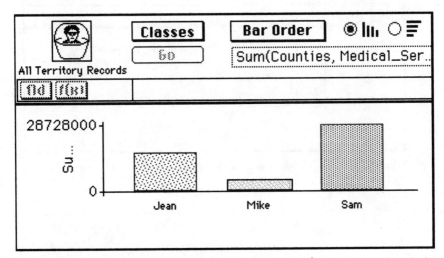

Figure 8-3. The sales potential within the current territories indicates a serious inequity in sales potential.[58]

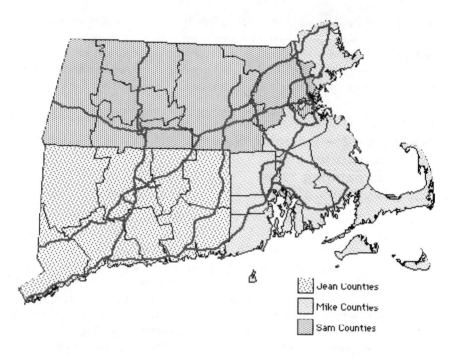

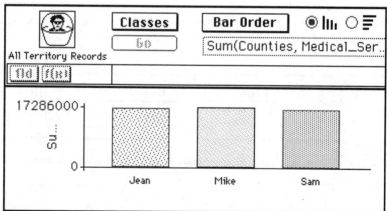

Figure 8-4. A sales territories and sales potential graph after a mapping session with Descartes.[59]

trally based at your corporate headquarters in Kansas City. A decision has been made to open several regional offices, and squabbles regarding territory assignments have already begun among the salespeople and sales managers. You are already familiar with market mapping tools and plan to use them to settle the disputes before they get serious and the salespeople start looking for openings with your competitors.

Offices will be opened in four major cities to reduce driving time, and a sales force will also be kept at your headquarters to handle customers in the Kansas City region. Offices will be opened in Denver, Dallas, Chicago, and Minneapolis. You need to work out sales territory arrangements for each city.

Step One—Define the Marketing Need

The first step is to define the project goal. The goals for this project are determined to be:

Primary Goal: "Define balanced sales territories by sales potential for each new office for the five salespeople that will work out of each office."

Secondary Goal: "Produce market maps that can be used to demonstrate the equity of the territory partitions to all salespeople and sales managers."

The results of this project will be used to clarify to the sales force the logic of the territory assignments. This will hopefully eliminate conflicts and gets the sales force to work faster because they'll spend less time quibbling over customer bases and more time selling.

Step Two—Identify and Acquire the Data Required to Create the Map

To perform the analysis, you must determine the geographic and attribute data you need to begin. There are two general types of data required to assemble this map. They are:

- A map of the Midwest complete with Interstate highways and counties.
- Attribute data showing the sales potential, by county, of the states in question.

In this case, a map of the contiguous United States is available from Strategic Mapping for Atlas GIS, the product to be used to support this research and analysis. The attribute data is acquired from government reports on farms in the area.

Step Three—Load the Cartographic and Attribute Data

After loading the map data, you load the attribute data which arrived in the format of delineated ASCII and was directly imported by Atlas GIS. You are now ready to define the relationships between the attribute data and the map.

Step Four—Define the Data Relationships

Now that data is available for Atlas GIS to use, you specify the relationships you want to see displayed. In this example, you want a simple comparison, by county, highlighting the sales potential of each for farm equipment.

Next, you define initial sales boundaries for each of the new sales offices, including Kansas City. The resulting map outlines the 200-mile radius of territories around each city and is used to create territories for each new office.

You start the territory assignment process by using the Kansas City office as your test case. You zoom to the center of the four-state region that this office will service, and Kansas City becomes the center of the map.

Initially your plan is to divide the territories by using the Interstate highways to partition the assignments. You then map the data with fill patterns to shows sales potential, by county, for the area.

This initial division of territories based on the Interstate highways creates territories that look approximately equal in size, but the attribute data shows that physical size and sales potential are not closely related. Atlas GIS has been set up to automatically calculate the total sales potential of each territory. It looks like partitioning territories by county may make more sense.

To accomplish balanced partitions, you reassign territories county-by-county by simply clicking on each area with your mouse until you reach an approximate balance among territories. Of course, the counties in each territory must be contiguous with each other or you will again have a drive time problem with salespeople commuting between distant parts of their territories to call on customers—so the relationship to the interstates is still considered as you choose the counties. Atlas GIS redraws a map showing sales territories that are balanced by sales potential, not by size.

Make a Decision

Following your session with Atlas GIS, you have a map that visually represents the territories and the hard data to back up your choice of counties. The salespeople study your maps and data in a presentation meeting and there are no disagreements whatsoever—a first for your company when

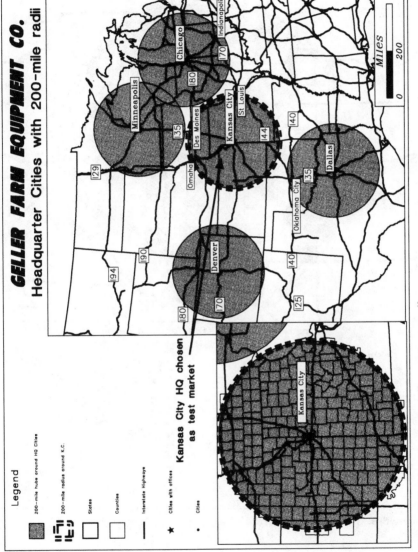

Figure 8-5. Map of new sales office service areas.[60]

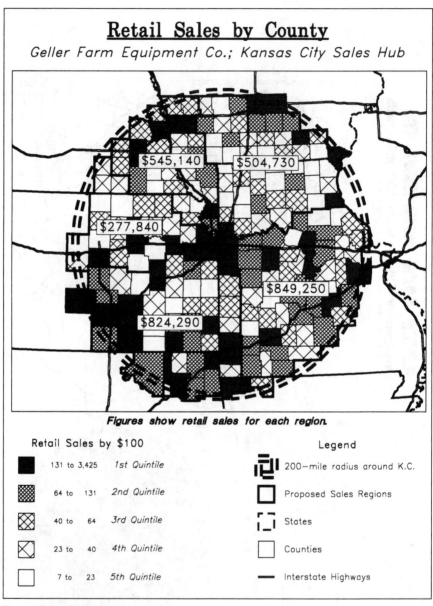

Retail Sales by County
Geller Farm Equipment Co.; Kansas City Sales Hub

$545,140 $504,730

$277,840

$849,250

$824,290

Figures show retail sales for each region.

Retail Sales by $100

■	131 to 3,425	*1st Quintile*
▓	64 to 131	*2nd Quintile*
⊠	40 to 64	*3rd Quintile*
◰	23 to 40	*4th Quintile*
□	7 to 23	*5th Quintile*

Legend

200—mile radius around K.C.

Proposed Sales Regions

States

Counties

—— Interstate Highways

Figure 8-6. The Kansas City area divided into territories by Interstate highways.[61]

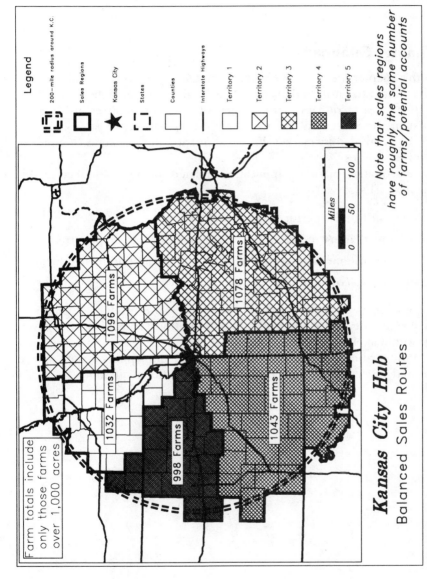

Figure 8-7. Kansas City territories partitioned equally by sales potential, not geographic features.[62]

assigning new sales territories. Not only that, but calling on customer accounts begins immediately, without the usual period of "adjustment" when individual salespeople argue for more territory or complain of unfair treatment.

Chapter Summary

In this chapter, we've shown how mapping analysis, coupled with reliable data, is used to clarify and justify politically awkward decisions such as reassigning sales territories. Similar types of mapping analyses are used to assist in the placement of new franchise operations or stores; related research can identify market share and distribution problems common to many businesses.

Other market mapping applications related to those described in this chapter include:

- Determining sales performance within a territory
- Analyzing delivery routes and other product distribution patterns
- Locating customer addresses and demographics around retail outlets
- Determining cost and profit margin differences across a sales territory

These types of analyses can be used to improve product distribution, change delivery routes, expand into new locations, and adjust sales coverage within a territory for maximum impact.

In the next chapter, we will look at ways market mapping is used to analyze and answer complex advertising and promotional questions.

9

Using Market Mapping for Advertising and Direct Mail Applications

Many American businesses spend more money on advertising and promotion than on any other single line item in their budgets. Using promotional funds for maximum effectiveness is the key to keeping costs in line and securing maximum profitability. Money wasted on ineffective promotions can be sizable if market segments, distributions, and demographics are not understood for the media used. Any kind of research that maximizes promotional effectiveness is an important asset to companies of all sizes, from small businesses to major corporations. With market mapping, poor media choices can be eliminated and promotional dollars can be used effectively to strengthen a campaign, to purchase additional media (placements), or to significantly improve the balance sheet.

There are countless research organizations that specialize in analyzing advertising media and direct mail programs for effectiveness and reach. Some of this research is done before programs commence. The effectiveness is then measured after ads are seen or direct mail is delivered. This kind of research is not only expensive, but also ineffective in many cases. Research that adds one-third more cost to an already overburdened promotional budget may push new firms and those running on tight margins to the breaking point. Fortunately, market mapping can be used to handle much of this work at a fraction of the cost of conventional research. Some progressive research organizations and advertising agencies use the same market mapping tools that you can. You can employ the tools yourself and save the mark-up and consulting fees.

Scenario #1—Analyzing Billboard Locations

In this case, you are the vice president of corporate communications for a large tobacco company. Recently you were given responsibility for a large, national advertising campaign to promote a new brand of low-cost cigarettes that require high-volume sales to be a successful product offering because of their slim profit margin. Because the advertising media available for promoting tobacco products are limited, the program includes a number of expensive ads in major magazines and the use of billboards scattered across the nation.

Unfortunately, the billboard selection process runs into minor but significant problems. The rental of billboard space (called *showings* in the industry) was arranged with a national billboard media broker, but you lack confidence in their selection criteria. The list of spaces means little to you and the crude photocopied maps provided by the company look more like arbitrary rentals of vacant billboards rather than a carefully tuned selection of appropriate space. In addition, the cigarette industry has been repeatedly criticized for placing billboard ads too close to "sensitive locations," such as hospitals and schools, and the photocopied maps don't contain information on the location of such facilities.

Conventional Location Analysis of Billboard Advertising

Conventionally, billboard showings are rented by the billboard provider who provides lists and maps of billboard locations and rates. Individual billboards are priced according to the estimated number of people who will see the locations each day. The more people exposed to the billboard, the higher the price. Larger billboards and those with lights for nighttime viewing are also more expensive because a larger size and night viewing increase the number of people who will see the billboard. Showings are often purchased as a package. The billboard sales representative or broker usually recommends a group of locations at a "special rate."

Because extensive research rarely goes into choosing the right billboards, it is largely a hit-miss affair, particularly when renting boards for a national campaign with thousands of showings. Even taking the time to study maps of each billboard location across the country tells you little about the quality of the space. In addition, placing showings away from schools and hospitals is difficult without comparing billboard locations to conventional road maps. This is a time-consuming process at best. Not surprisingly, some billboard companies (also called outdoor media suppliers) are offering market mapping capabilities to their customers to make the selection process easier.

Analysis of Billboard Locations with Market Mapping Tools

Instead of agreeing to a large, expensive program of showings to introduce your new line of cigarettes based solely on guesstimates and questionable recommendations, you use market mapping tools and data to analyze the locations and eliminate ineffective showings. You can also ask the software to flag schools and hospitals within one mile of prospective billboards to save you the trouble of checking each billboard against paper road maps of the entire country.

Market mapping takes the process much further. You set your maps up to display each showing vicinity with the demographics of the people who live or work there as well. Billboard selection along highways is easier too. The mapping software is set to color each highway according to the type of road it is. Otherwise, you may be purchasing overpriced space located next to a rural highway, long ago bypassed by a busy interstate.

Step One—Define the Marketing Need

While this project appears to have a number of requirements, you still attempt to keep the primary goal simple and fulfill the other objectives with secondary goals. Keeping the primary goal brief and to the point is the best way to keep focused on the project's ultimate objective while identifying data and assembling maps.

After careful consideration, the goals you develop for this project include the following:

Primary Goal: "Locate high visibility billboards on a national scale. In addition to freeway showings, identify ones located in areas where the demographics match those of the smoking population for the new product."

Secondary Goal: "Identify all schools and hospitals within target areas and draw a circle representing a one-mile radius around each. Color all billboard locations falling in this radius a different color than other available showings."

Step Two—Identify and Acquire the Data Required to Create the Map

There are four pieces of data required to assemble this mapping analysis. They are:

- Maps of major cities and their suburban vicinities. The maps should have zip codes and show arterial streets and highways as well. You may wish to use a map with complete street-level information to give you a better feel for billboard proximity to residential and industrial areas.

- Attribute data of the billboards for each city. The data should contain availability information as well.

- Attribute data of the demographics of the population in each city.

- Attribute data of the locations of schools and hospitals for each city.

For this analysis you have decided to use Tactician from Tactics, International to analyze the data because of the extensive map data available and because the program provides direct access to a wide range of data you already have in your company databases. Other data that is required is acquired from commercial data suppliers and the billboard company.

Step Three—Load the Geographic and Attribute Data

The next step is to make the data available to Tactician so the analysis can begin. After the geographic base maps for the United States and key cities to be studied are loaded, you zoom to Los Angeles and use this city area for creating the first map. Next, you add the attribute data for Los Angeles and prepare it for mapping.

			Billboard Data:Data		
Long Beach					
Target	041617				
Geocode	**Count**	**SMOKERS (1 MILE)**	**BILLBOARD LOCATION**	**CITY**	
◉ ➔ 041617	3	2710	Interstate 4055/Mile 234.5	Long Beach	
○ ➔ 041618	1	2797	Interstate 405/Mile 256.1	Long Beach	
○ ➔ 041621	3	2289	290045 North 53rd Avenue	Long Beach	
○ ➔ 041623	3	1823	Pacific Coast Hwy/Mile 762.5	Redondo Beach	
Sites					

Figure 9-1. Data with billboard locations and showing specifications.[63]

You then import the data provided by the billboard into a format compatible with the Tactician software. In this example, the data is on paper so you scan it with OCR software and import it after using a word processor to remove irrelevant information. Then, you geocode all of the data so the mapping software knows where billboards, schools, and hospitals are in relationship to Tactician's data on streets and highways. Finally, you geocode the population demographics and get ready to define the relationships between the data and the map.

Step Four—Define the Data Relationships

Now that the data is available for the mapping software to display, you define the attributes to be represented on the map. In this example, you want a map that shows the locations of available billboards while screening out locations with schools and hospitals in close proximity, so several functions must be used to define the display relationships. As part of the process, you also specify symbols and colors for the map, because this helps to better visualize the data relationships. Colors are also selected for the different kinds of streets and highways present in the map. Most street and

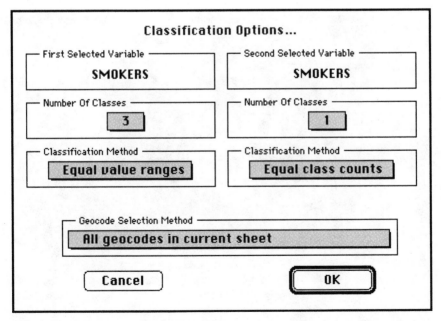

Figure 9-2. The data for available billboards is added to a base map of Los Angeles.[64]

highway data has a number attached to it in the data file that indicates road and highway types. For example, a quiet residential street might be numbered as a "1" class street. A major interstate might be a class "8." This allows the mapping software to differentiate between classes of roads, and you can ask the program to represent each road class differently on your map.

Step Five—Refine the Map

Because this map is so complex, you decide to refine it for easier comprehension by other managers. For example, you might simply eliminate the presence of schools and hospitals in the map by turning their layer off. Along with this, you can set the program to hide the circles around each one and remove all billboards that fall within the circle. This allows you to easily see where the target billboards are located in relation to each other.

Step Six—Add More Detail or Ask More Questions

In this step, you could choose to add more data to the map to help refine the analysis. All the data has already been loaded, but not all of it has been

Figure 9-3. A map is produced showing billboards and the location of schools and hospitals.[65]

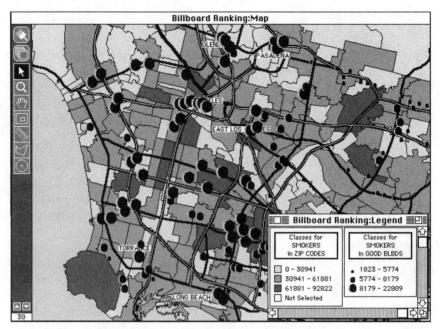

Figure 9-4. To add clarity to the map, billboard symbols are scaled in proportion to demographic profiles of the area they are located in.[66]

displayed on the map because there's too much to interpret at one time.

To get a better understanding of the billboard locations in relationship to the target market, you ask Tactician to color areas by market demographics. Billboards for this product that are located in low-income areas where people still smoke will be more effective than those located where the demographics reveal a population that contains far fewer smokers or one with upscale consumers who are likely to buy imported cigarettes or image brands. To clarify the map even further, you can ask the program to increase (or decrease) the size of each billboard symbol according to the number of people living or working within one mile of the showing. This helps you isolate poor showings located in sparsely populated areas around the fringe of the city.

You also notice a lack of showings in particular densely populated areas of the city. Since these might be within the one-mile radius around schools and houses rather than an anomaly of billboard locations, turn the circles back on if necessary to better understand the map. The Tactician program supports interactive analysis, quick access to on-line data, and simultaneous map displays that allow many questions to be answered and many possibilities to be explored in a single mapping session.

Make a Decision

Following your session with the mapping software, you identify all the billboards in the Los Angeles area appropriate and available for promoting the new low-priced cigarette product. You might also use data to plot the location of competing billboards. For example, an expensive showing located at a major intersection may look appealing initially, but data showing *all* the billboards at that location may point out ten other competitive showings. All the competitors and advertising density will seriously reduce the effectiveness of your billboards.

This analysis continues through the other cities as required. To communicate your choices to the billboard company, you delete the billboard symbols for showings that fail to meet your criteria and add street address labels to the billboard symbols you want to use. From these labels, the billboard company reserves space and draws up the contract.

As a result of the analysis, the ideal spaces are identified. This reduces the number of showings from the 220 originally proposed by the billboard company for Los Angeles to less than 150—a substantial savings in promotional dollars with better overall results. Your search also identifies several well-located billboards that the list from the billboard company failed to include! The resulting savings can be used for another program or to add money to the magazine ad media budget for promoting the new product. Now you can go on to use Tactician and market mapping to help choose the best media demographics for your magazine ads. But that's for another session. For the purposes of this book, let's look at another company and another challenge in marketing—how to effectively target a direct mail program for maximum impact and response.

Scenario #2—Targeting a Direct Mail Program for a Group of Department Stores in Chicago

In this hypothetical example, you are the vice president of marketing for a large group of department stores located in the Chicago metropolitan area. Your stores cater to moderately affluent households with customers mostly fifty years of age and older. In your role coordinating the marketing efforts for the company, you also are in charge of marketing communications for the company. While most of the hands-on communications projects are completed by an assistant and your advertising agency, you make most of the strategic promotional decisions yourself.

An unexpected increase in advertising rates for the city's major newspaper forced you to cut back on advertising, which, until now, was the major promotion vehicle for the stores. You have been looking for a more effective promotional vehicle that costs less than expensive full-page ads and is at least as effective. Direct mail looks like a good choice, but the only mailing list you own is one of the company's existing credit card holders. This group already gets monthly mailings for upscale goods such as perfumes and special sales.

Along with creating a series of high-impact mailers that stand out at the mailbox, you need a mailing list that fits the profile of most of your customers. Unfortunately, there are thousands of lists to choose from, priced from very inexpensive to very costly. Which one should you use?

Conventional Market Analysis of Direct Mail List Targeting

Conventionally, most mailing lists are rented from suppliers based on a selection of supposed demographic criteria that results in a targeted list. Depending on the list and the supplier, highly targeted lists can be rented, but these are usually the most expensive and in this example may contain large numbers of people who don't live close enough to one of your stores to shop there. Using such a list means paying a high premium for quality each time it's used and mailing to thousands of households with no interest in the mailer. This results in substantial waste because the worthless names must be paid for and the mailers and postage are mailed to uninterested recipients.

Another conventional alternative is to mail to a highly targeted mailing list of your own, in this case your list of existing credit card customers. Because the purpose of the mailer is to reach customers who normally read the ads and to attract new customers as well as existing ones, this list is only partially useful. The deficiency of the in-house list is reinforced because a recent research program disclosed that less than 40 percent of a day's typical customers owned or used the store's credit cards. Therefore, mailing to the credit card list won't build new business.

Mailing List Targeting with Market Mapping Tools

While purchasing an expensive, highly targeted list is useful for direct mail, it makes more sense economically if you purchase only the sections of the list you need. This saves on the list rental fees because you won't pay for useless names, fewer mailers need to be printed, and money is saved on postage. Since most list providers use computer programs to manipulate and sort their lists, you can rent names by street, zip code, county, or suburb. Market mapping tools can help you choose the right sections of the city for your mailings, so you buy only names of people living within reasonable proximity to one of your stores. This saves time and money. It also allows you to target mailings to different parts of the city. For example, if one of your stores is located in an affluent suburb, you might want to add an insert to the mailer for an exclusive line of expensive china. Whereas mailings to locations near a store located in a less-affluent suburb might not benefit from this same insert because there isn't a market for expensive fine china there, this target area might be influenced by a sale on fashion jeans or sports jackets.

Step One—Define the Marketing Need

In this example, defining the goal is straightforward. You want to effectively analyze your market as defined by store location and surrounding neighborhoods to include the households that live close enough to drive to your store, but that also have the income and age profile appropriate for purchasing your store's merchandise.

In this case, the primary goal is to "Identify by zip code areas surrounding each store a large number of potential customers with the right demographic profile. This analysis will be used to choose mailing lists."

To further refine the analysis, you also consider the size of each store in relationship to its trade area. Historically, the smaller stores attract customers from a smaller outlying radius than the largest stores, so you can limit your search to zip codes closer to the smaller stores.

Step Two—Identify and Acquire the Data Required to Create the Map

There are two general types of data required to assemble your map. They are:

- A map of the Chicago area that's compatible with the Tactician software you plan to use for this analysis. The map data should also include zip code boundary information and details of "driving zone" boundaries such as rivers, railroad tracks, and freeways.
- Attribute data showing the age and income demographics of the population of Chicago sorted by zip code.

In this case, the map data was available from Tactics International, the manufacturers of Tactician. For expediency, the attribute data on Chicago's consumer demographics was also purchased from Tactics International, even though it was available from other sources.

Geocode		FRACTION	AGE/INCOME INDEX	MEDIAN AGE	MEDIAN INCOME
46320		59	0.19	32.20	18945
46327		100	0.21	37.24	21908
46394		100	0.26	36.98	24078
60004		61	0.38	39.21	28561

ZIP Code Data:Data

21908

Figure 9-5. Demographic data attached to zip codes will be used in this map.[67]

Step Three—Load the Geographic and Attribute Data

After the geographic data is loaded for mapping, you zoom to an appropriate level so you can see the entire Chicago area in which you have retail stores. Next, you bring in the population data which, because it is provided by Tactician's manufacturer, is immediately ready for use by the program.

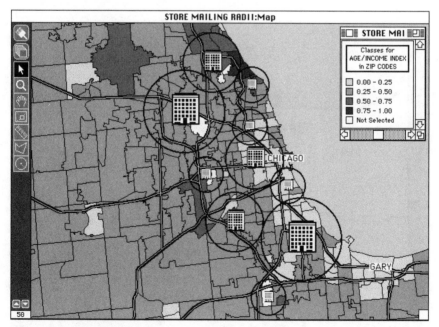

Figure 9-6. The map data shows each store's trade area and the income/age distribution in the surrounding areas by zip code.[68]

Step Four—Define the Data Relationships

In this example, you tie the attribute data to the map and ask the program to color each zip code by the age and income profiles from the data. In addition, you set the mapping parameters to represent each store based on its sales volume and size. In this example, larger stores are represented with larger store symbols. At a glance you see the relationship of each store's size and the mailing radius for that store.

Make a Decision

Using this simple technique, it's easy to see which zip codes that surround the stores are appropriate for the mailing. The areas that combine the right age group and income levels visually stand out from the ones that don't. By simply labeling the useful zip codes, you can request a highly targeted mailing list. Decisions can also be made regarding areas that are not immediately close to a store. For example, an affluent area with the right age group that's located midway between two stores, but a little out of driving range for each, may still be a good possibility for mailing. Yet, without the map-

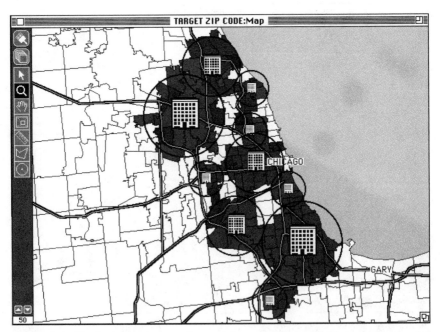

Figure 9-7. The finished map shows the zip code areas with the right demographics located within each store's trade area.[69]

ping software to create the visual representation of these households, you would never guess this.

As a result of this analysis, the expensive, but largely useless, names are eliminated from your mailings. The cumulative savings are substantial enough that you mail twice a quarter instead of just once. With the more frequent mailings bringing in better-qualified customers, you are able to effectively cut back on the newspaper advertising which is so expensive. Best of all, customers who weren't aware of your company before are visiting the stores. These people never read the newspaper and never saw the ads!

Chapter Summary

Mapping analyses can help control advertising and promotional costs because they show you exactly where the money *should* be spent for maximum impact. Map-based research minimizes the money spent on ineffective ad placements recommended by media salespeople with their commission in mind rather than your success. Direct marketing becomes less expensive because you eliminate the "shotgun" approach so standard in mailing programs and telemarketing campaigns. Best of all, because promotion is so expensive, increasing advertising effectiveness while decreasing the media required to reach a market cuts costs and improves the chance for a promotion to successfully influence the right segment of customers.

In addition to the examples in this chapter, other market mapping applications for promotional research include:

- Comparing the reach and demographics of various advertising media within the same geographic area

- Analyzing the demographics of new customers who have responded to a particular promotion or advertisement

- Establishing "cost per response" or "cost per sale" across geographic areas based on different promotions

- Measuring the response percentages for various promotions across geographic regions

These types of analyses can be used to explore a wide range of questions dependent on the geographic and demographic impact of promotional efforts. These include determining the best promotional media for a specific audience and establishing the best media for specific geographic and demographic criteria.

In the next chapter, we will explore the possibilities of international research with market mapping.

10
Using Market Mapping Tools to Evaluate International Market Potential

One of the most daunting tasks for companies distributing products internationally is to choose among countries and locations within countries. Which countries should be used to "grow" the market, and which lack potential or should be held off for a while? Without intense analysis of each individual economy and market, it's difficult to understand regional patterns in the marketplace. And, because many national economies are directly tied to the ones of their neighbors, regional trends are difficult to spot. For example, a slow growth year for one African country's economy may cause a slowing in its neighbor's economies beginning a year or two later. Without careful study of each region's economic figures, and an understanding of the geopolitical relationships, this analysis is very difficult.

In addition, not all products are received equally in all economies. This adds to the risk. While many parts of the world may love consumables such as American-style hamburgers or soft drinks, not all products have the same appeal across nationalities and cultures.

Another potential problem is the cost and quality of international research. There are a large number of data sources, research organizations, international consultants, and "experts" willing to provide advice on this topic. For major corporations, the fees for such services are not usually the problem. It is the usefulness of the data and advice that's questionable. Query three international market economists on a country's fiscal status, current and projected, and three different answers will likely be forthcoming. (Three invoices for the answers will materialize as well.)

While it is not a crystal ball, market mapping can help solve the international research dilemma, because entire regions of the world can be studied using visual comparisons of the results based on commonly available and credible international data. These maps can be used to show trends within regions, rather than just individual countries, and more effective global decisions can be made as a result.

The Scenario—Identify Potential Expansion Markets by Country

You are the vice president of international marketing for a large multinational corporation that sells soft drinks. Sales of your products in the domestic market have been flat for several years as the baby boomer population ages, and there are fewer people consuming soft drinks. The colas your company is known for are doing particularly poorly in the United States. To compensate, your board of directors has dictated a push on international expansion into new and existing markets.

You are nervous about the expansion because it involves a large sum of money. The members of the board want your recommendations, but they also want to make the final decision on their own. You know how to identify the right markets, but since the board wants an answer in less than a week, you lack the time to prepare traditional research, let alone make a comprehensive report. The multitude of data required is nearly impossible to explain to the board of directors, so the decisions they make will be based more on instinct than logic. You need a quick method for analysis that can also be used to convince the board that some economies may look ripe for expansion, but could potentially sour in a couple of years.

You already have access to reams of data describing market economies worldwide—so much in fact that the useful and up-to-date information is buried among the tangential research and reports. You also have access to an army of consultants, but the last time you asked for reports on regional economic trends from four of them, the analysis provided was largely contradictory and confusing.

Conventional Analysis of International Markets for Expansion Possibilities

Conventionally, expansion into new countries with a major product line, using increased promotion and distribution, is decided by analyzing each individual country's economic picture. This may include a detailed study of printed reports with pages of numbers, verification of government data against numbers provided by consultants, and use of your gut instinct to determine if the country's economy is ready for expansion and poised for growth. Such analysis takes months to prepare and verify, and it rarely takes into account regional trends that may shake the country under review, even though there is no indication of future problems right now.

Choosing the wrong country or countries for expansion can be devastating. It might mean the construction of an expensive new manufacturing facility, hiring and training staff, spending large sums on advertising and promotion, and importing a fleet of trucks for distribution. If the product fails to sell, this effort (and substantial expense) will be fruitless, and a major charge may have to he taken against corporate earnings.

Market Mapping Analysis of International Markets for Expansion Possibilities

Market maps are powerful tools for evaluating international expansion potential, market-by-market. Unlike conventional methods, market maps can be used to graphically display economic and potential product growth, not just in one country, but for entire regions. The results of this analysis can be used to demonstrate regional or continent-wide trends to other managers. Because the data used for creating a market map is broken out from irrelevant information that only clouds the issues, maps can add clarity to the data and the decisions not available with any other tool.

Step One—Define the Marketing Need

As usual, the first step is to define the project goal. While this project could entail the use of literally thousands of numbers and data, summation data of economic growth and product sales with each country and region under consideration are all that's required for the initial analysis. The goals for this project are:

Primary Goal: "Identify countries where a combination of increasing soft drink (cola) consumption and economic growth is occurring. Look for negative regional growth trends that could negatively influence the expansion."

Secondary Goal: "Produce market maps that can be used to convince the board of directors that certain countries have much brighter expansion prospects than others, and demonstrate regional trends that could materially affect the success of the expansion program."

The results of this project not only clarify the best possibilities in an unassailable manner, but also allow the decision makers to see where seemingly unimportant economic trends in neighboring countries may cause problems in the near future for the expansion. Based on the analysis supported with your mapping tools, the expansion can go ahead only in countries with the right mix of cola consumption and positive economic growth potential, and situated away from countries where economic problems may damage bordering economies.

Step Two—Identify and Acquire the Data Required to Create the Map

To perform the analysis, you must determine the geographic and attribute data you need to begin the analysis. There are three pieces of data required to assemble this map. They are:

- A map of the world as up-to-date as possible, so it accurately reflects recent global border changes.
- Attribute data that shows the economic growth of all countries for the last five years (real GNP).
- Attribute data of the per capita consumption of carbonated soft drinks of all kinds. If it's available, consumption data of colas specifically would be even more useful.

In this case, the global map is available from Tactics International for Tactician, the product used to support this research and analysis. The other data is acquired from major international data suppliers, corporate databases, and the global news weekly, *The Economist*.

Step Three—Load the Cartographic and Attribute Data

Your next step is to load the data into the mapping program so the analysis can begin. The first data to load is the map data. In this example, you zoom to Europe to study new markets in newly formed Eastern Bloc republics. Next, the attribute data is added for all the countries of Europe. In this example, the economic data is available in the format of delineated ASCII saved on a microcomputer-compatible diskette so importing it is comparatively easy. The per capita beverage consumption is acquired in paper format, but not that many countries are involved, so directly typing it into Tactician's integrated database takes only a few minutes.

Geocode	POP GROWTH	YR 2000 POP	YR 2020 POP	%GNP GROWTH	COLA SALES ($ MILL)
AFGHANISTAN	2.36%	24.50	39.12	1.54%	14.48
ALBANIA	2.07%	3.79	4.62	3.44%	3.15
ALGERIA	3.20%	33.71	49.41	4.26%	24.19
AM.SAMOA	3.86%	0.05	0.06	1.75%	0.04

Country Data:Data

2.36

Figure 10-1. Worldwide data is used, including each country's economic profile.[70]

Step Four—Define the Data Relationships

Now that the data is available for the mapping software, you specify the relationships you want to see displayed. In this example, you want a simple comparison by highlighting the countries that have the most positive economic growth over the last five years, along with a high per capita consumption of soft drinks.

Once defined, the data draws a map highlighting the countries with the most potential for expansion possibilities. A second criteria may need to be

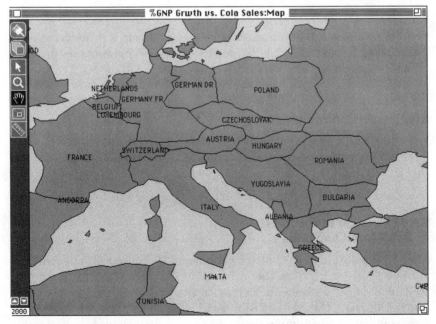

Figure 10-2. Europe is a potential market, so you zoom directly to the area with Tactician.[71]

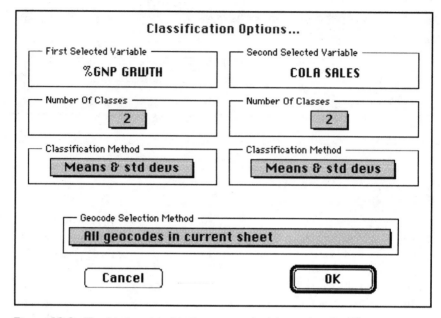

Figure 10-3. The data is matched to the map to provide a visual analysis.[72]

considered as well—countries with good economic potential, where residents consume a maximum amount of your company's products already. These areas should not be highlighted for expansion because they probably do not represent markets with much growth potential.

Step Five—Refine the Map

You may wish to zoom the map to show only the countries and regions in question. Countries that marginally meet the criteria may by eliminated by slightly refining the formula used to select prospective economies.

Step Six—Add More Detail or Ask More Questions

After seeing the initial results of your query, there are other secondary attributes you decide to ask about. For example, adding information on the availability of raw ingredients such as sugar and diet sweeteners may come into the analysis. A landlocked country with good economic growth and the right soft drink consumption level may require further study to determine if supplies can be readily shipped there. An unmodernized country may lack the electric power required to support a modern bottling plant. Market maps can be created almost instantaneously to reflect the answers to these questions by querying the on-line databases you have available through the direct network linkage Tactician has with your mainframe computer databases.

Make a Decision

Following your work with the mapping software, you have a map that graphically displays economic trends by country and region and also clearly reflects per capita consumption of soft drinks. The next step is to check your work and assemble the maps into a format you can present to the company's board of directors. The maps and the supporting data used to create them are used to assist them in their decision process and choose the right countries for expansion while bypassing those that look risky because of local or regional trends.

As a result of the analysis, the board picks the same countries you would have chosen for the expansion. The market maps made the choices clear,

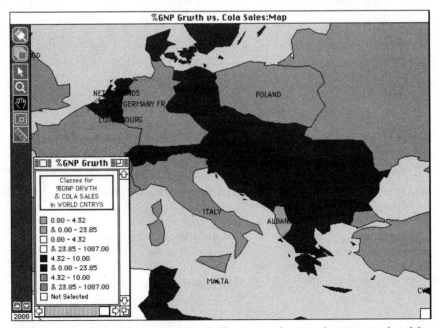

Figure 10-4. The finished map graphically illustrates each country's expansion desirability based on economic information and growth potential.[73]

and your addition of data regarding ingredients, labor costs, and power sources clinched the choices. One board member, who was unusually enthusiastic about expanding into a particular East European country, fell silent when she saw the map showing the country's slow economy and serious lack of electrical power.

Chapter Summary

International marketing issues are some of the toughest to understand, especially if you are unfamiliar with the locations and cultures you must analyze. Market mapping software fed with accurate data can take the complexity out of the process, and also reduce dependence on outside consultants and uninformed guesswork. Effective maps, used in a formal presentation or an interactive war room session, can be used to convince everyone involved, including marketing managers, board members, and even the salespeople in the field, about the best international opportunities.

Additional market mapping applications for international research include:

- Comparing the demographics, buying patterns, ethnic composition, educational levels, and economic conditions in international markets
- Analyzing worldwide markets by ethnic group and/or by geographic region, regardless of national boundaries
- Assessing promotional coverage of international media
- Determining the availability of manufacturing capabilities and raw materials across geographic areas
- Establishing product pricing parameters and monetary fluctuations across geographic regions and political boundaries
- Displaying distribution options by region and nation
- Mapping competitors' distribution channels and customer demographics in worldwide markets

These analyses can be used to determine new market opportunities, define distribution channels, and establish new marketing programs in markets anywhere in the world.

The example in this chapter concludes our presentation of mapping scenarios and our discussion of market mapping in general. However, the examples do not even begin to scratch the surface of market mapping possibilities. The extent of market mapping research is dependent only on your own curiosity about your markets, competitors, and customers.

There are no limits to the number of locations and new combinations of data you can consider.

Now that you have a basic understanding of the potential of market mapping analysis, you can begin to formulate your own questions and start using the power of geographic visualizations to make a difference for your business and your career. In the next section of the book, we have provided a wealth of sources and contacts to get you started on your mapping explorations of the marketing world. At this point, it's up to you to start mapping and explore the world of opportunities available to your company!

PART 3
Resources for Market Mapping

Desktop Mapping Software Companies

The following companies manufacture or distribute desktop mapping software products. This is by no means a comprehensive list. There are many other companies and products out there, and more are being added every day. The ones here are either products we have worked with or ones that have been recently reviewed in computer literature. Because companies are constantly improving their product offerings, the products listed for a particular company may not be comprehensive.

A listing in this book should not be considered a testimonial for the functionality or suitability of any product. The listings are provided to get you started in your own evaluation of mapping software.

COMGRAPHIX INC.
620 E St.
Clearwater, FL 34616
(813) 443-6807
fax (813) 443-7585
ComGraphix is a graphics software company that markets MapGraphix GIS, a full-featured GIS product; MapLink, a translation module for importing and exporting different data formats; and MapGraphix Display, an inexpensive runtime version of the full GIS product.

DONNELLEY MARKETING INFORMATION SERVICES
70 Seaview Avenue
P.O. Box 10250
Stamford, CT 06904
(800) 866-2255
(203) 353-7267
fax (203) 353-7276
A major demographic and business data supplier and marketing research firm, Donnelley Marketing Information Services (DMIS) also offers a proprietary mapping environment for displaying their own data called Graphic Profile and a desktop marketing information system called CONQUEST that provides visual displays of DMIS' vast array of databases.

ENVIRONMENTAL SYSTEMS RESEARCH INSTITUTE, INC.
380 New York Street
Redlands, CA 92373
(714) 793-2853
fax (714) 793-5953
Environmental Systems Research Institute, Inc., usually referred to as ESRI, has been developing and marketing geoprocessing tools for over 20 years. The ARC/INFO software released in 1981 was one of the first powerful database-oriented GIS systems developed. ESRI specializes in very sophisticated GIS products with special-purpose extensions used by environmental researchers,

universities, government agencies, and business planners. ESRI supports a number of base map structures, including detailed topographical maps and raster maps. The company's sophisticated spatial analysis and display products, and add-on modules, run on a number of UNIX-based workstations, VAX minicomputers from Digital Equipment Corporation (DEC), and IBM mainframes. In addition, PC ARC/INFO and modules for digitizing, overlaying, networking, viewing, and data modeling bring the power of ESRI's mapping systems to desktop computers.

FACILITY MAPPING SYSTEMS, INC.
38 Miller Avenue, Suite 11
Mill Valley, CA 94941
(800) 442-FMSI
Facility Mapping Systems markets a full-featured GIS for use with AutoCAD that works on DOS-based computers or Sun Microsystem SPARCstation workstations called FMS/AC. The customizable templates provided in FMS/AC for topological-based spatial and network analysis are especially useful for land-use planning and municipal GIS applications.

GEOQUERY CORPORATION
475 Alexis R. Shuman Blvd.
Suite 385E
Naperville, IL 60563-8453
(708) 357-0535
fax (708) 717-4254
GeoQuery Corporation developed and markets GeoQuery, a Macintosh-based analysis-level mapping program that is affordable and full-featured. The company also markets data to support GeoQuery-based analyses.

GOLDEN SOFTWARE, INC.
809 14th Street
Golden, CO 80401
(800) 972-1021
(303) 279-1021
fax (303) 279-0909
Golden Software produces a number of quality, low-cost graphics products for IBM PCs and compatibles. Surfer is a contour mapping and three-dimensional graphics program that creates impressive visual representations of surface structures. MapViewer, which works with Windows, is a capable presentation-level mapping program that supports analysis-level functions. The product supports color output, multiple map layers, numerous thematic map types, and custom symbols.

HAWTHORNE SOFTWARE COMPANY, INC.
P.O. Box 35
Hawthorne, NJ 07507
(201) 304-0014
Hawthorne Software offers PINMAP, a PC-based mapping program for displaying zip code and county-level data.

HYPERDYNE INC.
4004 Woodland Road
Annandale, VA 22003
(703) 354-7054
Hyperdyne markets Mapix, a raster-based mapping system that facilitates access to a number of paper and digital map libraries and linkages to spreadsheets, database files, and other data. Presentation graphics are not supported in the package, but if descriptive street- and route-level analysis is important, the product is very powerful.

LANTERN CORPORATION
63 Ridgemoor Drive
Clayton, MO 63105
(314) 725-6125
Lantern Corporation developed and markets Voyager, an expertly engineered product that permits temporal comparisons of maps to view the changes in data variables and boundaries over time, as well as database linkages that support a variety of map views. The program supports some presentation-level features, in addition to the advance analysis-level functions. The product works with Windows.

MAPINFO CORPORATION
200 Broadway
Troy, NY 12180
(518) 274-8673 (in New York)
(800) FAST-MAP
fax (518) 274-0510
As one of the leaders in desktop mapping technology, MapInfo Corporation markets its MapInfo software system on a number of platforms, including IBM PCs and compatibles, PCs with Windows, Macintosh computers, and Sun Microsystems and Hewlett Packard workstations. MapInfo combines database management, presentation, and GIS functions in its products. In addition, custom mapping applications can be created using the MapCode programming language developed by the company for some platforms. MapInfo also markets a catalog of geographic and attribute data to support its mapping software, in addition to support and training services.

PC GLOBE, INC.
4700 South McClintock
Tempe, AZ 85282
(602) 730-9000
fax (602) 968-7196
PC Globe, Inc., recently purchased by Broderbund Software, specializes in the development and marketing of electronic atlases and geographic education products, including MacGlobe, PC Globe, PC USA and more. In addition, they market Descartes, an analysis-level mapping product for businesses that runs on Macintosh computers. They offer a wide range of commercial data to use with Descartes through National Planning Data Corporation.

SAMMAMISH DATA SYSTEMS
1813 130th Avenue, NE, Suite 216
Bellevue, WA 98005-2240
(206) 867-1485
Sammamish Data Systems offers two mapping software products, one designed specifically for market mapping and another for sales territory research. GeoSight integrates database information with multiple geographic layers. Territory Management System allows territories to be interactively defined on a wide range of geographic levels. Data from Market Statistics is compatible with these systems.

SOFTWARE PUBLISHING CORPORATION
1901 Landings Drive
P.O. Box 7210
Mountain View, CA 94039-7210
(415) 962-8910
Software Publishing Corporation is an international supplier of business productivity software for IBM PCs and compatibles. Harvard Geographics is a DOS-based presentation-level mapping program designed for individuals who need to create customer maps for inclusion in presentations and reports. The maps are compatible with Harvard Graphics, the company's popular graphics program, and a number of other commonly used graphic files formats. (Software Publishing Corporation has no connection with Harvard University.)

STRATEGIC MAPPING, INC.
4030 Moorpark Ave.
Suite 250
San Jose, CA 95117
(408) 985-7400
fax (408) 985-0859
Strategic Mapping, Inc. is a pioneer developer of desktop mapping software. Founded in 1983, the firm offers a complete range of professional desktop mapping products from thematic mapping programs to full-featured GIS software, including Atlas MapMaker, Atlas Pro, and Atlas GIS. It offers products for DOS-based personal computers, Windows-based personal computers, and the Macintosh. It also offers Atlas Script, a customization programming language for Atlas Pro and Atlas GIS. In addition, Strategic Mapping provides training and customization services. The company also markets a diverse range of data products, both proprietary and from general government and commercial sources, to use with their products.

TACTICS INTERNATIONAL LIMITED
16 Havervill Street
P.O. Box 4016 BV
Andover, MA 01810
(508) 475-4475
(800) WAR-ROOM
fax (508) 475-2136

Tactics International builds decision technology for corporate marketers and executives. Tactics' flagship product is the award-winning Tactician, a sophisticated analysis-level mapping product with GIS-level features that integrates database management, mainframe data access, decision support system functions, and much more. There are versions of Tactician for personal computers that use Windows and for the Macintosh. The company offers a significant number of data choices for domestic and international research from diverse commercial and governmental sources. The company also provides consulting for developing corporate "war rooms" and other training and support services.

TYDAC TECHNOLOGIES, INC.
1655 North Fort Myer Drive, Suite 320
Arlington, VA 22209
(703) 522-0773
SPANS is a PC-based GIS marketed by TYDAC Technologies that includes data modeling, networking, and address matching. The system has interfaces to a variety of databases.

URBAN DECISION SYSTEMS, INC.
2040 Armacost Ave.
P.O. Box 25953
Los Angeles, CA 90025
(800) 633-9568
(213) 820-8931
fax (213) 826-0933
Urban Decision Systems, Inc. started as a supplier of demographic, lifestyle, financial, and other data. Their diverse data offerings are available as printed reports and in computer formats for use with many mapping products. UDS is now finalizing the development and release of Scan/US, a high-end analysis-level mapping product that runs on PCs with Windows. The product combines decision support, database management, and geographic information functions.

For More Vendor and Product Information

As we mentioned before, there are many more software vendors in the mapping marketplace. If you need more in-depth information on GIS products and the desktop mapping industry, Daratech, Inc. is a market research and technology assessment firm that markets an annual subscription to an industry-specific report titled *GIS Markets and Opportunities* that analyzes more than 65 GIS vendors and over 200 GIS-related products, and documents trends in mapping applications and research. Information on obtaining a subscription to this report is available from:

DARATECH, INC.
140 Sixth Street
Cambridge, MA 02412
(617) 354-2339
fax (617) 354-7822

Geographic Data Companies

The following companies are primarily sources of geographic data, although some provide or market their own desktop mapping products as well.

AMERICAN DIGITAL CARTOGRAPHY, INC.
715 West Parkway Blvd.
Appleton, WI 54914-2645
(414) 733-6678
fax (414) 734-3375
American Digital Cartography (ADC) offers digital maps, including TIGER, terrain relief, contour line, digital line graph (DLG), digital elevation model (DEM), and geodetic control point maps for use on PCs and workstations. Many of these map products are designed for use in CAD environments, particularly AutoCAD, as well as by popular GIS software packages. The company also markets Mentor Software's Tralaine PC-based coordinate data conversion program that allows geographic data to be compatible with popular desktop mapping programs and maps database fields to ADC's maps.

CHADWYCK-HEALEY
1101 King Street
Alexandria, VA 22314
(800) 752-0515
Chadwyck Healey offers Supermap, a CD-ROM program for displaying 1980 census and other data. Users can also enter their own data for mapping.

GEOGRAPHIC DATA TECHNOLOGY, INC.
13 Dartmouth College Highway
Lyme, NH 03768-9713
(603) 795-2183
GDT markets boundary and street data for use with mapping software, in additional to GeoSpreadsheet, a mapping program.

INTELLIGENT CHARTING, INC.
600 International Drive
Mt. Olive, NJ 07828
(201) 691-7000
This company offers custom-generated maps from your own data, which can be delivered overnight if required.

MPSI SYSTEMS, INC.
8282 South Memorial Drive
Tulsa, OK 74133
(918) 250-9611
MPSI offers an international mapping product, called Geographic Information System, and markets data for use with the system. MPSI also generates custom data files for specific geographic areas.

RAND MCNALLY
8255 North Central Park Avenue
Skokie, IL 60076-2970
(800) 332-7163
(312) 673-9100 ext. 3477
Rand McNally is a standard source for atlas data, both published and in computer database formats.

WESTERN ECONOMIC RESEARCH COMPANY, INC.
8155 Van Nuys Boulevard
Suite 100
Panorama City, CA 91402
(818) 787-6277
This company is known for its zip code maps, and also provides demographic data. Their data is available as reports, on disk, or as maps.

United States Government Information and Data Sources

The following United States government agencies provide data in a variety of formats for public use. There are also other divisions in most of the agencies that are not listed in this section, but we have tried to list the most relevant information numbers here, so you can request details on the information available and the prices of the data.

United States Bureau of the Census

United States Department of Commerce
Washington, DC 20233

Census Helplines

General Information   (301) 763-4100
Data User Services   (301) 763-1584
Ask about CENDATA, The Census Bureau Online available through DIALOG and CompuServe, in addition to the other data available from the Bureau.

Office of Congressional Affairs	(301) 763-2446
Public Information Office	(301) 763-4040
1990 Census Promotional Office	(301) 763-1990

Geographic Concepts and Products

1970/1980 Census Map Information	(301) 763-5720
1980 Census Map Orders	(812) 288-3192
1990 Census Maps	(301) 763-4100
Cartographic Operations	(301) 763-3973
Computer Mapping	(301) 763-3973
Metropolitan Areas (MSAs)	(301) 763-5158
Outlying Areas	(301) 763-2903
Statistical Areas	(301) 763-3827
TIGER System Applications	(301) 763-1580
TIGER System Products	(301) 763-4100
Urban/Rural Residence	(301) 763-7962
Voting Districts	(301) 763-3827
Zip codes	(301) 763-4667

University Data Centers

These university centers are members of the National Clearinghouse for Census Data Services. They offer research services and access to census data.

Center for Applied Demography and Survey Research
University of Delaware
Newark, DE 19716
(302) 451-8406

Census Access Program
University of Florida Libraries
Department of Reference
University of Florida
Gainesville, FL 32611
(904) 392-0361

Michigan State University
Computer Laboratory
East Lansing, MI 48824
(517) 355-4684

Mississippi State University
Department of Sociology
P. O. Box Drawer C
Mississippi State, MS 39762
(601) 325-2495

University of Missouri-St. Louis
Computer Center
8001 Natural Bridge Road
St. Louis, MO 63121
(314) 553-6014

CUNY Data Service
Graduate School and University Center
City University of New York
33 West 42nd Street, Room 1446
New York, NY 10036
(212) 642-2085

Memphis State University
Bureau of Business and Economic Research
Memphis, TN 38152-0001
(901) 678-2281

The Bureau of the Census is the primary provider of demographic data in the United States. The Bureau records domestic and international data. Some of the data from the Bureau is available from commercial data suppliers that reformat the data to be easier to use or to be compatible with specific computer products.

United States Department of Agriculture

1301 New York Ave., NW
Washington, DC 20005

Economic Research Service	(202) 786-1512
Family Economics Research	(301) 436-8461
Group Child Raising Costs	(301) 436-8461
Human Nutrition Information Service	(301) 436-8474
Income Studies Group	(202) 786-1527
Information Division	(202) 786-1504
Population Group	(202) 786-1534
Savings & Investment	(301) 436-8461
Free Mailing List on New Publications	(800) 999-6779

The USDA provides reports and research services on farm, nutrition, family-oriented, and income data.

Department of Commerce

Economics and Statistics Administration
Office of Business Analysis
Room H4878, HCH Building
Washington, DC 20230

National Trade Data Bank (on CD-ROM)   (202) 377-1986

The NTDB database on CD-ROM contains more than 90,000 documents from 15 federal agencies including basic export information and country-specific information. The information is released monthly, and is especially valuable for companies that have international marketing and exporting interests.

Bureau of Economic Analysis

United States Department of Commerce
1401 K Street, NW
Washington, DC 20230

Public Information Office	(202) 523-0777
Economic Projections, State & Metropolitan Areas	(202) 523-0971
Economic Information Staff	(202) 523-0966

Income data from the BEA is different from Census Bureau data. The BEA is an important source for per capita income statistics and employment data.

Office of Educational Research and Improvement (National Center for Education Statistics)

Education Information Branch
United States Dept. of Education
555 New Jersey Ave., NW
Washington, DC 20208

General Information	(800) 424-1616
In metro Washington area	(202) 626-9854
Common Core of Data	(202) 357-6335
Data Tapes/Computer Products	(202) 357-6528
	(202) 357-6522
Elementary & Secondary Education	(202) 357-6614
Longitudinal Studies	(202) 357-6774
International Education	(202) 357-6740
Library Surveys	(202) 357-6642
Post-Secondary Education	(202) 357-6354
Private Schools	(202) 357-6333
Projections	(202) 357-6581
School District Tabulation	(800) 424-1616

According to the NCES, one in four Americans is involved in the formal educational system in some way. NCES reports on all aspects of education and people involved in education.

Energy Information Administration

National Energy Information Center
Forrestal Building
1000 Independence Ave., SW
Washington, DC 20585
(202) 586-1174

The EIA records information and makes forecasts on American energy usage.

Equal Employment Opportunity Commission (EEOC)

EEOC Survey Division
Office of Program Research
1800 L St., NW, Rm. 9608
Washington, DC 20507
(202) 633-4920

The EEOC tracks the status of women and minorities, who will account for five out of six additions to the work force in the 1990s. The agency provides a number of free reports on job patterns.

National Center of Health Statistics

Scientific and Technical Information Branch
National Center for Health Statistics
United States Department of Health and Human Services
3700 East-West Highway, Room 157
Hyattsville, MD 20782

The NCHS provides health data and vital statistics, including data on births, deaths, marriages, and divorces.

Department of Housing and Urban Development

451 Seventh Street, NW
Washington, DC 20410
(202) 755-6374

HUD completes a biennial American Housing Survey and makes this data on housing, neighborhoods, demographics, and financial information available for the United States and by regions.

Immigration and Naturalization Service

Statistical Analysis Branch
425 Eye Street, NW, Room 5020
Washington, DC 20536

Telephone contacts
Deportations, Required Departures, & Exclusions   (202) 376-3015
Emigration   (202) 376-3008
Immigrants   (202) 376-3066
Nonimmigrants   (202) 376-3015
Refugees, Naturalization, & Derivative Citizenship   (202) 376-3046

In the future, the majority of United States population growth is expected to come from immigration. The INS tracks the people who enter the United States as immigrants, nonimmigrants, children of immigrants, and refugees.

Internal Revenue Service

Statistics of Income
Division, R-S
1111 Constitution Ave., NW
Washington, DC 20224
(202) 376-0216

IRS data, which includes an annual report of individual income, is a good source of demographic data and can be used to examine migration and population trends between censuses.

Bureau of Justice Statistics

633 Indian Ave., NW
Washington, DC 20531
(202) 724-7759

Correctional Statistics   (202) 724-7755
Judicial Statistics   (202) 724-7774
Law Enforcement Statistics   (202) 724-7770
National Crime Survey   (202) 724-7774

The BJS provides free reports of demographic data about criminals, crime, and law enforcement in the United States.

Bureau of Labor Statistics

441 G Street, NW
Washington, DC 20212

Inquiries & Correspondence   (202) 523-1221
Recorded Message:
    Consumer Price Index (CPI), Producer Price
    Indexes (PPI), & Employment Situation   (202) 523-9658

Consumer Expenditure Survey (Data and Tapes)	(202) 272-5060
Consumer Expenditure Surveys	(202) 272-5156
Consumer Price Index Detail	(202) 523-1239
Demographic Studies	(202) 523-1944
Economic Growth and Employment Projections	(202) 272-5328
Family & Marital Characteristics of	(202) 523-1371
Local Area Unemployment Statistics	(202) 523-1002
Microdata Tapes & Analysis	(202) 523-1776
Occupational Outlook	(202) 272-5282
Occupational Projections—National	(202) 272-5382
Producer Price Index Detail	(202) 523-1765
State & Local Area Demographic Data	(202) 523-1002

The BLS provides a wealth of employment and unemployment information, but even more importantly for most market research, the BLS also provides extensive reports on consumer spending, price indexes, and economic projections.

National Park Service

Denver Service Center, T-N-T
P.O. Box 25287
Denver, CO 80225

NPS maintains information on the millions of people who visit the parks and sites maintained by the NPS. Reports on attendance and usage are available on a monthly and yearly basis.

National Technical Information Service

5285 Port Royal Road
Springfield, VA 22161

Request for NTIS General Catalog	(703) 487-4650
Economic Bulletin Board	(202) 377-1986

The following commercial on-line sources offer access to the NTIS bibliographic database, either on-line or on CD-ROM:

BRS Information Technologies	(800) 345-4277
DATA-STAR	(800) 221-7754
DIALOG Information Services, Inc.	(800) 334-2564
ORBIT Search Service	(800) 421-7229
In Virginia	(703) 442-0900
STN International	(800) 848-6533
In Ohio and Canada	(800) 848-6538
SilverPlatter Information, Inc.	(800) 343-0064
Online Computer Library Center, Inc. (OCLC)	(800) 848-5878
In Ohio	(800) 848-8286

The NTIS, a clearinghouse for government data, sells information in a variety of formats. NTIS supports itself from the sale of its data products.

Social Security Administration

Office of Research & Statistics
United States Department of Health & Human Services
4301 Connecticut Ave., NW
Washington, DC 20008

The Social Security Administrations offers data on more than retired people, including data on international social security systems and broad economic data for people receiving unemployment compensation, workers' compensation, and other maintenance income.

Department of Veterans Affairs

Office of Planning and Management Analysis
Statistical Service (043C2)
810 Vermont Ave., NW
Washington, DC 20420

Secretary of Veterans Affairs Annual Report	(202) 233-2525
Patient Treatment File & Annual Patient Census	(202) 233-6807
Population Estimates & Projections	(202) 233-2458
Surveys of Veterans	(202) 233-6811
Veterans Receiving Compensation or Pension & Veterans Receiving Educational Benefits	(202) 233-6815
Veterans Unemployment, Labor Force Status, Income	(202) 233-6813

The VA tracks health, welfare, and demographic data on the 27 million living United States veterans, gathered from a variety of surveys and research estimates.

State and Local Government Agencies

The scope of this book does not allow us to list the state and local governmental agencies that maintain public-access data that can be useful in market mapping research. The governmental listings in a local telephone book will direct you to general information numbers where you can request information on the data available from various local agencies.

Primary Demographic and Business Data Suppliers

CACI
Information Products
9302 Lee Highway, #310
Fairfax, VA 22031
(800) 292-2224
(703) 218-4400

CACI Marketing Systems provides a range of international demographic information and source books. They offer an on-line data service and a data ordering service called SITELINE. ACORN is CACI's lifestyle classification system, and they offer reports classified by standard geographic, demographic, and ACORN segments. Insite•USA is their PC-based geographic information system.

CLARITAS
201 N. Union Street
Alexandria, CA 22314
(703) 683-8300
Claritas markets the PRIZM and P$YCLE market segmentation cluster systems and Compass, a PC-based marketing system for targeting, profiling, site locations, and planning. The company also offers several financial services data products.

DATAMAP, INC.
6436 City West Parkway
Eden Prairie, MN 55344
(800) 533-7742
(612) 941-0900
Since 1975, Datamap has offered custom mapping services and data services. They also sell small-area demographics and insurance industry data, in addition to offering CAM-1+, a software product that assists in site planning and target marketing.

DISCLOSURE INFORMATION RETRIEVAL AND DELIVERY SERVICES
5161 River Road
Bethesda, MD 20816
(800) 638-8241
(212) 581-1414
Since 1968, Disclosure has been providing data. Current products include CD-ROM databases and document retrieval services, information on Security and Exchange Commission filings, government research data, and international business information.

DONNELLEY MARKETING INFORMATION SERVICES
70 Seaview Ave.
Stamford, CT 06904
(800) 866-2255
(203) 353-7474
In addition to offering a desktop marketing and mapping system, Donnelley is a major supplier of business, market segment, lifestyle, financial, and demographic data, as well as marketing research and analysis services. DMIS provides access to information from Dun and Bradstreet Corporation as well.

DOW JONES & COMPANY, INC.
Information Services Group
P.O. Box 300
Princeton, NJ 08543-0300
(609) 520-4649
fax (609) 520-4660

The Dow Jones News/Retrieval Service is available on-line through major network providers, including Tymnet and SprintNet, among others. The service is a major source of full-text business data from news wires services and major business publications, including *The Wall Street Journal, Business Week, Forbes, Fortune,* and hundreds of regional and industry-specific publications.

DUN'S MARKETING SERVICES
A Company of The Dun & Bradstreet Corporation
Three Sylvan Way
Parsippany, NJ 07054
(201) 605-6000
(800) 526-0651
Dun and Bradstreet specializes in maintaining business data. Duns Million Dollar Disc is a CD-ROM that provides access to quality information on the largest public and private companies in the United States, derived from the company's proprietary database of eight million companies. The company offers a number of other data services, directories, and software access products.

DRI/MCGRAW-HILL
Executive Offices
24 Hartwell Avenue
Lexington, MA 02173
(617) 863-5100
A major international supplier of business, financial, and government information for more than 20 years, DRI/McGraw-Hill has offices across the United States, Canada, and in many foreign locations. The company specializes in providing strategic and tactical decision-making expertise, in the forms of consulting, data products, research, and custom PC applications for data analysis. Some of the company's data is offered in computer-readable formats, including CD-ROM.

EQUIFAX MARKETING DECISION SYSTEMS
(formerly National Decision Systems)
539 Encinitas Boulevard
Encinitas, CA 92024
(800) 877-5560
(619) 942-7000
Specializing in demographic and market cluster data, Equifax produces Infomark, a PC-based information system on three CD-ROMs, among other consumer and marketing data products.

INFORMATION ACCESS COMPANY
362 Lakeside Drive
Foster City, CA 94404
(415) 378-5206
(800) 441-1165
Information Access Company is a major supplier of periodical reference products, both printed and on-line. The company provides indexes of domestic and

international magazines, newspapers, and a variety of specialty publications. In addition, the company offers access to a variety of industry-specific databases and competitive information.

MARKET STATISTICS
633 Third Avenue
New York, NY 10017
(212) 986-4800
Market Statistics produces an annual buying power survey and other information on sales and marketing. Data is available in a variety of formats.

MEAD DATA CENTRAL, INC.
9393 Springboro Pike
P.O. Box 933
Dayton, OH 45401
(513) 865-6800
(800) 227-4908
Mead Data Central offers LEXIS, a full-text legal database, and NEXIS, a full-text news and business database. The company also offers a financial information service, a country information service, and a patent and trademark database, among other information products.

NATIONAL PLANNING DATA CORPORATION
P. O. Box 610
Ithaca, NY 14851-0610
(607) 273-8208
(800) 876-NPDC
Since 1969, NPDC has been a supplier of significant demographic data and business information products, including special reports on markets, mailing lists, credit summaries, health care, labor statistics, and much more. The company also markets custom reports, on-line information access products, and mapping programs.

PITNEY BOWES
Software Systems
1200 Roosevelt
Glen Ellyn, IL 60137-6098
(800) MAILERS
(708) 932-7000
Pitney Bowes, famous for their postage meter and other office products, also provides geographic information, demographic information, and software products for managing mailing lists.

SLATER HALL INFORMATION PRODUCTS
1522 K Street, N.W.
Washington, D.C. 20005
(202) 682-1350
SHIP markets information on business, agriculture, and census data on CD-ROMs. The company also includes SEARCHER, a software product for formatting and finding data with their CD-ROM products.

THOMAS REGISTER ONLINE
One Penn Plaza
New York, NY 10119
(212) 290-7291
Thomas Register Online is a comprehensive database available through the DIALOG Business Information Service (listed under On-Line Services), on CD-ROM, or through fax requests that contain information from the current edition of the Thomas Register of American Manufacturers, a major source of contact and product information for more than 148,000 United States and Canadian companies.

URBAN DECISION SYSTEMS, INC.
2040 Armacost Ave.
P.O. Box 25953
Los Angeles, CA 90025
(800) 633-9568
(213) 820-8931
UDS provides a wide range of small-area demographics and financial services data, packaged in computer-readable and printed formats. UDS is also in the final development stages of Scan/US, a sophisticated mapping program for PCs running Windows.

Special Interest Data Suppliers

Brand-name Marketing Data

MARKETING EVALUATIONS TVQ, INC.
14 Vanderventer Avenue
Port Washington, NY 11050
(516) 944-8833

Economic Research and Population Projections

DATA RESOURCES, INC.
24 Hartwell Avenue
Lexington, MA 02173
(617) 863-5100

DEMO-DETAIL (County-Level Data)
2303 Apple Hill Road
Alexandria, VA 22308
(703) 780-9563

NPA DATA SERVICES, INC.
1424 16th Street, NW
Suite 700
Washington, DC 20036
(202) 265-7685

THE WEFA GROUP
Wharton Econometric Forecasting Associates
150 Monument Road
Bala Cynwyd, PA 19004
(215) 896-4927

WOODS & POOLE ECONOMICS
1794 Columbia Road, NW
Washington, DC 20009
(202) 332-7111

Electronics, Home Electronics, and Electronic Information

LINK RESOURCES CORPORATION
79 Fifth Avenue
New York, NY 10003

Gay and Alternative Lifestyles

OVERLOOKED OPINIONS, INC.
3712 N. Broadway, Suite 277
Chicago, IL 60613
(800) 473-3405

Household Data and Forecasts

ANALYSIS AND FORECASTING, INC.
P.O. Box 415
Cambridge, MA 02138
(617) 491-8171

Labor Data and Affirmative Action

PRI ASSOCIATES, INC.
1905 Chapel Hill Road
Durham, NC 27707
(919) 493-7534

Media Specialists—Print, Radio, and Television

THE ARBITRON COMPANY
142 West 57th Street
New York, NY 10019
(212) 887-1300

BIRCH/SCARBOROUGH RESEARCH
12350 NW 39th Street
Coral Springs, FL 33065
(305) 753-6043

DIRECTORY DATA
One Post Road
Fairfield, CT 06430
(203) 254-1410

INFORMATION RESOURCES, INC.
150 N. Clinton Street
Chicago, IL 60606
(312) 726-1221

MEDIAMARK RESEARCH, INC.
708 Third Avenue
New York, NY 10017
(212) 599-0444

MENDELSOHN MEDIA RESEARCH, INC.
Marketing
352 Park Avenue South
New York, NY 10010
(212) 684-6350

NIELSEN MEDIA RESEARCH
Nielsen Plaza
Northbrook, IL 60062-6288
(708) 498-6300

Political and Election Data

ELECTION DATA SERVICES, INC.
1522 K Street, NW
Suite 626
Washington, DC 20005
(202) 789-2004

Race and Ethnic Market Data

WESTERN ECONOMIC RESEARCH CO., INC.
8155 Van Nuys Blvd., Suite 100
Panorama City, CA 91402
(818) 787-MAPS
(818) 787-6419

STRATEGY RESEARCH CORPORATION (Hispanic Data)
100 NW 37th Avenue
Miami, FL 33125
(305) 649-5400

Real Estate Data

DANTER COMPANY
40 West Spruce Street
Columbus, OH 43215
(614) 221-9096

FULTON RESEARCH, INC.
11351 Random Hills Road
4th floor
Fairfax, VA 22030
(703) 359-1720

SOCIOECONOMICS
17004 26th Avenue, NE
Seattle, WA 98155
(206) 382-9658

Sports Data

AMERICAN SPORTS DATA, INC.
243 North Central Avenue
Hartsdale, NY 10530
(914) 328-8877

Supermarket and Retailing Data

MARKET METRICS
P.O. Box 10097
Lancaster, PA 17605-0087
(717) 397-1500

Senior Citizen and Mature Market Segments

PRIMELIFE MARKETING
Marketing Division
The Data Group
2260 Butler Pike, Su. 150
Plymouth Meeting, PA 19462
(215) 834-3003

Travel and Employee Relocation

RUNZHEIMER INTERNATIONAL
Runzheimer Park
Rochester, WI 53167
(414) 534-3121

U.S. TRAVEL DATA CENTER
1133 21st Street, NW
Washington, DC 20036
(202) 293-1040

Western United States Market Data

CENTER FOR CONTINUING STUDY OF THE CALIFORNIA ECONOMY
610 University Avenue
Palo Alto, CA 94301
(415) 321-8550

Youth and Teenage Market

TEENAGE RESEARCH UNLIMITED
601 Skokie Boulevard
Northbrook, IL 60062
(708) 564-3440

General Market, Public Opinion, and Lifestyle Research Firms

FIND/SVP
Communications
625 Avenue of the Americas
New York, NY 10011
(212) 645-4500

FROST & SULLIVAN, INC.
106 Fulton Street
New York, NY 10038
(212) 233-1080

THE GALLUP ORGANIZATION
100 Palmer Square
Suite 200
Princeton, NJ 08542
(609) 924-9600

IMPACT RESOURCES
125 Dillmont Drive
Columbus, OH 43235
(614) 888-5900

LANGER ASSOCIATES, INC.
19 West 44 Street
New York, NY 10036
(212) 391-0350

MARKET OPINION RESEARCH
243 West Congress
Detroit, MI 48226
(314) 963-2414

NFO RESEARCH, INC.
2700 Oregon Road
Box 315
Toledo, OH 43691-0315
(419) 666-8800

THE NPD GROUP, INC.
900 West Shore Road
Port Washington, NY 11050-0402
(516) 625-2302

NATIONAL DEMOGRAPHICS & LIFESTYLES, INC.
1621 Eighteenth Street
Denver, CO 80(202) 1211
(800) 525-3533
(303) 292-5000

OPINION RESEARCH SERVICE
P. O. Box 9076
J.F.K. Station
Boston, MA 02114
(617) 482-1534

PACKAGED FACTS
274 Madison Avenue
Suite 202
New York, NY 10016
(212) 532-5533

THE ROPER ORGANIZATION
205 East 42nd Street
New York, NY 10017
(212) 599-0700

SIMMONS MARKET RESEARCH BUREAU
380 Madison Avenue
New York, NY 10017
(212) 926-8900

VALUES AND LIFESTYLE (VALS) PROGRAM
333 Ravenswood Avenue
Menlo Park, CA 94025-3493
(415) 859-4324

YANKELOVICH CLANCY SHULMAN
8 Wright Street
Westport, CT 06880
(203) 227-2700
(212) 752-7500

Direct Marketing and Mailing Lists

R.L. POLK & CO.
List Services
6400 Monroe Blvd.
Taylor, MI 48180-1814
(313) 292-3200

SALES EVALUATION ASSOCIATES
780 Third Avenue
Suite 1603
New York, NY 10017
(212) 758-2990

SMARTNAMES, INC.
176 Second Avenue
Waltham, MA 02154
(800) 424-4636
(617) 890-8900

STANDARD RATE AND DATA SERVICE, INC.
National Register Publication Company
5201 Old Orchard Road
Skokie, IL 60076

SURVEY SAMPLING, INC.
One Post Road
Fairfield, CT 06430
(203) 255-4200

Academic Demographic Information Sources

CENTER FOR HUMAN RESOURCES RESEARCH
NLS Public Users Office
Suite 200
921 Chatham Lane
Columbus, OH 43221
(614) 442-7300

CENTER FOR MATURE CONSUMER STUDIES
Georgia State University
University Plaza
Atlanta, GA 30303
(404) 651-4177

JOINT CENTER FOR URBAN POLICY RESEARCH
Rutgers University
Douglas Campus
New Brunswick, NJ 08903
(201) 932-6703

POPLINE
Population Information Program
School of Hygiene and Public Health
John Hopkins University
624 North Broadway
Baltimore, MD 21205
(301) 955-8200

POPULATION ASSOCIATION OF AMERICA
1429 Duke Street
Alexandria, VA 22314
(703) 684-1221

PRINCETON-RUTGERS CENSUS DATA PROJECT
Princeton University
Computer Center
87 Prospect Avenue
Princeton, NJ 08540
(609) 452-6052

RUTGERS UNIVERSITY
Center for Computer and Information Services
P. O. Box 879
Piscataway, NJ 08854
(201) 932-2483

THE ROPER CENTER FOR PUBLIC OPINION RESEARCH
P.O. Box 440
Storrs, CT 06268
(203) 486-4440

SURVEY RESEARCH CENTER
Institute for Social Research
P.O. Box 1248
University of Michigan
Ann Arbor, MI 48106
(313) 763-5224

Industry and Nonprofit Organizations with Market and Demographic Data

AMERICAN CHAMBER OF COMMERCE RESEARCH ASSOCIATION
4323 King Street
Alexandria, VA 23302
(703) 998-4172

AMERICAN INSTITUTE OF FOOD DISTRIBUTION
28-12 Broadway
Fair Lawn, NJ 07410
(201) 791-5570

AUTOMOTIVE MARKETING
201 King of Prussia Road
Radnor, PA 19089
(215) 964-4395

THE CONFERENCE BOARD
Consumer Research Center
845 Third Avenue
New York, NY 10022
(212) 759-0900

EMPLOYEE BENEFIT RESEARCH INSTITUTE
2121 K Street, NW
Suite 600
Washington, DC 20037
(202) 659-0670

HISPANIC BUSINESS
360 South Hope Avenue, Suite 300c
Santa Barbara, CA 93105
(805) 682-5843

MARKETING SCIENCE INSTITUTE
1000 Massachusetts Ave.
Cambridge, MA 02138-5396
(617) 491-2060

MATURE MARKET INSTITUTE
20 Chevy Chase Circle, NW
Washington, DC 20015
(202) 363-9644

NATIONAL ASSOCIATION OF HOME BUILDERS
Economic Division
15th and M Streets, NW
Washington, DC 20005
(800) 368-5242
(202) 822-0292

NATIONAL OPINION RESEARCH CENTER
1155 East 60th Street
Chicago, IL 60637
(312) 702-7200

Data tape available from:
The Roper Center
University of Connecticut
Storrs, CT 06268
(203) 486-4882

NATIONAL RESTAURANT ASSOCIATION
1200 17th Street, NW
Washington, DC 20036
(800) 424-5156
(202) 331-5900

NATIONAL SPORTING GOODS ASSOCIATION
Information & Research
1699 Wall Street
Mt. Prospect, IL 60056
(708) 439-4000

NEWSPAPER ADVERTISING BUREAU
1180 Avenue of the Americas
New York, NY 10036
(212) 921-5080

POINT-OF-PURCHASE ADVERTISING INSTITUTE
Education Relations Manager
66 North Van Brunt Street
Englewood, NJ 07631
(201) 894-8899

THE POPULATION RESOURCE CENTER
500 East 62nd Street
New York, NY 10017
(212) 888-2820

PREVENTION MAGAZINE
33 East Minor Street
Emmaus, PA 18098
(215) 967-5171

PROGRESSIVE GROCER
Maclean Hunter Media, Inc.
Four Stamford Forum
Stamford, CT 06901
(203) 325-3500

SUNSET'S WESTERN MARKET ALMANAC
Research Services
Lane Publishing Company
80 Willow Road
Menlo Park, CA 94025
(415) 321-3600

THE TRAFFIC AUDIT BUREAU FOR MEDIA MEASUREMENT
114 East 32nd Street
Suite 802
New York, NY 10016
(212) 213-9640

THE UNITED WAY OF AMERICA
Market Research Products & Services
701 North Fairfax Street
Alexandria, VA 22314-2045
(703) 836-7100

THE URBAN INSTITUTE
2100 M Street, NW
Washington, DC 20037
(202) 857-8547

WOMEN'S RESEARCH & EDUCATION INSTITUTE
1700 18th Street, NW
Suite 400
Washington, DC 20009
(202) 328-7070

WORLD FUTURE SOCIETY
4916 Saint Elmo Avenue
Bethesda, MD 20814
(301) 656-8274

Canadian Information Sources

CANADIAN MARKET ANALYSIS CENTER (CMAC)
International Institute for Market Analysis
3430 Mansfield Road
Falls Church, VA 22041
(800) 829-3004
(703) 824-0200

Canadian address:
P.O. Box 2749
Station "A"
Toronto, Ontario
CANADA M5W 9Z9

COMPUSEARCH MARKET AND SOCIAL RESEARCH LIMITED
Marketing
330 Front Street West, Suite 1100
Toronto, Ontario M5V 3B7
Canada
(416) 348-9180

STATISTICS CANADA
R.H. Coats Building
Tunney's Pasture, Ottawa
Ontario K1A 0T6
Canada

Media information	(613) 951-4636
Statistical information	(613) 951-8116
Library	(613) 951-8219
National sales line (outside Canada)	(613) 951-9276
Publication sales office	(613) 951-8742

TETRAD COMPUTER APPLICATIONS LIMITED
1445 West Georgia Street
Vancouver, British Columbia
Canada V6G 2T3
(604) 685-2295

International Information Sources

CENTER FOR INTERNATIONAL RESEARCH
(United States Bureau of the Census)
Washington, DC 20233
(301) 763-4014

Country/Subject Specialists:

Africa, Asia, Latan/North America, and Oceania	(301) 763-4221
China	(301) 763-4012
Europe	(301) 763-4022
Russian States (formerly Soviet Union)	(301) 763-4022
Demographic techniques	(301) 763-4086
Health studies	(301) 763-4086
International database	(301) 763-4811

EAST-WEST CENTER
Research Information Specialist (Asia and Pacific Information)
Population Institute
1777 East-West Road
Honolulu, HI 96848
(808) 944-7450

ESOMAR (European Society for Opinion and Marketing Research)
Central Secretariat
J.J. Viottastraat 29
1071 JP Amsterdam
Netherlands
31-20-664-21-41

EUROMONITOR
87-88 Turnmill Street
London ECIM 5QU
England
071-251-8024

Many titles available in the United States through:

Gale Publications
Dept. 77748
Detroit, MI 48277
(800) 223-4153

THE EUROPEAN COMMUNITY
2100 M Street, NW
Suite 707
Washington, DC 20037
(202) 862-9500

Publications available from:
UNIPUB
4611-F Assembly Drive
Lanham, MD 20706
(301) 459-7666

INSTITUTE FOR RESOURCE DEVELOPMENT, INC. (IRD)
8850 Stanford Boulevard
Columbia, MD 21045
(301) 290-2800

LATIN AMERICAN DEMOGRAPHIC CENTER (CELADE)
Casilla 91
Santiago, Chile
011-56-2-485051

MACFARLANE & COMPANY
Suite 450, One Park Place
Atlanta, GA 30318
(404) 352-2290

MANAGEMENT HORIZONS
570 Metro Place North
Dublin, OH 43017
(614) 764-9555

THE ORGANIZATION FOR ECONOMIC COOPERATION
 AND DEVELOPMENT (OECD)
2001 L Street, NW
Suite 700
Washington, DC 20036-4905
(202) 785-6323

POPULATION INDEX
21 Prospect Avenue
Princeton, NJ 08544
(609) 258-4949

POPULATION REFERENCE BUREAU, INC. (PRB)
777 14th Street, NW
Suite 800
Washington, DC 20005
(202) 639-8040

UNITED NATIONS

Public Inquiries Unit
Public Services Section
Dept. of Public Information
United Nations
(Room GA-057)
New York, NY 10017
(212) 963-4475

Demographic & Social Statistics Branch
Public Inquiries Office
Statistical Office
New York, NY 10017
(212) 754-7721

Dept. of International Economic and Social Affairs
United Nations Secretariat
(Room DC2-1950)
New York, NY 10017
(212) 963-3179

SIS INTERNATIONAL, INC.
172 Madison Avenue, Suite 306
New York, NY 10016
(212) 725-4550
fax (212) 725-5954

THE WORLD BANK
Customer Service
World Bank Publications
1818 H Street, NW
Washington, DC 20433
(202) 473-2943

WORLD HEALTH ORGANIZATION (WHO)
Distribution and Sales
Avenue Appia
1211 Geneva 27
Switzerland
791-21-11

On-line Information Networks

BRS INFORMATION TECHNOLOGIES
8000 Westpark Drive
McLean, VA 22102
(800) 289-4277

COMPUSERVE INFORMATION SERVICES
5000 Arlington Center Blvd.
P.O. Box 20212
Columbus, OH 43220
(800) 848-8199

DIALOG INFORMATION SERVICES, INC.
3460 Hillview Ave.
Palo Altos, CA 94304-1321
(800) 334-2564

NEWSNET (Independent Publications)
945 Haverford Road
Bryn Mawr, PA 19010
(800) 345-1301
fax (215) 527-0338

Usenet
UUNET Technologies
Falls, Church, VA
(703) 876-5050

Other Marketing and Business Information Resources

General Marketing Resources
Demographics Publications

AMERICAN DEMOGRAPHICS MAGAZINE
P.O. Box 68
Ithaca, NY 14851
(800) 828-1133

In addition to the monthly magazine, American Demographics produces a number of useful almanacs, reports, and books on demographics and consumer trends.

General Business References

DATA SOURCES FOR BUSINESS AND MARKET ANALYSIS
The Scarecrow Press, Inc.
52 Liberty Street
Box 656
Metuchen, NJ 08840

Useful Publications and Directories on Media Research

STANDARD DIRECTORY OF ADVERTISING AGENCIES
National Register Publications Company, Inc.
5201 Old Orchard Road
Skokie, IL 60076

ADVERTISING RESEARCH FOUNDATION
3 East 54th Street
New York, NY 10022

AUDIT BUREAU OF CIRCULATION
123 N. Wacker Drive
Chicago, IL 60606

AYER DIRECTORY OF PUBLICATIONS
IMS Press 426 Pennsylvania Avenue
Fort Washington, PA 19034

AYER GLOSSARY OF ADVERTISING AND RELATED TERMS, 2nd Edition
IMS Press
426 Pennsylvania Avenue
Fort Washington, PA 19034

GUIDE TO ADVERTISING RESEARCH SERVICES
Advertising Research Foundation, Inc.
3 East 54th Street
New York, NY 10022

JOURNAL OF ADVERTISING RESEARCH
Advertising Research Foundation, Inc.
3 East 54th Street
New York, NY 10022

STANDARD RATE AND DATA SERVICE
National Register Publication Company
5201 Old Orchard Road
Skokie, IL 60076

Business Associations and Organizations

AMERICAN MANAGEMENT ASSOCIATION
Marketing Division
135 West 50th Street
New York, NY 10020

AMERICAN MARKETING ASSOCIATION
222 South Riverside Plaza
Chicago, IL 60606

BUSINESS AND PROFESSIONAL ADVERTISING ASSOCIATION (BPAA)
41 East 42nd Street
New York, NY 10017

UNITED STATES SMALL BUSINESS ADMINISTRATION (SBA)
P.O. Box 15434
Forth Worth, TX 76119

Glossary

Some of the terms listed in this glossary are related to maps and cartography in general; others are computer terms you will find used in desktop mapping programs; and some terms are related to marketing research and demographics. Together, these terms provide the requisite terminology to get started in market mapping research.

Active layer: The layer in a map document window that receives all input. In most software, only one layer can be active at a time. Layers are used to partition a map document into various overlays.

Aerial mosaic: A pattern of overlapping photographs taken from the air, often used as the basis for creating maps.

Antarctic Circle: Line of latitude 66½° south of the equator.

Arctic Circle: Line of latitude 66½° north of the equator.

Area: A closed object capable of representing data contained in a worksheet. An area consists of a boundary line, an optional fill pattern, and a identification code used to link the area to a data value in a worksheet or database. This data value is used to modify the appearance of the area in thematic maps.

ASCII: American Standard Code for Information Interchange. A standard code used in most microcomputers, computer terminals, and printers for representing characters as numbers. It includes not only printable characters, but also control codes to indicate carriage return, backspace, and so forth.

Atlas: A book of maps.

Attribute data: Data that describes characteristics about a population or market such as the population of a census, the traffic volume of a highway, or the number of products sold. Attribute data is generally stored in a database format where each record represents a set of data fields on a specific entity and each field is a variable or attribute about the entity or feature.

Axis: Graduated lines bordering the plot area. Location coordinates are measured relative to the axes. By convention the x-axis is horizontal and the y-axis is vertical.

Azimuth: Bearing direction, normally in degrees.

Baby boom generation: An identifier for the large number of Americans born between 1946 and 1964. The children of the baby boom generation are called baby boomlets or the echo boom.

Base map: An outline map on which other maps can be based. In mapping software, a base map is usually a type of map that displays areas as boundaries only. Fill patterns or colors may be displayed independently of any attribute data to indicate boundary areas. Boundary editing is best done on a base map. Examples of base maps include road maps and geological maps.

Bearing: The direction of one point from another as determined with a compass.

Bitmap: A screen image displayed as an array of dots or "bits." Software usually generates either bit-mapped (raster) or object-oriented (vectored) files.

Blocks: Administrative areas of the United States census, equal to approximately a city block in area.

Block group: Groups of blocks with an average population of about 1,000 to 1,200. More census data is available for block groups than for individual blocks.

Boundary: The lines which define any area, curve, or point. In maps, the limit or dividing line between one area or point and another. Borders enclose regions. A single boundary can incorporate multiple polygons. For example, Indonesia is a single boundary but consists of multiple polygons.

Boundary file: A file containing information about map boundaries for areas, curves, and points. The file contains identification codes associated with the area or point, and the set of points (x-y coordinates or latitude-longitude coordinates) used to define the area boundaries on a map.

Boundary survey: Survey to establish the position of a boundary line on the ground.

Buffer: A region of a specified radius around a map feature. A buffer around a line feature is known as a corridor. A buffer around a point feature is known as a ring. For example, you might create a buffer ring of five miles around the center of a city.

Bureau of the Census: The Bureau of the Census, popularly called the United States Census Bureau, is an operation of the United States government that collects census data and reports on it in a variety of forms by government areas, divisions, regions, tracts, and other statistical areas.

Cardinal points: N (north), S (south), E (east), and W (west) on a compass or map.

Cartesian coordinates: The conventional representation of geometric objects by x and y values on a plane.

Cartographic accuracy: Cartographic accuracy refers to the degree to which map features on the map are located with respect to defined geographical positions. A map using a map projection and a coordinate system allows for the accurate placement of map features.

Cartography: The science and art of making maps.

Census: The official reporting of demographic, social, and economic information on the population of a specific area, usually a country or a state. A complete United States census is collected and reported every 10 years (a decennial census).

Census Bureau (United States Census Bureau): See Bureau of the Census.

Census divisions: In the United States, there are nine census divisions that include combinations of states. The nine divisions include Pacific, Mountain, West North Central, East North Central, West South Central, East South Central, South Atlantic, Middle Atlantic, and New England.

Census tract: Statistical subdivisions of metropolitan statistical areas (MSAs) with average populations of 4000, but ranging in population from 2500 to 8000, depending on the population density in the MSA.

Centroid: The calculated geographic center of a region or centers of populations. For example, there are zip code centroids and block group centroids used to define the boundaries of data from the United States census.

Clip art: Drawings or scanned images in a digital format commonly used in word processing or desktop publishing documents. Clip art examples include portraits of people, logos, and border designs.

Clipboard: A data exchange storage area for information that is cut or copied from an application. The data can then be imported into other applications, or other positions within the same application.

Complex area: An area composed of more than one polygon. Complex areas can contain either islands (included regions) or lakes (excluded regions).

Contour: A line on a map passing through places of the same elevation.

Contour interval: Difference in elevation between two contour lines on a map.

Control station: Point on the ground, with a known position, used as a base for surveying.

Coordinate: A pair of numeric values based on map axes. Coordinates are used to define the position of a point on a map. A coordinate may be in either page units, boundary units, or projection units.

Coordinate system: A coordinate system is used to create numerical representations of geometric objects. Each point in a geometric object is represented by a pair of numbers. Those numbers are the coordinates for that point. *See also* Cartesian coordinates and Spherical coordinates. Also a grid system applied to a map projection and used as a means of identifying unique positions across the map surface. For example, the Universal Transverse Mercator (UTM) coordinate system is applied to the Transverse Mercator projection. Any location on the map is identified by an *x-y* coordinate with values corresponding to the UTM grid.

DAL: The acronym for Data Acquisition Language, a system developed by Apple computer and employed by some mapping products that allows Macintosh computers to send and receive data from minicomputers and mainframes with the Mac handling the translation and format incompatibilities for the mainframe.

Database: A compilation of records or organized collection of data. The term is often used to refer to a single file or table of information used as attribute data with mapping programs.

Data file: A file containing a set of data variables, which can be both numbers and text. Data files are used by most mapping software to link data in a worksheet or database to areas or points on a map. Data files may also contain variable names that identify the type of data contained in a spreadsheet or database column, and other attribute data.

Data value: A single statistic for a map area, such as the "average household size of Colorado." Occupies a single cell in the spreadsheet or a single field in a database.

Data variable: The name of a set of data values based on the same statistic. For example, state population could be a data variable listed for each state.

Decimal degree: Some mapping programs use decimal degrees to specify latitude and longitude, instead of the standard notation. One decimal degree equals one ordinary degree. But distances smaller than a degree are indicated in decimal form, where the standard system uses degrees, minutes, and seconds.

Demographics or Demography: A social science that focuses on the study of populations—including their size, distribution, structure, and changes. The word demographics is also used as a noun meaning the structure or attributes of a target population.

Density map: A map using dots to display data. The number of dots drawn in an area is proportional to the data variable represented for that area. Each dot is placed randomly within the area and represents a specific quantity.

Desktop marketing system or desktop demographic system: A personal computer system, including specific application software and hardware, that allows multiple marketing databases and demographic attributes to be charted, mapped, or reported. The term is often used synonymously with desktop mapping or market mapping, although a desktop marketing system is really more generic in function, and may or may not include mapping functions. Sophisticated mapping programs can be considered desktop marketing systems because they include the ability to analyze a wide range of databases and produce reports and charts, in addition to maps.

Dialog box: A box that allows you to enter additional information or change settings related to a specific command.

Distance: The interval between two points, such as between two cities or along a stream, expressed in a measurement such as feet or miles.

DOS: An acronym for disk-based operating system. Also the commonly used abbreviation to refer to the operating system on the IBM PC (PC-DOS) and compatible computers (MS-DOS).

Driver: A general term used to describe software that enables a program to run a particular peripheral device, such as a printer. In most cases, each driver will run only one specific device by a specific manufacturer.

Edit: To make changes to a map by altering map objects, text, or parameters.

Electronic atlas: Digital images of pieces of geography, such as North America or London, England, depicting physical features, political boundaries, infrastructure, and place names. These software representations of maps are used for general reference and are not designed for what-if analysis or the representation of unique attribute data.

Field: A field is a specific type of information contained in a database or file, such as NAME, AGE, or DATE OF BIRTH. Fields are combined to make records, and records are combined to make a file or database.

Fill pattern: The design and color used to fill a closed object.

FIPS code: The "Federal Information Processing Standards" code, published by the National Bureau of Standards, for representing and organizing the large number of named geographic areas in data files for computer processing.

Flow maps: Maps that show the direction of movement of something across the area of the map. Transportation maps showing shipping routes or air routes are examples of flow maps.

Font: A character set or typeface based on a particular style and size. Fonts have names like Garamond, Helvetica, Times Roman, and many others to identify them. A variety of fonts are useful for annotating and designing maps used in presentations and publications.

Geocode or Geocoding: The process of adding geographic coordinates to a file or database so the attribute information or objects can be displayed on a map. In geocoding, mapping programs take textual information and associate it with geometric information. For example, text descriptors like

STATE, COUNTRY, or ZIP CODE contained in a database must be geocoded into coordinates that are represented on a map in the correct locations.

Geographic data: The data that describes the location and shape of map features (regions, lines, or single locations). Map features are defined by a series of latitude-longitude or *x-y* coordinates connected together.

Geographic information system (GIS): A sophisticated software-based system designed to capture, store, manipulate, analyze, report on, and print geographically referenced or geo-relational information. GIS technology was originally developed for environmental monitoring and natural resource assessments, and rapidly expanded into applications for facilities management, public planning, and governmental applications. Today, GIS systems and related desktop mapping systems are being used in business to complete a wide range of research assignments based on geo-relational data.

Geo-relational: The geographic relations of features or data as displayed on a map. For example, does the road cross the zip code? How many school buildings are within one mile of the city park? How many census tracts border the river? Computerized mapping technology is often called geo-relational technology.

Graticule: The grid formed by the lines of latitude (parallels) and the lines of longitude (meridians). The graticule is also referred to as the earth's coordinate system.

Great circle: A circle on a sphere, or through the globe, such that the plane containing the circle passes through the center of the sphere; also, the line of shortest distance between two points on the surface of the earth.

Grid: A series of regularly spaced, crossing lines that are drawn on a map and used for reference. These lines can represent projection lines or specific boundary lines on a map.

Grid reference: Numbered location identified by referring to the numbered grid lines across the top and sides of a map.

Hatch map: A thematic map that displays fill colors and patterns for areas as a way to represent data ranges.

Hemisphere: Half the globe, usually divided at the equator.

Hole: An excluded region or "lake" within a complex area that allows underlying objects to show through. In some mapping programs, holes are isolated polygons contained entirely within the boundary of a complex area, and are considered to be part of that area. Any operation performed on this type of complex area is not be applied to the hole if the software supports this concept.

Island: A single polygon included as part of a complex area. Islands are isolated polygons which are grouped in a single complex area with no outer boundary. Any operation performed on this type of complex area is applied to each island if the software supports this concept. For example, Hawaii is a complex area that consists of several islands.

Large-scale map: Map on a scale large enough to show significant detail.

Latitude: Used to describe the north-south position of a point as measured in degrees above or below the equator. Latitude lines are the horizontal lines (east-west) on a map that increase from 0 degrees at the Equator to 90 degrees at both the north (+90 degrees) and south (−90 degrees) poles.

Latitude-longitude: The spherical coordinate system used to define positions on the earth's surface. Lines of latitude (also known as parallels) run in an east-west direction. Lines of longitude (also known as meridians) run in a north-south direction. Positions are measured in degrees-minutes-seconds or decimal degrees.

Layer: A method of grouping similar map features in a mapping system. For example, all land parcels might be on one layer and all roads on another layer. All features on a layer can be manipulated together.

Legend: An explanation of the data representations, symbols, and features on a map.

Line or line feature: A map feature characterized by a series of coordinates connected together that extend across a map. Examples of line features are roads, streams, and topographic lines.

Line survey: Survey based on a line of known position and length.

Longitude: Used to describe the east-west position of a point. The position is reported as the number of degrees east (to −180 degrees) or west (to +180 degrees) of the prime meridian (0 degrees) and represented by lines running from the north to south poles. Lines of longitude are farthest apart at the Equator and intersect at both poles, and are, therefore, not parallel. Lines of longitude are negative for the United States.

Magnetic azimuth: The direction of the magnetic north pole.

Map features: Map features are graphic symbols that represent entities in the real world. There are three fundamental types of map features represented in mapping software: regions (zip codes, districts, etc.), lines (roads, streams, etc.), and points (stores, hospitals, fire hydrants, etc.).

Map projection: The transformation of a spherical surface, such as the earth, to a flat surface. A projection uses lines on a map to represent a corresponding system of imaginary lines on the surface of the earth. There are three basic projection surfaces—planar, conical, and cylindrical. Each type of projection has different areas of distortion, depending on the size of the area projected and the tangent (area touching) the projection surface.

Market mapping: In this book the primary application of GIS and desktop mapping research in business is called market mapping. Market mapping is the display of market, customer, and other attribute data on thematic and other types of display-oriented maps to better visualize the relationships, trends, and business opportunities in a geographical area.

Mercator's projection: A method of projecting a map so latitude and longitude lines are square to each other. The result is severe exaggeration of the size in the polar regions. The chief advantage is that compass directions appear as straight lines, so this type of map is useful for navigation.

Meridian: A line or portion of a line running from the north to the south pole. A longitudinal line, which is a great circle on the surface of the earth passing through the poles, has the same longitude on all points.

Miller projection: A cylindrical projection method that reduces areal exaggeration by lengthening the distance between lines of latitude away from the equator. Distortion in the areas increases away from the equator.

Modified projection: The basic geometric projections (planar, cylindrical, and conic) can be modified mathematically to hold overall distortion to a minimum or to make a map look good. The best or most accurate areas from various projections are combined or spliced together, or a global projection is interrupted so noncritical areas absorb the most distortion and important features are displayed accurately.

Nautical mile: One minute of latitude (6080 feet).

Neatline: The border between the map and its margin.

Node: When dots on a map are connected to make a polygon, these dots are often referred to as nodes.

One-sided link: The process of placing one map over another map which covers the same geographic area in order to compare the two maps in some manner. For example, you might overlay a map of soil data over a map of parcels to determine the intersection of soil types and parcels.

Orientation: The relationship between a map and the part of the earth's surface being represented.

Orthographic projection: A type of planar projection that produces realistic-looking globes, as if viewing the earth from a point far out in space. In orthographic projections, distortion is least around the tangent point (the center of the circle) and greatest at the ends of the circle.

Orthophotomaps: Maps made of color-enhanced photographic images.

Parallel of latitude: A line parallel to the equator through all points with the same latitude.

Physical map: A map that features elevations and natural features.

Pie map: A thematic map that displays a representation of two or more data variables for each area. The variables are presented in pie charts centered on the specific area to which the data is assigned.

Pin map: A map which uses symbols to show the point locations for a set of data, such as office locations or residents with past-due bills. The symbols are usually overlaid on a base map such as a street network.

Pixel: An acronym for picture element. The smallest addressable element or dot on a graphics monitor or output by a printer. Each character, object, or line on the screen is composed of numerous pixels.

Point: A map feature representing a single location, characterized by a single coordinate. Examples of point features are crime locations, fire hydrants, and hospitals.

Pointer: The arrow that moves on the screen when moving the mouse. The pointer is used to select objects, commands, and options by positioning the tip over the desired position on the screen and clicking with a mouse or other pointing device.

Point size: A measurement used for measuring the size of a character or font. There are 72.27 points per inch, although many software manufacturers specify 72 points per inch for convenience.

Political map: A map that shows borders, cities, place names, roads, or countries, usually without contours and physical features.

Polygon: A closed two-dimensional figure consisting of three or more straight line sides. In many mapping programs, areas are polygons constructed with straight lines connected at the vertices (corners or nodes) to form a closed figure or bounded region.

Polyline: A line that can have more than two nodes. Polyline drawing tools available in some mapping programs are used to create polygons on maps.

Prime meridian: Longitude 0° at the meridian of Greenwich, England.

Prism map: A thematic map that presents areas as three-dimensional prisms. The height of each prism is proportional to a data value associated with the area.

Projection: A mathematical method for converting spherical latitude-longitude coordinates (on a globe) to two-dimensional coordinates (on a flat map). Projections usually result in some degree of size or shape distortion.

Quadrangle: A four-sided area bounded by meridians of longitude and parallels of latitude.

Quadrantal points: Northeast, southeast, southwest, and northwest on a compass or map.

Query: To ask a question. In mapping software, to query something is to ask for specific information to be displayed from a database or file according to the textual attributes of the data. Usually, specific commands like

Select or Define Query are used to specify the desired information or report that will display on a map, table, or graph.

Raster font: A type of font consisting of a matrix of dots. This type of font cannot always be scaled or rotated without some distortion. Raster fonts give a much cleaner look at small sizes and plot much faster than vector fonts. Raster fonts cannot be reproduced on vector devices such as plotters.

Raster map: A map made up of a matrix of cells. Map features are defined by assigning a value to each cell within a feature. For example, a Landsat satellite image is composed of cells that are each 80 meters by 80 meters in size.

Record: The information about one object in a database, file, or table is a record. Thus, a record about Jane Smith in a personnel database would contain Jane's name, social security number, address, data of birth, start date, etc.

Region: A map feature characterized by a series of coordinates connected together where the first and last coordinate are the same, thus closing the region. Regions are known as polygons or areas. Sometimes the term is used synonymously with the term boundary. Examples of region features are census tracts, districts, and zip codes.

Relational database: A type of database representation used by some computer programs that conceptually represents data in tables, usually as rows and columns of data.

Scale: Relation between a distance on a map and the distance it represents on the surface of the earth.

Segment: In a street-level map, a segment is a single section of the street. In urban-level maps, segments are generally one block long. Address ranges are often stored at the segment level in mapping programs.

Sliver: A small gap between the common border of two adjacent areas.

Small-scale map: Map of a large area that is too small to allow much detail to be represented.

Snap: To align objects exactly with ruler or grid divisions. When creating new objects with the pointer, or moving/sizing existing objects, the tip of the pointer or edge of the object jumps between adjacent ruler divisions or grid lines.

Spatial information: Information that can be related to a location in some space such as the earth. The information can define the location, such as the coordinates of a school district boundary, or it can be about the location. For example, the number of students in a school district relates to the location of the school district.

Spherical coordinates: A coordinate system that uses latitude and longitude values to represent objects on the surface of the globe.

Spooling: To send a page to a file before printing. When spooling is complete, the page prints when the printer is available and you may return to work with the software or select another print operation.

SQL: Acronym for Structured Query Language. SQL is a standard language for analyzing information stored in computer databases. People also refer to SQL as "sequel" in conversation.

Standard deviation: A measure of the variation of a set of data values around the mean. Technically, a measure of the dispersion of a frequency distribution that is the square root of the arithmetic mean of the squares of the deviation of each of the class frequencies from the arithmetic mean of the frequency distribution.

Street-based map: A pin map using a base map of streets. *See* pin map.

Symbol map: A thematic map that displays a representation of a single data variable for each area. The variables are presented as proportionally sized (based on the data values) symbols centered on the specific area to which the data is assigned.

System 7: As of the writing of this book, the latest version of the operating system for the Apple Macintosh line of computers, that employs a sophisticated graphic user interface with icons, pull-down menus, multiple fonts, and consistent operating functions across applications.

Table: A representation or listing of data in rows and columns.

Text cursor: A blinking vertical bar that indicates where typed characters will appear.

Thematic map: A map that presents the distribution of attribute data (a theme) across a set of map features. This is done by filling a map object—points, lines, or boundaries—with a color, shape, or fill pattern, to indicate something about the object (i.e., population, rainfall, sales volume, etc.). Through the use of color, patterns, shading, or size, the relative value of feature characteristics and their geographic relationships can be displayed. For example, you might display per capita income by census tracts to see the location of different income groups and observe the boundaries between high- and low-income areas. Thematic maps can be quantitative, meaning they illustrate statistical data, or they can be qualitative, meaning they illustrate distributions in which no percentages, ratios, or other absolute quantities are involved, such as the distribution of climate, soils, or vegetation.

TIGER file: Stands for Topologically Integrated Geographic Encoding and Referencing. A digital map of street segments, usually covering a county, developed by the United States Census Bureau. Each segment also contains attribute data such as zip code or county code on each side of the street. Developed for the 1990 census, these files cover the entire United States and some outlying areas such as Puerto Rico.

Toolbox: A collection of icons, each of which represent a different drawing tool. The toolbox is positioned along the left edge of the map document window.

Topographic map: A map presenting the vertical and horizontal positions of features on the surface of the earth.

Tropic of Cancer: Parallel of latitude 23½° north.

Tropic of Capricorn: Parallel of latitude 23½° south.

Two-sided link: The attribute data can be queried from both the database and the map display. Thus, you can query the data based on a geographic query or view the geography based on an attribute query.

Vector map: A map made up of regions, lines, and points. Each map feature is defined by a series of x-y coordinates. Examples of vector maps include parcel maps, land use maps, soil maps, and crime incident maps.

Vertex: The connecting point between two straight line segments of an area or curve.

Window: A box or rectangle on the screen. Windows contain title bars and control buttons along the top, and may contain menu options in a menu bar. Windows can be moved, minimized, or maximized.

Windows: A graphical user interface product marketed by Microsoft Corporation that works with its MS-DOS operating system. Many mapping programs for IBM PC and compatible computers require Windows to be installed to operate. The Windows interface uses icons, windows, and pull-down menus, somewhat similar to those employed by the operating system developed earlier for the Macintosh by Apple Computers.

World geographic reference system: Worldwide position reference system, primarily used on aeronautical charts.

x-y coordinates: A single x-y coordinate represents a location on a two-dimensional grid or coordinate system. Most maps are based on a map projection and a specific coordinate system.

Zip code: A five-digit code (with four-digit extension option for finer location specification) established by the United States Postal Service to facilitate mail delivery. The first digit refers to one of the 10 geographic areas into which the United States is divided. The second digit refers to a state, a collection of sparsely populated states, or a portion or a heavily populated state. The third digit refers to a major post office location. The fourth and fifth digits refer to the local delivery area.

Zoom: The process of magnifying or reducing a region within a map window displayed on a computer monitor.

Bibliography

Crispell, Diane. *The Insider's Guide to Demographic Know-How: How to Find, Analyze, and Use Information About Your Customers.* 2d ed. Ithaca, New York: American Demographics Press, 1990.

Maloney, Elbert S. *Piloting & Small Boat Handling.* 59th ed. New York: Hearst Marine Books, 1989.

Renner, Sandra L., and W. Gary Winget. *Fast-Track Exporting: How Your Company Can Succeed in the Global Market.* New York: AMACOM, 1991.

Map Product Credits

[1] MapInfo—MapInfo, Corporation
[2] MapInfo—MapInfo, Corporation
[3] MapViewer—Golden Software, Inc.
[4] Descartes—PC Globe, Inc.
[5] MapInfo—MapInfo, Corporation
[6] Tactician—Tactics International Limited
[7] MapViewer—Golden Software, Inc.
[8] MapViewer—Golden Software, Inc.
[9] MapInfo—MapInfo, Corporation
[10] MapInfo—MapInfo, Corporation
[11] MapInfo—MapInfo, Corporation
[12] MapInfo—MapInfo, Corporation
[13] MapInfo—MapInfo, Corporation
[14] Tactician—Tactics International Limited
[15] MapInfo—MapInfo, Corporation
[16] MapInfo—MapInfo, Corporation
[17] Tactician—Tactics International Limited
[18] MapInfo—MapInfo, Corporation
[19] Tactician—Tactics International Limited
[20] MapInfo—MapInfo, Corporation
[21] Tactician—Tactics International Limited
[22] MapViewer—Golden Software, Inc.
[23] Tactician—Tactics International Limited
[24] Tactician—Tactics International Limited
[25] Arc/Info—ESRI
[26] Scan US—Urban Decisions Systems, Inc.
[27] MapInfo—MapInfo, Corporation
[28] Atlas GIS—Strategic Mapping, Inc.
[29] Atlas GIS—Strategic Mapping, Inc.
[30] MapInfo—MapInfo, Corporation
[31] MapInfo—MapInfo, Corporation
[32] MapInfo—MapInfo, Corporation
[33] MapInfo—MapInfo, Corporation
[34] MapInfo—MapInfo, Corporation

[35] MapInfo—MapInfo, Corporation
[36] MapInfo—MapInfo, Corporation
[37] MapInfo—MapInfo, Corporation
[38] MapInfo—MapInfo, Corporation
[39] MapInfo—MapInfo, Corporation
[40] MapInfo—MapInfo, Corporation
[41] MapInfo—MapInfo, Corporation
[42] MapInfo—MapInfo, Corporation
[43] MapInfo—MapInfo, Corporation
[44] MapInfo—MapInfo, Corporation
[45] MapInfo—MapInfo, Corporation
[46] MapInfo—MapInfo, Corporation
[47] MapInfo—MapInfo, Corporation
[48] MapInfo—MapInfo, Corporation
[49] Descartes—PC Globe, Inc.
[50] Descartes—PC Globe, Inc.
[51] Descartes—PC Globe, Inc.
[52] Descartes—PC Globe, Inc.
[53] Atlas GIS—Strategic Mapping, Inc.
[54] Atlas GIS—Strategic Mapping, Inc.
[55] Atlas GIS—Strategic Mapping, Inc.
[56] Descartes—PC Globe, Inc.
[57] Descartes—PC Globe, Inc.
[58] Descartes—PC Globe, Inc.
[59] Descartes—PC Globe, Inc.
[60] Atlas GIS—Strategic Mapping, Inc.
[61] Atlas GIS—Strategic Mapping, Inc.
[62] Atlas GIS—Strategic Mapping, Inc.
[63] Tactician—Tactics International Limited
[64] Tactician—Tactics International Limited
[65] Tactician—Tactics International Limited
[66] Tactician—Tactics International Limited
[67] Tactician—Tactics International Limited
[68] Tactician—Tactics International Limited
[69] Tactician—Tactics International Limited
[70] Tactician—Tactics International Limited
[71] Tactician—Tactics International Limited
[72] Tactician—Tactics International Limited
[73] Tactician—Tactics International Limited

Index

About the Authors

SUNNY BAKER founded Microsoft University while she was
general manager and director of marketing for Microsoft
Corporation. She has held similar positions at Intel and
National Semiconductor. She is currently a marketing and
computer consultant, with clients including Microsoft, Apple
Computer, Rolm, and Telenet.

KIM BAKER is a writer and marketing communications
consultant, specializing in desktop applications. He has been
an executive in both advertising agencies and marketing
communications departments for high-tech firms.